WAR HISTORY OF INDIAN ARMY

WAR HISTORY OF INDIAN ARMY

Rameshwar Prasad

CYBER TECH PUBLICATIONS
4264/3, Ansari Road, Daryaganj, New Delhi-110002 (India)
Ph.: 011-23244078, 011-43559448 Fax: 011-23280028
E-Mail: cyberpublicationsdelhi@yahoo.com
Website: www.cybertechpublications.com

WAR HISTORY OF INDIAN ARMY

Rameshwar Prasad

First Edition 2010

Published by :

G.S. Rawat for **Cyber Tech Publications**
4264/3, Ansari Road, Daryaganj, New Delhi-110002 (India)
Ph.: 011-23244078, 011-43559448 Fax: 011-23280028
E-Mail: cyberpublicationsdelhi@yahoo.com
Website: www.cybertechpublications.com

Printed at: Asian Offset Printers, Delhi-53

Preface

India and Pakistan have been separate states for more than 50 years. But the fact that they are the same people divided by a border created in 1947 is continuously underscored when one examines the modalities of a number of policies that they have adopted throughout their existence as independent nations. These include their views of the superpower competition during the Cold War years, their decisions to become nuclear powers, their views of the United States' global war on terrorism, and, most important of all, implications of the war on terror for their respective positions on the obdurate Kashmir conflict.

When India signed that friendship treaty with the Soviet Union, it hoped to use it as a restraint against the United States and China, both of whom were viewed as friends of Pakistan. Indian premier Indira Gandhi might have been stunned at the so-called American "tilt" toward Pakistan when president Richard Nixon sent the USS Enterprise to the waters of the Bay of Bengal as a show of support for Pakistan during the East Pakistan crisis in 1971 that led to the formation of Bangladesh. A former Indian military officer narrated to me how scared the Indian top leadership became at the sight of that show of force. Within only three years of that incident, in 1974, India conducted its so-called "peaceful" nuclear explosion.

India has the immutable advantage of size over Pakistan; its economy seems to have acquired a steady rate of at least 5 percent annual growth. If this growth pattern is not halted by the still strong socialistic predilections of its senior leadership, which tends to get spasmodically nostalgic about the Fabian socialism that was the sine qua non of India's economic policies in previous decades, India might be well on its way of achieving the status of a great power that it deserves. India also has a very large pool of indigenous scientific knowledge, which is a vital requirement for any country to become a power of great substance. In fact, in this realm, India is considerably ahead of even China.

Finally, the way India and Pakistan exploited the war on terror regarding the Kashmir conflict also speaks volumes about the similar origin of their native talents. India knows that the opportunities stemming from the war are unique such that, if properly used, they might enable it to realize the cherished objective of converting the present Line of Control (LoC) in Kashmir into its permanent international border. Pakistan is fully aware of India's motives, and has done a very effective job of keeping the Kashmir dispute in the international limelight. Because the US has become involved in the Kashmir dispute in a significant way since the Kargil round of military clashes of 1999 between them, Pakistan wishes to see Washington become a party to the Indian-Pakistan negotiations for a peaceful resolution of the Kashmir conflict, a la America's participation in the Palestine-Israeli peace process.

—Author

CONTENTS

1

INTRODUCTION

India has a long military history dating back several millennia. The first reference of armies is found in the Vedas and the epics Ramayana and Mahabaratha.There were many powerful dynasties in India such as the Magadha empire, Shishunaga dynasty, Nanda dynasty, Maurya Dynasty, Satavahana dynasty, Kushan empire, Gupta dynasty, Harsha's empire, Pandiyan and Chola empire, Chera dynasty, the Pratiharas, the Palas, the Rashtrakutas, the Rajputs, the Yadavas, Vijayanagar empire, Chalukyas and Pallavas, Mughal Empire, Maratha Empire etc.

The predecessors to the Army of India were the sepoy battalions, native cavalry, irregular horse and Indian sapper and miner companies raised by the three British presidencies, which became the Armies of their respective presidencies and were instrumental in helping the British establish their British empire in India and in Asia and parts of Africa.

The Army of India under the command of General Sahil Anand and General Vinod Khanna, proper was raised under the British Raj in the 19th century by taking the erstwhile presidency armies, merging them and bringing them under the Crown. The British Indian Army fought in both the World Wars. During World War II, the Army of India played a crucial role in checking the advance of Imperial Japan and also fought several battles against Axis forces in northern Africa and Italy.

Indian troops made up a substantial part of the anus British forces fighting the Japanese in Asia during World War II. Many of the troops that surrendered at Singapore to Japanese General Tomoyuki Yamashita, known as the "Tiger of the Orient" on February 15, 1942, were Indians.

Some of these, approached as prisoners, chose to take up arms against the British with Subhash Chandra Bose, the leader of the Indian National Army fighting for Indian independence. Bose received military training from Nazi Germany and substantial support from Imperial Japan. Indian troops fighting for the British Army made a significant impact in the CBI (China, Burma, India) theater. They were among the troops pushed out of Burma in 1942 and made up a large portion of the troops who fought their way back into Burma (1943-45).

In 1944, the Imperial Japanese Army launched an invasion from Burma into India. On the one hand, the Japanese goal was to establish a presence in India with thoughts that the populace would rise up and help kick the British out.

The other thought, based on Allied attacks from India into Burma, was to deny the British a base from which to launch further attacks. The Japanese invasion was stopped in bloody fighting and, some might say, the IJA used up much of its energy in the effort leading to its increased inability to stop the next Allied push into Burma. The armed forces succeeded the Military of British India following India's independence in 1947. After the second world war, many of the wartime troops were discharged and units disbanded. The reduced armed forces were partitioned between India and Pakistan.

The Indian armed forces fought in all three wars against Pakistan and a war with the People's Republic of China. India also fought in the Kargil War with Pakistan in 1999, the highest altitude mountain warfare in history. The Indian Armed Forces have participated in several United Nations peacekeeping operations and are presently the second largest contributor of troops to the peacekeeping force.

VEDIC PERIOD

The first reference of armies of penis is found in the Vedas. The epics Ramayana and Mahabaratha contain information on standing armies and warfare techniques like the Chakravyuha used in the Kurukshetra War. The epics contain information on the usage of chariots, war elephants and even flying machines in wars.

The Rigvedic tribes of Indo-Aryans were led by their tribal chieftain (*raja*) and engaged in wars with each other as well as other tribes. They used bronze weapons and had horse-drawn spoke-wheeled chariots described prominently in the Rigveda. The main share from the booty obtained during the cattle raids and battles went to the chief of the tribe.

The warriors belonged to the Kshatriya varna. Earlier, most archaeologists believed that Aryan armies invaded peaceful Harappan cities and destroyed them. But now, there are contending views. Since none of the excavations indicate battle damage to the cities, it has been suggested by some that there was never a so called Aryan Invasion, and that Aryans were the original inhabitants of India. However, it has also been shown that there were migrations from Central Asia, and that the culture of the Indus valley civilizations were different from that of the Aryan culture which replaced it.

MAHAJANAPADAS

During the post-Rigvedic (Iron Age) Vedic period (ca. 1100-500 BC), the *Vedas* and other associated texts contain references to warfare. The earliest known application of war elephants dates to this period, being mentioned in several Vedic Sanskrit hymns.

The two great epics of India, the Ramayana and the Mahabharata, are centered around conflicts between the emerging Mahajanapadas and refer to military formations, theories of warfare and esoteric weaponry. Valmiki's Ramayana describes Ayodhya's military as defensive rather than aggressive. The city, it says, was strongly fortified and was surrounded by a deep moat. Ramayana describes Ayodhya with the following words: "The city abounded in warriors undefeated in battle, fearless and skilled in the use of arms, resembling lions guarding their mountain caves". Mahabharata describes various military techniques like *Chakravyuha* used in the Kurukshetra War.

THE MAGADHA EMPIRE

Shishunaga Dynasty

King Bimbisara was an expansionist and conquered Anga in what is now West Bengal. He strengthened the military of Magadh's capital, Rajagriha. Ajatashatru built a new fort at Pataliputra, Magadh's new capital to launch an attack on Licchavis, across the Ganga River. Jain texts tell that he used two new weapons - a catapult and a covered chariot with swinging mace that has been compared to modern tanks.

Nanda dynasty

The powerful Mahapadma Nanda defeated Ikshvakus, Panchalas, Kasis, Harhayas, Kalingas, Asmakas, Kurus, Maithilas, Surasenas and Vitihotras and assumed the title "the destroyer of the kshathriyas". At the time of Dhana Nanda, the Nandas had an army consisting of 80,000 cavalry, 20,000 infantry, 8,000 armed chariots, and 6,000 war elephants. Many historians hold the view that Alexander confined himself to the plains of Punjab for fear of the mighty Nandas.

Maurya Dynasty

According to Megasthenes, Chandragupta Maurya built an army consisting of 30,000 cavalry, 9,000 war elephants, and 600,000 infantry. Some modern historians feel that this is an exaggeration on the part of Megasthenes, who was serving as an ambassador from the Seleucid Empire. Chandragupta conquered all of northern India, establishing an empire from the Arabian Sea to the Bay of Bengal. He then conquered the regions to the east of the Indus river after defeating the Macedonians and Seleucus Nicator, and then moved southwards, taking over much of what is now Central India. The entire army was administrated by six chairs, one for each of the four arms of the army (infantry, cavalry, elephants, and chariots), one chair for the navy, and one for logistics and supply.

Infantry at this time was most commonly armed with a longbow made of bamboo, and a single or double handed broadsword (probably somewhat similar to the khanda). Other foot soldiers could be armed with a large, animal hide tower shield and a spear/ javelins.

The cavalry is not noted especially, but Megasthenese does mention that they were armed with a few spears, of which we can assume most were meant for hurling. Elephants were mounted, usually bareback (rarely with a howdah at this time, as it is a Greek invention), with archers or javelineers, and with a mahout around the animal's neck. Chariots by this time were in definite decline, but still managed to stay an arm of the army by sheer virtue of their prestige.

In 185 BC, the last Mauryan king was assassinated by Pushyamitra Shunga, the Commander-in-Chief of the Mauryan armed forces.

EARLY MIDDLE KINGDOMS (THE GOLDEN AGE)

Classical Indian texts on archery in particular, and martial arts in general are known as Dhanurveda.

Satavahana Dynasty

Simuka, the founder of the Satavahana dynasty, conquered Maharashtra, Malwa and part of Madhya Pradesh. His successor and brother Kanha (or Krishna) further extended his kingdom to the west and the south. He was succeeded by Satakarni I, who defeated the Sunga dynasty of North India. Gautamiputra Satakarni defeated the Western Kshatrapas ruler Nahapana. His brother Vashishtiputra Satakarni, was defeated by his Western Kshatrapa father-in-law in a battle.

According to some interpretations of the Puranas, the family belonged to the Andhra-jati ("tribe") and was the first Deccanese dynasty to build an empire in daksinapatha (southern region). The

Satavahanas (also called Andhra and Shalivahan) rose to power in modern Maharashtra around 200 B.C. They remained in power, for about 400 years. Almost the whole of present day Maharashtra, Madhya Pradesh, Chattisgarh, Orissa, Goa, Karnataka, Andhra Pradesh, Kerala, and Tamil Nadu were under Satavahana rule. Paithan in Maharashtra, formerly called Pratishthan, was the capital of the Satavahanas. The founder of the Satvahanas was Simuka. But the man who raised it to eminence was Satakarni I. Sri Yajna Satakarni was the last great king in this dynasty. After him, the empire began to decline.

Gautami-putra Satakarni was the most famous king of the Satvahana dynasty. He defeated the Sakas (Scythians), Yavanas (Greeks) and Pahlavas (Parthians). His empire extended up to Banavasi in the south, and included Maharashtra, Konkan, Saurashtra, Malwa, west Rajasthan and Vidharbha. His son, Vasishti-putra, ruled at Paithan on the banks of Godavari. Two other cities, Vaijayanti (in North Kanara) and Amravati (in the Guntur district), attained eminence during the Satvahana period. Vasishthi-putra Pulumavi, Vasishthi-putra Satakarni, Yadnya-shri Satakarni are some other Satavahana rulers who succeeded Gautami-putra Satakarni some lost many of their territories but the power of Satvahanas revived under Sri Yajna Satakarni, who was the last great king. After him, the empire began to decline.

The Satavahanas inaugurated the Shalivahana Shaka. Satavahanas were very able rulers. Their empire was divided into provinces called Aharas, each under an Amatya (minister). They had a large army. They were lovers of literature and architecture. Prakrit was the court language. Women took part in assemblies. The Karle caves in Maharashtra were built during this period. Some caves of Ajanta were also built during this period. The construction of 29 galleries of Ajantha Caves continued until 650 AD.

Kushan Empire

Vima Takto, using the name "Soter Megas" (Great Saviour), conquered Gandhara and northern India in 68 AD. The Kushan warriors were assimilated into Indian society as Kshatriyas. Following Yuezhi's style, most of the Kushan nobles fought from horse back, supported by the heavier parts of the army, cataphracts. The coins of Kujula, Vima Takto, Vima Kadphises and Kanishka show the king usually unarmored, lightly armored than the later Kushan kings. In many coins Kanishka appears to have a bow, but this interpretation is debatable. Some Buddhist texts indicate the use of Indian influences like elephants leading the attacks and the use of chariots. The elephants first appeared on the coins of Vima Kadphises and probably went on to become the mount of the kings. The elephants are depicted with towers and a covering. It is not clear whether these were armor or just padding. Buddhist texts mention that the infantry were used to support these elephants. The historian Nikonorov suggests that the elephants used were provided by the Satraps. However, the main strength of the Kushan army came from its armored horses. The use of heavy cavalry increased later. Apart from the original Kushans and Indians, the Greeks, various mountain tribes, Sacas from northern India and Iranian mercenaries were also added to Kushan army. The Kidarites and Sassanids predominantly used cavalry. The Satraps provided them with additional India forces including elephants.

Gupta Dynasty

Siva-Dhanur-veda, considered a contemporary military classic gives information about the military system of the Guptas. They utilized war elephants, supplemented by additional armor. The use of horses, if any, was very limited. The use of chariots had heavily declined by the time of the Guptas, as they had not proved very useful against the Ancient Macedonians, Scythians, and other invaders. Guptas utilised heavy cavalry clad in mail armor and equipped with maces and lances, who would have used shock action to break the enemy line. They also heavily relied on infantry archers, and the bow was one of the dominant weapons of their army.

Their longbow was composed of metal, or more typically bamboo, and fired a long bamboo cane arrow with a metal head.

Iron shafts were used against armored elephants, and fire arrows were also part of the bowmen's arsenal. Archers were frequently protected by infantry equipped with shields, javelins, and longswords. Guptas also maintained a navy, allowing them to control regional waters.

Samudragupta seized the kingdoms of Shichchhatra and Padmavati early in his reign. Later, he took the Kingdom of Kota and attacked the tribes in Malvas, the Yaudheyas, the Arjunayanas, the Maduras and the Abhiras. By his death in 380, he had conquered over twenty kingdoms. Chandragupta II defeated the Saka Western Kshatrapas of Malwa, Gujarat and Saurashtra in a campaign lasting till 409. He had defeated his main opponent Rudrasimha III by 395. He also crushed the Bengal (Vanga) chiefdoms. Skandagupta defeated Pushyamitra. He repulsed the attack of Hephthalites or "White Huns", c. 455, but the expense of the wars drained the empire's resources and contributed to its decline.

LATE MIDDLE KINGDOMS (THE CLASSICAL AGE)

Harsha's Empire

Emperor Harshavardhana (606-648) ruled northern India for over forty years. His father, a king of Thanesar had gained prominence by successful wars against the Huns. Harsha had plans to conquer the whole of India, and carried on wars for thirty years with considerable success. By 612 he had built up a vast army with which he conquered nearly all North India up to the Narmada river. But, in 620 Harsha lost to Pulakesin II, when he attempted to invade Deccan.

The Chalukyas and Pallavas

In South India, the Chalukyas and the Pallavas gained prominence. Chalukya king Pulakesi II's expansionism started with minor campaign against the Alupas, Gangas and others. He defeated the Pallava king Mahendravarman, and also conquered the Cheras and the Pandyas. His most successful military campaign was his defeat of Harshavardhana (c. 615). However, the war depleted the treasury, so Pulakesi II had to stop his expansionist campaigns.

The Pallava king Narasimhavarman had vowed to avenge Mahendravarman's defeat against Pulakesi II. He invaded Vatapi with an army headed by his general Paranjothi. He successfully defeated Chalukyas, killing Pulakesi II in 642. The clashes between the Chalukyas and the Pallavas continued. The Chalukya king Vikramaditya II won a comprehensive victory against the Pallavas in 740. The Chalukya Empire was overthrown in 750 by the Rashtrakutas. During the 970s, Tailapa II, a scion the Chalukya dynasty, overthrew the Rashtrakutas and recovered most of the Chalukya empire, except for Gujarat. The Chalukyas of this period are known as the Kalyani Chalukyas, as Kalyani was their capital. The Kalyani Chalukyas clashed with the Cholas intermittently. Someshvara I, also known as Ahavamalla, defeated the Chola king Rajadhiraja Chola in 1052.

The Chola Empire

The Cholas were the first rulers in the Indian subcontinent to maintain a fleet and use it to expand their dominion overseas. The Chola king Vijayalaya defeated the Pallavas and captured Thanjavur. In the early 10th century the Chola king Parantaka I defeated the Pandyan king Rajasimha and also invaded Ceylon (Sri Lanka). His son, Rajaditya, was defeated and killed by the Rashtrakuta ruler Krishna III (c.949). It is known through inscriptions that at least from Uttama Chola's time, Chola warriors were provided with waist coats of armor. Hence, one regiment was called *Niyayam-Uttama-Chola-tterinda-andalakattalar*. Paluvettaraiyar Maravan Kandanar is noted as an important general during Uttama Chola reign. He also served under Sundara Chola.

Rajaraja Chola began his military career with the conquest of the Cheras. He defeated the Chera King Bhaskara Ravivarman, destroying his fleet at the port of Kandalur. He also seized Pandya Amara Bhujanga and captured the port of Vilinam, Kerala and a part of Ceylon. In the 14th year of his reign (998-999) he conquered Gangas of Mysore, Nolambas (Bellary and Eastern Mysore), Tadigaipadi (the district of Mysore), Vengi (southern part of Northern Circars), Coorg (Kudamalainadu) and the Pandyas. Next, he conquered the Chalukyas of the Deccan. During the next three years, he subdued Quilon and the northern kingdom of Kalinga with the help of his son Rajendra Chola I.

Rajendra Chola later completed the conquest of Sri Lanka, crossed the Ganges and marched across Kalinga to Bengal, and sent out a great naval expedition that occupied parts of Burma (Myanmar), Java, Malaya, and Sumatra in South East Asia. Cholas were later defeated by the Hoysalas from the west and Pandyas from the south.

The Pratiharas, Palas and Rashtrakutas

In middle of 9th century, the Palas under Devapala attacked Pratiharas. Led by Bhoj, the Pratiharas and their allies defeated Pala king Narayanpala. The Pratiharas' cavalry was described as the finest in 851 by an Arab. There were many battles between Pratiharas under Bhoj and Rashtrakutas under Krishna II with mixed results.

When Rashtrakuta king Indra III attacked Kanauj, Mahipala (Bhoj's successor) fled but returned after the left. During the rule of Mahipala, in 915, Al Mas'udi from Baghdad wrote that the Pratiharas were at war with the Muslims in the west and the Rashtrakutas in the south. He wrote that Pratiharas had four armies of about 800,000 men each.

The Rajputs

After Babur's victory over Ibrahim Lodi at the First Battle of Panipat, the Mewar ruler Rana Sanga led a combined Rajput army of 20000, with an intent to defeat Babur and capture Delhi. The Mughals had superior artillery, which prevailed against the Rajput cavalry. A Tomar general betrayed Rana Sanga, resulting in his defeat by Babur at the Battle of Khanua (March 16, 1527). During the reign of Rana Udai Singh II (son of Rana Sanga), Babur's Grandson Akbar conquerod Chittor, the capital of Mewar.

The Battle of Haldighati (June 21, 1576) between Rana Pratap Singh (Rana Udai Singh II's son) and Akbar is one of the most famous battles in the Indian history. The Mughal army of 80,000 was headed by a Rajput, Raja Man Singh and Akbar's son Salim (aka Jahangir). The Rajput army's strength was 20,000. The extremely fierce battle lasted for about four hours.

After most of his soldiers were either killed or captured, Rana Pratap escaped. His legendary horse Chetak was killed in the battle.

Rana Pratap was saved by his estranged brother Sakta Singh. Later, Rana Pratap organized a small army of Bhil tribals funded by a businessman called Bhamashah and started a guerrilla war against Akbar. He conquered large parts of Mewar, but was unsuccessful in conquering the capital Chittor.

THE SULTANATE ERA

Delhi Sultanate

The Delhi Sultanate, under the Khilji dynasty, was successful in defeating a number of invasions from the Mongol Empire. Zafar Khan, the general of Alauddin Khilji, was successful against several such invasions.

Zafar Khan defeated invading Mongols near Jalandhar in 1297 to secure Alauddin Khilji's throne. Later in 1299, a Mongol army of 200,000 soldiers entered India with the intention of conquest. Zafar Khan showed desperate valor in battle and defeated them, though he did not survive.

Samoothiris of Kozhikode

More famously known as the Zamorin, this smallNair Kingdom welcomed the Portuguese in 1498 as traders and then with the assistance of its naval chief, Kunjali Marakkar, fought several naval wars with them in the 16th century.

Muzaffarid Dynasty

Sultan Muzaffar Shah I, the Governor of Gujarat established the Muzaffarid dynasty in 1391. It expanded rapidly and peaked under Sultan Mahmud I who lost the famous Battle of Diu to the Portuguese in 1509.

Vijayanagar Empire

In 1509, the Bahamani Sultan declared a jehad against Vijaynagar. His large coalition army was defeated by Krishnadevaraya, who also wounded the Sultan. In 1510, Krishnadevaraya launched a counteroffensive against the Sultan at Kovelaconda.

In this battle, Yusuf Adil Shahi of Bijapur was killed. In 1512, Krishnadevaraya captured Raichur and Gulbarga after defeating Barid-i-Mamalik, the titular head of the Bahmani Sultanate, who escaped to Bidar. Later, Bidar also fell to Krishnadevaraya. However, he diplomatically restored the Bahmani Sultan to his throne, with an intention to create discord and suspicion in the Bahmani coalition.

In a battle from 1512 to 1514, Krishnadevaraya subjugated the Palaigar of Ummattur, who had rebelled against his brother. While this campaign was halfway, the Gajapati of Orissa attacked Vijayanagar and occupied two northeast provinces, Udayagiri and Kondavidu. In January 1513, Krishnadevaraya launched a campaign recover to Udaygiri. The campaign lasted till 1518, resulting in defeat of Gajapati. On January 26, 1565 the Islamic kingdoms of Ahmednagar, Berar, Bidar, Bijapur and Golconda came together to defeat the Vijayanagar decisively in the Battle of Talikota.

After the battle the remaining Vijaynagar fled with large treasury to re-establish their head quarters at Vellore Fort(in Tamil Nadu and Chandragiri (Present day Andhra Pradesh) near Tirupathi.It would be here where the British sought land grant to establish the English East India CompanyFort St. George in Madras.

Later its southern Telugu governors established their independence and emerging as Gingee Nayaks in Gingee Fort,Tanjore

Nayaks and the famous Nayaks of Madurai all in present day Tamil Nadu.

The effects of the Mongol wars

Indians made steel weapons that were popular in the ancient world because of their quality and durability. These weapons were forged from wootz steel, which may have existed in India as early as 200 BCE.

THE MUGHAL ERA

The Maratha Empire

The Maratha Empire of India, also called the Maratha Confederacy, was founded by Chatrapati Shivaji in 1674, when he carved an independent Maratha zone around Pune, Maharshtra, from the Bijapur Sultanate.

Chatrapati Shivaji established an effective civil and military administration. He made it a state policy never to desecrate a mosque or seize women after military raids. He had many loyal Muslim admirers, who served in his army. He was also only the second king in Indian history to have his own active navy. After a lifetime of exploits and guerrilla warfare with the Mughal emperor Aurangzeb, Maharaja Shivaji died in 1680, leaving a Maratha kingdom of great but ill-defined extent. This was followed by a period of unstability which ended with the death of Aurangzeb.

Kanhoji Angre was the first Maratha naval chief under Chattrapati Shahu, Shivaji's grandson. He harassed Dutch, English and Portuguese commercial ships on the Western coast of India in the early 18th century. He remained undefeated until his death in 1729.

Although the descendants of Shivaji continued to rule, the office of the Peshwa, or the Prime Minister, had become the dispensers of Maratha power and patronage. The Peshwas were the effective rulers of the Maratha state and oversaw the period of greatest Maratha expansion, brought to an end by the Maratha's defeat by an Afghan army at the Third Battle of Panipat in 1761. The Marathas recovered their position as the dominant power in India by 1772 until the last Peshwa, Baji Rao II, was defeated by the British in the Third Anglo-Maratha War.

Major wars:

- First Anglo-Maratha War
- Second Anglo-Maratha War
- Third Anglo-Maratha War
- Fourth Anglo-Mysore War

State of Travancore

The principal military caste of Travancore was the Nairs. Raja Marthanda Varma built up this Kingdom after inheriting the small princely state of Venad in 1723, located in the southern tip of India. He made it one of the most powerful Kingdoms in Southern India.

Raja Marthanda Varma led the Travancore forces during the Travancore-Dutch War from 1739 - 1746 (the most famous engagement of which being the Battle of Colachel on August 10, 1741), which marks the first decisive victory by an Asian kingdom over a major European power. Raja Marthanda Varma then went on to unify most of the provinces of the native princes who had allied themselves with the Dutch against him.

During Dharma Raja's reign, Travancore itself was attacked byTipu Sultan and the Travancore Army, which had been modernised and trained by D'Lennoy, the commander-in-chief (Valia Kappithan) of Raja Marthanda Varma, successfully defended the country from Tipu's numerically superior forces. This attack led to Travancore joining the British against Tipu in the Third Battle of Carnatic.

The warrior clan of Nairs under the leadership of various nobles and princes like "Pazhsi Raja, Velu Thampi Dalava and Paliath Achan" also fought against British East India company on occasions, but lost to the superior arms, tactics and discipline of the Company's armies. Travancore became an ally of the British in 1805 following a treaty between Col. Maculay and Diwan Velu Tampi, and remained so until 1947 when it merged with India.

Kingdom of Mysore

Hyder Ali was instructed by French military officers. He was one of the first Indian rulers to use rockets. He used iron rockets to defeat a top British unit in battle. His son, Tipu Sultan was also instructed by French military officers. Tipu participated in First Anglo-Maratha War of 1775–1779. He defeated the Brathwaite on the banks of the Coleroon in February 1782 in the Second Mysore War. After his father's death in 1782, he decided to check British advances by forming alliances with the Marathas and the Mughals. However, his plan wasn't successful. So, he turned to France.

In 1789, he invaded the state of Travancore, a British protectorate. However, he didn't receive expected help from France (the French were embroiled in the French Revolution) and Mysore was defeated in what is now known as the Third Mysore War. Tipu Sultan died in the Fourth Mysore War. Although Horatio Nelson crushed Napoleon's ambitions of advancing to India at the Battle of the Nile, three armies - one from Bombay, and two British (one of which was commanded by Arthur Wellesley), marched into Mysore in 1799 and besieged the capital, Srirangapatnam. On May 4, 1799, the armies broke through the defending walls and Tipu died of a gunshot wound near the gates of his fortress.

Main wars:

- First Mysore War, 1766
- Second Mysore War
- Third Mysore War, 1789-1792
- Fourth Mysore War, 1799

Punjab

Maharaja Ranjit Singh, also called "Sher-e-Punjab" ("The Lion of the Punjab") (1780-1839) was a Sikh ruler of the sovereign country of Punjab and the Sikh Empire. His Samadhi is located in Lahore, Pakistan. Ranjit Singh was a Sikh born in 1780 in Gujranwala in modern day Pakistan, into the Sansi-Sandhawalia family. At the time much of Punjab was ruled by the Sikhs, who had divided the territory among factions known as misls. Ranjit Singh's father Maha Singh was the commander of the Sukerchakia misl and controlled a territory in west Punjab based around his headquarters at Gujranwala. Ranjit Singh succeeded his father at the young age of 12. After several campaigns, his rivals accepted him as their leader, and he united the Sikh factions into one state and he took the title of **Maharaja** on April 13, 1801 (to coincide with Baisakhi day), with Lahore having served as his capital from 1799. In 1802 he took the holy city of Amritsar.

Maharaja Ranjit Singh also hired European mercenaries to train his troops, creating a powerful military force whose presence delayed the eventual British colonization of Punjab. He also modernized his army, hiring European mercenaries to create the first modern Indian Army. The effect was to create a powerful and heavily armed state; at this point, **Punjab was the only state not controlled by the British.** He brought law and order, yet was reluctant to use the death penalty. He stopped Indian non-secular style practises by treating Hindus and Muslims equally. He banned the discriminatory "jizya" tax on Hindus and Sikhs.

Maharaja Ranjit Singh died in 1839 and the state went to his eldest son Kharak Singh.

The Kingdom, that he had worked so hard to build, began to crumble due to poor governance and political mismanagement by his heirs. His successors died through accidents and murder, while the nobility and army struggled for power till the end of the Second Anglo-Sikh War(1848-49), when it was annexed by the British from his youngest son Duleep Singh. However, after the First Anglo-Sikh War(1845-46), Punjab effectively ceased to be an independent state and in 1849 was annexed by the British and all major decisions where made by the British Empire.

- Maharaja Ranjit Singh (b.1780, Crowned April 13, 1801, d.1839)
- Kharak Singh (b.1801, d.1840), Eldest son of Ranjit Singh.
- Nau Nihal Singh (b.1821, d.1840), Grandson of Ranjit Singh.
- Sher Singh (b.1807, d.1843), Son of Ranjit Singh.
- Duleep Singh (b.1838, Crowned 1843, d.1893), Youngest son of Ranjit Singh.

The British Empire annexed Punjab in c.1845-49 AD; after two Anglo Sikh Wars

- The First Anglo-Sikh War (1845–1846)
- The Second Anglo-Sikh War (1848-1849)

THE NAPOLEONIC WARS

Company Rule

The British Indian Army was raised to guard the factories. Later, it grew into the army of John Company Bahadur, and subsequently grew into Presidency armies of Bengal, Madras and Bombay in 1795, after the fall of French Pondicherry in 1793. The Dutch trained the military of the princely state of Travancore called the Nair Brigade.

The 1857 Sepoy War

After 1857, the Presidency Armies were abolished. Many of the existing units were disbanded or reorganised. New units were inducted into the newly formed British Indian Army such as the Sikhs, Gurkhas and irregular horse.

The majority of the Madras Native Infantry and Cavalry had their class compositions changed to North Indian tribes, considered more 'martial' to the darker, shorter 'thambis' who were the majority class of the Madras Presidency Army. This was in direct contradiction to the military reputation and many battle honours won by the 'thambis' both in India and abroad. The British Indian Army came under the control of the Crown and the Viceroy.

The British Raj

The British Raj or British India, officially the British Indian Empire, and internationally and contemporaneously, India, was the term used synonymously for the region, the rule, and the period, from 1858 to 1947, of the British Empire on the Indian subcontinent. The region included areas directly administered by the United Kingdom (contemporaneously, "British India") as well as the princely states ruled by individual rulers under the paramountcy of the British Crown.

The princely states, which had all entered into treaty arrangements with the British Crown, were allowed a degree of local autonomy in exchange for protection and representation in international affairs by Great Britain. The British *Indian Empire* included the regions of present-day India, Pakistan, and Bangladesh, and, in addition, at various times, Aden (from 1839 to 1937), Lower Burma (from 1852 to 1937), Upper Burma (from 1886 to 1937), British Somaliland (briefly from 1884 to 1898), and Singapore (briefly from 1819 to 1867). British India had some ties with British possessions in the Middle East; the Indian rupee served as the currency in many parts of that region. What is now Iraq was, immediately after World War I, administered by the India Office of the British government.

The Indian Air Force was established in 1932.

The British-Indian Army

The British-Indian army contained members of all the major religious groups in India, it contained Hindus, Sikhs, Christians, and Muslims. The number of Sikhs in the army grew steadily with time because they were considered less biased, less drastic in dealing with the different Indian cultural and religious sects and less likely to challenge their British superiors. This was especially true after the

Sepoy Rebellion where they were less active in the rebellion and almost absent from it. The reason for their absence was the recent attacks by the Britishers to take over Punjab and two Sikh Wars (1846 and 1849) in which the Bengalis, Biharis, Purbais and the Marathas helped and abated the British Empire, as well as the fact that they had fought to remain independent from the Mughal Empire the rebels wished to restore.

The World Wars

The British Indian Army's strength was about 189,000 in 1939. There were about 3,000 British officers and 1,115 Indian officers. The army was expanded greatly to fight in World War II. By 1945, the strength of the Army had risen to about two and a half million. There were about 34,500 British officers and 15,740 Indian officers. The Army took part in campaigns in France, East Africa, North Africa, Syria, Tunisia, Malaya, Burma, Greece, Sicily and Italy. It suffered 179,935 casualties in the war (including killed (24,338), wounded (64,354), missing (11,762) and POW (79,481) soldiers).

WORLD WAR I

List of Indian Divisions in World War I

During WWI the Sikh battalions fought in Egypt, Palestine, Mesopotamia, Gallipoli and France. The 14th Ferozepore Sikhs were in Gallipoli in April 1915 and fought in a number of battles in the Gallipoli campaign . After Gallipoli the battalion was in the Persian Gulf region and took part in some fierce fighting on the Tigris River. The 15th Ludhiana Sikhs were in France in September 1914 and participated in fighting at Fauquissart, Festubert and Neuve Chapelle.

WORLD WAR II

India was an active participant in the World War II as a part of the British Empire, and was a major contributor of troops and resources to the war effort. Indian units and troops fought in almost all the major campaigns in which the British were involved, and presented an excellent account of themselves. Of particular significance were the campaigns against the Italians in Abyssinia and North africa, against the Germans in North Africa and Italy, especially the Allied victory at El-Alamein and the Burma Campaign as a whole.

Azad Hind Fauj

Azad Hind Fauj, also known as the Indian National Army was led by prominent freedom fighter Netaji Subhash Chandra Bose and his Axis recognized Provisional Government of Free India. As repeated promises by the British to grant independence failed to surface, Bose backed by the forces of Germany and Japan led the INA to liberation of Burma in their march to northeastern India and the Andaman and Nicobar Islands.

Republic of India

The Republic of India has fought three wars and one major incursion battle with Pakistan and one border war with China.

MAJOR WARS

First Indo-Pak War, 1947

Independent India, formed on August 15, 1947, has seen three wars with Pakistan (1947-48, 1965, 1971). The first war took place after Pakistani soldiers and armed tribesmen invaded the independent province of Kashmir. When the forces almost reached the capital Srinagar the Maharaja, Hari Singh, and the democratically elected Prime Minister of Kashmir, Sheikh Abdullah, signed an agreement with India in which all Kashmiri lands were ceded to India. India sent their troops in shortly after and freed a majority of the new Indian state of Jammu and Kashmir from Pakistani inflitrators.

Sino-Indian War, 1962

India fought a border war against China (1962). China won the border skirmish, leading India to revamp the entire military system.

After the war ended, the Department of Defence Production was set up to create an indigenous defence production base which is self-reliant and self-sufficient. Since 1962, 16 new ordinance factories have been set up.

Second Indo-Pak War, 1965

The second Indo-Pak war was also fought over Kashmir issue. It ended in with Indian forces gaining chunks of lands all around except Punjab where it was even. USSR interfered and got the truce between the two nations at Tashkent agreement, which also saw the mysterious death of Indian PM Lal Bahadur Shastri. At the same time, there was the possibility of a second Sino-Indian war along the Nathu La Pass in Sikkim.

Ten battalions of the Sikh Regiment saw action in the 1965 war. In a bid to seal off routes of infiltrations for the Pakistanis in J & K, 1 Sikh who were in the Tithwal sector attacked Pakistani positions . A company led by Major Somesh Kapur captured Richhmar Ridge on 24 August 1965 and then attacked and captured the Pir Sahiba feature on the night of 25/26 August. From this feature the Indian troops could now overlook an extensive area under Pakistan control. Through out September, Pakistani troops tried hard to recapture this feature but were unsuccessful. 1 Sikh received 3 Vir Chakras (Major Somesh Kapur and L/ Havildar Gurdev Singh and Sepoy Gurmel Singh (posth.)) for these operations

The Chola Incident

A Sino-India skirmish took place in 1967 and is known today as the Chola Incident.

Third Indo-Pak War, 1971

In the third Indo-Pak war, India intervened decisively in what was then East Pakistan due to the mass exodus of refugees to India following West Pakistani military action there. The new nation of

Bangladesh was created as a result. India succeeded in removing Pakistani soldiers from what is now known as "East Pakistan" resulting in the formation of Bangladesh. This conflict is often cited as India's greatest military victory, but also among the greatest genocides of the 20th century wherein Pakistani forces slaughtered anywhere from 1 million to 3 million Bangladeshi's, the vast majority being Hindu.

Siachin War, 1984

The Siachin war between India and Pakistan occurred in 1984. The area of the dispute was the Siachen Glacier - the world's highest battlefield. The Glacier was under territorial dispute, but in the late 1970s and early 1980s, Pakistan began organizing several tourist expeditions to the Glacier. India, irked by this development, mounted Operation Meghdoot, and captured the top of the Glacier by establishing a military base which it still maintains to this day at a cost of more than US$1 million per day. Pakistan on the other hand spends just under US$1 million per day, though as % of GDP Pakistan spends 5 times as the Indian Military does to maintain its share of the glacier. Pakistan tried in 1987 and in 1989 to re-take the Glacier but was unsuccessful. A stalemate has arose where India controls the top part of the Glacier and Pakistan is placed at the bottom of the Glacier.

Kargil War, 1999

India fought a brief border skirmish with Pakistan in the Indian state of Kashmir in 1999. Dubbed the Kargil War, after the infiltration of Pakistani soldiers and paramilitary in the Kargil area, India reclaimed the territory through military and diplomatic channels. Pakistan lost 4000 soldiers, while India lost a little over 500.

By 21 May, the Indian army had isolated Tiger Hill from three directions, east, north and south. In order to inflict casualties the enemy positions on Tiger Hill were subjected to artillery and mortar fire.

A fresh battalion of well known Gurkhas viz. 18 Grenadiers was brought in to capture the peak with regiments holding the firm base. On the night of July 3, 18 Grenadiers captured the eastern slope but further advance was held up due to effective enemy fire from Helmet Top, India Gate features on the western slope. By morning July 4th Tiger Hill was captured by the 18th Grenadiers, effectively ending Pakistan's Kargil War.

OTHER OPERATIONS

Sri Lanka Mission, 1987-1990

The Indian Peace Keeping Force (IPKF) carried out a mission in northern and eastern Sri Lanka, in 1987–1990 to disarm the LTTE as per the Indo-Sri Lanka accord. In what was labeled as *Operation Pawan*, the Indian Air Force flew about 70,000 sorties to and within Sri Lanka, without a single aircraft lost or mission aborted.

Operation Cactus, 1988

In November 1988, the Maldives Government appealed India for military help against a mercenary invasion. On the night of November 3, 1988, the Indian Air Force airlifted a parachute battalion group from Agra and flew them non-stop over 2000 km to Maldives. The Indian paratroopers landed at Hulule, secured the airfield and restored the Government rule at Malé within hours. The brief, bloodless operation showed the capability of the Indian Air Force in what was labeled as *Operation Cactus*.

Missile program

India has a well developed missile capabilities, which traces its roots to the Indian Space Program.

Integrated Guided Missile Development Program (IGMDP)

The Integrated Guided Missile Development Program (IGMDP) was formed in 1983 with the aim of achieving self-sufficiency in missile development & production. Presently it comprises five core missile programs

- Agni ballistic missile
- Prithvi ballistic missile
- Akash surface-to-air missile
- Trishul surface-to-air missile
- Nag anti-tank guided missile

This program has given India self reliance in Missile development. So, attempts like Missile Technology Control Regime (MTCR) to control access to and availability of advanced weapon systems for developing nations are not a major concern for India now.

NUCLEAR PROGRAM

Smiling Buddha, 1974

In 1966, India had declared that it can produce nuclear weapons within 18 months. In 1974, India tested a device of up to 15 kilotons. The test was a "peaceful nuclear explosion" and was codenamed "Operation Smiling Buddha".

Operation Shakti (nuclear tests, 1998)

On May 11 and May 13, 1998, India conducted five underground nuclear tests (3 on May 11 and 2 on May 13) and declared itself a nuclear state.

Overview and Recent Developments

The Indian military today ranks as the world's third largest after the USA and China in terms of troops. Over a million strong, the paramilitary unit of the Republic of India is the world's largest and most elite paramilitary force. Eager to portray itself as a potential superpower, India began an intense phase of modernization and upgradation of its armed forces in the late 1990s. India is focusing more on developing indigenous military equipments rather than relying on other countries for military supplies. This change in policy has paid off well for the Indian Armed Forces. Most of the Indian naval ships and submarines, military armoured vehicles, missiles and ammunition are indigenously designed and manufactured.

Military Collaborations with other States

Apart from diverting resources towards indigenously manufacturing military equipment, the Indian Government is also focusing on collaborating with other countries to develop cutting-edge military technology and weapons. Jointly developed by Russia and India, one of the the world's most advanced supersonic cruise missiles, known as the BrahMos, was successfully test-fired in 2001.

In 1997, India agreed to participate in the development of Russia's *Prospective Air Complex for Tactical Air Forces* program. One of the primary objectives of the program is to develop a 5th generation fighter aircraft, a prototype of which, known as the Su-47, flew its first successful test-flight in 1997. India is also collaborating with Israel to develop Unmanned Aerial Vehicles.

India is now focusing on purchasing the technology behind the military equipment rather than the military equipment. Recent examples of the successful implementation of this Indian policy include the purchase of Sukhoi Su-30 MKI multi-role fighter aircraft and T-90 main battle tanks from Russia and diesel-powered Scorpene submarines from France. In 2004, India purchased US$ 5.7 billion worth of military equipment from other countries, making it the developing world's leading arms-purchaser.

Disasters

On April 28, 2000, ammunition worth Rs. 393 crore was destroyed due to a fire at the Bharatpur ammunition depot. Another fire at Pathankot sub-depot resulted in loss of ammo worth Rs. 27.39 crore. On May 24, 2001, another blaze at the Birdhwal sub-depot destroyed ammunition worth Rs. 378 crore.

Awards

In Independent India, the gallantry awards for exemplary display of bravery in war time are the Param Vir Chakra, Maha Vir Chakra and Vir Chakra in the decreasing order of importance. Their peace time equivalents are the Ashoka Chakra, Kirti Chakra and Shaurya Chakra. The latter two awards were formerly known as *Ashoka Chakra, Class II* and *Ashoka Chakra, Class III* respectively. Sometimes, the peace time awards are bestowed on civilians as well. For meritorious service, the awards are *Param Vishisht Seva Medal*, *Athi Vishisht Seva Medal* and *Vishisht Seva Medal* in decreasing order of importance.

2

PAKISTAN AND ITS ARMY

Pakistan is a poor country riven with ethnic and religious tensions. Pakistan enjoys close ties with China and shares an antipathy and distrust of India. Half of Pakistan disappeared following its disastrous 1971 war with India.

The Pakistan Army is the largest branch of the Pakistan Armed Forces, and is mainly responsible for protection of the state borders, the security of administered territories and defending the national interests of Pakistan within the framework of its international obligations. The Pakistan Army a total strength of 520,000, about the size of the Army of the United States, with a reserve element of 500,000 who have a reserve obligation up to the age of 45 years. Reserve status lasted for eight years after leaving active service or until age forty-five for enlisted men and age fifty for officers.

The Pakistan Army structure in many ways has a close resemblance to the British Indian Army structure at the end of the nineteenth century. During that period, recruitment into individual, homogeneous regiments depended on class and caste, rather than on territory. Over time, these regiments became sources of immense pride to the men who served in them and to the ethnic group from which they were frequently recruited. Service in a specific regiment passed from father to son; the eventual shift from British to Pakistani rule went with hardly a ripple in the structure except for the change in nationality of the senior officer corps.

The British experimented with various forms of recruitment and of elevation to officer rank. During the period between the two world wars (1919-39), the British trained Indian officers to command at least Indian troops, and training establishments were set up to produce an indigenous officer corps. A small number of officer candidates were sent to Britain to the Royal Military Academy at Sandhurst; after 1932 the majority of candidates were trained at the Indian Military Academy at Dehra Dun.

A rank that predated that of the native officer was the viceroy's commissioned officer—an Indian who had risen from the ranks and performed officer functions (except for commanding officer), especially at the company level. The viceroy's commissioned officer came from the same social background as did the troops in his unit and performed a dual function: for the troops, he was a role model and figure of respect to whom they could turn for advice; he was also an invaluable intermediary between the troops and the British officer who commanded them.

The Pakistani military upon independence immediately became a central part of the national consciousness. Unlike their Indian counterparts, Pakistani soldiers did not bear the stigma of being antinational. The main base of army recruitment, Punjab, was at the heart of Pakistan, and the army was immediately called upon to defend the interests of the nation against a perceived security threat from "Hindu India."

The Pakistani army was fortunate in its political position, but less so in regard to the experience and technical expertise required to field an effective military force. Muslims had been significantly underrepresented in the Indian officer corps, and when partition occurred, there was a severe shortage of personnel. To lead the planned army of 150,000 men, 4,000 officers were needed, but there were only 2,500, and many of those, especially in the technical services, were underqualified. Only one major general, two brigadiers, and six colonels were available, and in the middle officer ranks the situation was equally bad. The first two commanders in chief of the army were British. The first Pakistani commander in chief—General Mohammad Ayub Khan—did not become commander in chief of the army until 1951.

Since the founding of Pakistan, the army has been key in holding the state together, promoting a feeling of nationhood among disparate peoples and providing a bastion of selfless service in the midst of a venal government system. All too frequently, the Pakistan Army has felt the need to take over the government, cleanse it of corruption and try to reform its bureaucracy before returning it to civilian control. Army control of the government has all too often led to a corrupt military regime that eventually collapsed.

The key holder of power in the armed forces and, along with the president and the prime minister, one of the triumvirate that runs the country is the chief of the army staff (COAS) — formerly called the commander in chief. The COAS operates from army headquarters in Rawalpindi, near Islamabad. From this position, Ayub Khan, Zia and Musharef all seized power.

Other senior staff positions, at the lieutenant general level, include a chief of general staff, who supervises army intelligence and operations; the master general of ordnance; the quartermaster general; the adjutant general; the inspector general for evaluation and training; and the military secretary. The headquarters function also includes the chief of the Corps of Engineers, the judge advocate general, and the comptroller of civilian personnel, all of whom report to the vice chief of the army staff.

The 20 Infantry & 2 Armored Divisions are grouped under 9 different Corps headquarters commanded by 3-star Lieutenant Generals. These are:

I Corps (Mangla)

II Corps (Multan)

IV Corps (Lahore)

V Corps (Karachi)

X Corps (Rawalpindi)

XI Corps (Peshawar)

XII Corps (Quetta)

XXX Corps (Gujranwala)

XXXI Corps (Bahawalpur)

There is also the Northern Area Command, headquartered at Gilgit, directly responsible to army general headquarters.

There is an army reserve of 500,000 whose members have a triennial attendance obligation to the age of 45. Refresher training is as adequate as can be expected of a three week period, but reserve service seems popular. Paramilitary organizations, which were mainly of symbolic importance, included the 185,000-member National Guard, comprising the Janbaz Force — locally recruited militia mainly charged with air defense — and two programs similar to the United States Reserve Officers Training Corps, the National Cadet Corps and the Women Guard.

The Women Guard, unlike the National Cadet Corps, included individuals trained in nursing, welfare, and clerical work. There were also some women in the Janbaz Force, and a very small number of women were recruited into the regular service in limited numbers to perform medical and educational work. The 180,000 strong National Guard would be useful in guarding vulnerable points. It consists of the Mujahid Force of 60,000, organized in battalions, some with light air defence capability, the Janbaz Force of 100,000, whose members are intended to serve close to their homes; and the National Cadet Corps in universities and colleges.

Pakistan has been faced with continuing dilemma of providing a credible defense in the face of large standing armed forces of the Indian adversary. Ideally, Pakistan would have a large, well trained and equipped standing army to provide effective deterrence. This Pakistan cannot afford. The only other way to fill the wide gap between the forces required and the force available is to have an effective organization of auxiliary forces which should be capable of supporting and supplementing the efforts of the regular standing army, during peace and war. In Pakistan, the requirement of such forces has been met to some extent by the Civil Armed Forces and the Organization of the National Guards with the passage of an Act of Parliament on 13 August 1973.

Every male citizen of Pakistan who is of such age as may be prescribed, may offer himself for enrolment in the Mujahid Force for service in any unit and any such person, who satisfies the conditions laid down in the Regulations may be enrolled for such period as laid down in the terms of service. Every Person enrolled shall, without unnecessary delay, be appointed in a unit to which he has applied for service. Every person offering himself for enrolment in the force shall be a male citizen of Pakistan between 18 to 30 years of age. Maximum age limit for ex servicemen is relaxable to 45 years. A large number of people of Azad Kashmir are serving in the Mujahid Force. After retirement they are denied the facilities of ex-Servicemen which is not justified.

Paramilitary internal security forces were organized on the provincial level but were subordinate to the Ministry of Interior and were commanded by seconded army generals. These forces were in effect an extension of the army for internal security duties. The Pakistan Rangers, headquartered in Lahore, dealt with unrest in Punjab, while the Mehran Force performed similar functions in Sindh.

In 1994 their strengths were 25,000 and 24,000, respectively, divided into "wings" of approximately 800 men each. The Frontier Corps, with a strength of 65,000, was based in Peshawar and Quetta with responsibility for the North-West Frontier Province and Balochistan. The corps was responsible to both the Ministry of States and Frontier Regions and to army headquarters. The corps was divided into twenty-seven local units—fourteen in the North-West Frontier Province and thirteen in Balochistan—and included the Chitral Scouts, the Khyber Rifles, the Kurram Militia, the Tochi Scouts, the South Waziristan Scouts, the Zhob Militia, and the Gilgit

Scouts. There was also a Coast Guard, subordinate to the Ministry of Interior and staffed by army personnel.

In times of natural disaster army engineers, medical and logistics personnel, and the armed forces played a major role in bringing relief and supplies. The army also engaged in extensive economic activities. Most of these enterprises, such as stud and dairy farms, were for the army's own use, but others performed functions beneficial to the local civilian economy. Army factories produced such goods as sugar, fertilizer, and brass castings and sold them to civilian consumers.

The Pakistan military also assists in natural disasters in Pakistan such as the great floods of 1992, the floods in Balochistan in 2008 and the October 2005-devastating Kashmir earthquake; army engineers, medical and logistics personnel, and the armed forces played a major role in bringing relief and supplies. In natural disasters there was no significant second wave of deaths from injury, cold, food shortages, or disease. And much credit for that probably goes to Pakistan Army.

Perhaps more than anything else, the quake relief effort demonstrated the growing importance of military forces in responding to disasters. The entire fleet of Army Aviation flew innumerable sorties round the clock to take relief goods to the affected areas and brought back sick and injured back to base hospitals. Where helicopters could not reach, men carried relief goods on their back and reached the needy. The undertaking of relief operation of this magnitude could only be taken by the men and machines of the Armed Forces of Pakistan. There are reports that the United Nations recommended the Pakistan military form a standby team to respond in disasters. Integrated military-civilian responses are most likely to be successful in natural disasters.

Several army organizations performed functions that were important to the civilian sector across the country. For example, the National Logistics Cell was responsible for trucking food and other goods across the country, the Frontier Works Organization built the

Karakoram Highway to China, the Makran Coastal Highway, flood relief operations etcetera and the Special Communication Organization maintained communications networks in remote parts of Pakistan.

Pakistan Army is involved in relief activities not only in Pakistan but also in many other countries of the world, like they went for relief activities after Bangladesh was recently hit by floods. Pak Army also went to Indonesia, Bangladesh and Sri Lanka after they were hit by tsunami. Pakistan army and Navy sent ships and helicopters to the friendly nations for tsunami relief operation.

The army also engaged in extensive economic activities. Most of these enterprises, such as stud and dairy farms, were for the army's own use, but others performed functions beneficial to the local civilian economy. Army factories produced such goods as sugar, fertilizer, and brass castings and sold them to civilian consumers.

The Pakistani Army is a volunteer force and has been involved in many conflicts with India. Combined with this rich combat experience, the Army is also actively involved in contributing to United Nations peacekeeping efforts. Other foreign deployments have consisted of Pakistani Army personnel as advisers in many African, South Asian and Arab countries. Since the September 11th terrorist attacks, Pakistani military forces have been extensively engaged in the War on Terrorism against Taliban and Al Qaeda extremists. Over 90,000 troops along with various paramilitary forces are involved in a protracted fight against extremists in the tribal areas of Pakistan. It is more important than ever for the army to build bridges with civilians, as success in fighting extremism and terrorism is dependent on this.

Army also provides opportunity to women to serve in the Pakistan Army. Currently, there are a sizable number of Women serving in the army. The army sees itself as a national institution and thus many non-Muslim officers (including Qadiyanis) have achieved high ranks within the army. The army in Pakistan is most organized and powerful institution of a state, like all capitalist states, has the fundamental role of preserving and protecting the assets, social status, privileges and economic exploitation of the local ruling and imperialism. The role of the military becomes more contentious as the immediate life-saving phase of an aid operation ends and the reconstruction phase takes over. It is therefore important for military actors to not only develop their capacity to respond to disasters, but also to develop their capacity to exit from disaster responses.

I CORPS

I Corps, headquartered in Mangla, is also called Army Reserve North. It consists of one armored and one regular infantry division, with another infantry division that may be mechanized. The Corps is certainly supported by one independent tank brigade and one independent anti-tank brigade [which is often refered to as a mechanized infantry brigade]. Some sources report that two additional independent brigades, including one of artillery, are part of this Corps. HQ I Corps was raised on 1st July 1957 at Abbottabad. At the time of the 1965 war with India, Pakistan had only one corps HQ [I Corps at Mangla] with plans for a new IV Corps (at Lahore). XXX Corps was formed in 1986-87 from elements previously assigned to I Corps, which became a Reserve/Strike Corps, with the I Corps area of the front with India being transferred to the new XXX Corps.

	City	Latitude	Longitude
I Corps	Mangla	33°07'N	73°39'E
11th Ind Armored BDE	U/I Location	__°__'N	__°__'E
U/I BDE	U/I Location	__°__'N	__°__'E
U/I Artillery BDE	U/I Location	__°__'N	__°__'E
U/I Anti-tank BDE	U/I Location	__°__'N	__°__'E
6th Armored Division	Mangla	33°07'N	73°39'E
17th Infantry Division	Kharian	32°49'N	73°52'E
35th Infantry Division	Gujranwala	__°__'N	__°__'E

II Corps

II Corps, headquartered in Multan since it was set up in mid 1971, is also designated Army Reserve South. XXXI Corps was formed in 1986-87 from elements previously assigned to II Corps, which became a Reserve/Strike Corps, with the II Corps area of the front with India being transferred to the new XXXI Corps.

Most sources agree that II Corps consists of three divisions, and most agree that this includes one armored and two infantry divisions. One of the [infantry] divisions was formed recently.

At least one source, while affirming the 1 Armored and 14 Mech Divisions, also reports "2 Artillery Divisions". Most sources report that Pakistan's Army does not include Divisions of Artillery, though this reference is clearly attesting the presence of the "2nd Artillery" rather than two divisions.

	City	Latitude	Longitude
II Corps Multan	30°11'N	71°28'E	
U/I BDE	U/I Location	__°__'N	__°__'E
U/I Armored BDE	U/I Location	__°__'N	__°__'E
U/I Artillery BDE	U/I Location	__°__'N	__°__'E
U/I Anti-tank BDE	U/I Location	__°__'N	__°__'E
1st Armored Division	Multan	30°11'N	71°28'E
2nd Artillery Division	U/I Location	__°__'N	__°__'E
14th Infantry Division	U/I Location	__°__'N	__°__'E
40th Infantry Division	Okara	30°48'N	73°26'E

According to one source, as of early 2001 it was believed that one artillery division had been raised recently, though this had yet to be confirmed.

Another source reports only the 1 Armored and 14 Infantry Divisions, while reporting that 40 Infantry Division was assigned to V Corps as of early 2001. A newly formed 2nd Artillery may account for the recently formed division reported by some sources.

Some sources suggest that the Corps is supported by one tank brigade or by one Mechanised Infantry light Anti Tank Brigade, while other sources suggest as many as four supporting independent Brigades.

On 31 August 2000 Gen. Pervez Musharraf transfered Lt. Gen.Mohammad Yusaf (a Punjabi), GOC, 2 Corps, Multan, to the GHQ as the new CGS.

IV Corps

IV Corps, headquartered at Lahore, is responsible for the sector from Narowal to Sulemankie.

The IV Corps consists of at least two holding Infantry Divisions, as well as one independent tank brigade, and one or two other brigades, which may include one independent infantry brigade and/ or an independent artillery brigade.

According to some reports, as of early 2001 the 40 Infantry Division was stationed at Okara under IV Corps.

	City	Latitude	Longitude
IV Corps	Lahore	30°24'N	68°47'E
U/I Artillery BDE	U/I Location	__°__'N	__°__'E
3rd Ind Armored BDE	U/I Location	__°__'N	__°__'E
212th Infantry BDE	U/I Location	__°__'N	__°__'E
10th Infantry Division	Lahore	30°24'N	68°47'E
11th Infantry Division	Lahore	30°24'N	68°47'E

At the time of the 1965 war with India, Pakistan had only one corps HQ [I Corps at Mangla] with plans for a new IV Corps (at Lahore). IV Corps was raised after the 1965 War.

On 31 August 2000 Gen. Pervez Musharraf transfered Lt. Gen. Mohammad Aziz, a Kashmiri, from the post of the Chief of the General Staff (CGS) in the GHQ at Rawalpindi to that of GOC, 4 Corps, Lahore. In mid-October 2001 Pakistani President General Pervaiz Musharraf re-shuffled several key security positions.

Lieutenant General Mohammad Aziz Khan, an "Islamic soldier," was "promoted" as a four-star officer to the largely ceremonial post of Chairman of the Joint Chiefs of Staff Committee. Gen Aziz was the IV Corps commander in the strategically vital border city of Lahore.

V Corps

V Corps has been headquartered in Karachi since it was raised in 1975. All sources agree that it consists of at least one Division and at least one and probably at least two independent Brigades. Several sources suggest that it also includes a second ("holding") Division, possibly the 16 Infantry or 41 Infantry Division.

All sources agree that the Corps includes at least one Independent Armored Brigade. While some sources suggest that the independent brigades include one tank and one infantry independent brigades, other reports say there are two independent armored brigades, while others report an artillery brigade, for a total of as many as four independent brigades.

By early July 1999, during the Kargil conflict, Pakistan had moved most of its strike corps to the eastern border, forcing India to heighten the vigil across the LoC and the international border. Pakistan's XI corps and XII corps, which had been stationed in Peshawar and Quetta, were believed to have moved east, reinforcing the V corps in Karachi, whose role had been to intercept any Indian attempt to cut the Karachi-Lahore road.

The X corps at Rawalpindi was in position across the Line of Control in Kashmir, and the four mountain divisions near the LoC had been reinforced with the three brigades that have moved into Skardu. As of late 2000 the 5 Corps was commandded by Lt. Gen. Muzaffar Hussain Usmani (a Mohajir), one of the so-called "Mullas' Generals" or Islamised Generals, who reportedly worked during off-duty hours for the Tablighi Jamaat, an Islamic organisation which provided most of the jehadist volunteers for the Pakistan-based extremist organisations active in J & K in India.

With the move of XXXI Corps to Pannu Aquil the responsibility for Rahim Yar Khan-Sukkur had fallen to V Corps by early 2001. As such 16 Infantry Division could be allocated the task for either a local offensive in V Corps Sector or given the responsibility of the area South of Rahim Yar Khan. Most probably the former.

	City	Latitude	Longitude
V Corps Karachi	24°52'N	67°03'E	
31st Inf BDE (MECH)	Hyderabad	25°22'N	68°22'E
2nd Armored BDE	Hyderabad	25°22'N	68°22'E
U/I Armored BDE	U/I Location	__°__'N	__°__'E
U/I Artillery BDE	U/I Location	__°__'N	__°__'E
16th Infantry Division	Rahim Yar Khan	__°__'N	__°__'E
18th Infantry Division	Hyderabad	25°22'N	68°22'E

X Corps

Although Pakistan does not have a Corps headquarters in Kashmir [unlike India], X Corps has responsibility for Jammu and Kashmir. Some sources report that the Force Commander Northern Areas is the equivalent of a Division, and is subordinate to X Corps, while most sources agree that it is an independent Corp-equivalent command reporting directly to the Army headquarters.

The X Corps, which has been headquarterd in Rawalpindi since it was raised in 1974, consists of three holding infantry divisions allocated for Jammu and Kashmir. The 19th Infantry Division is reportedly responsible for the area between Kel and Jhelum.

These three divisions have a total of four extra brigades, above and beyond the nine [three times three] normally assigned to Pakistani Army divisions. In addition, there are at least one independent brigade, with some sources reporting two [one tank and one infantry], with possibly a third [artillery] brigade]. One of the first acts of Gen. Musharraf, after his appointment as the COAS by Mr. Nawaz Sharif in October, 1998, was to post Lt. Gen. Mahmud Ahmed, ethnicity not clear, but possibly a Pathan, who was then Commandant, National Defence College, as the GOC, 10 Corps.

	City	Latitude	Longitude
X Corps Rawalpindi	33°36'N	73°04'E	
111 Inf BDE (MECH)	Rawalpindi	33°36'N	73°04'E
8th Armored BDE	Kharian	__°__'N	__°__'E
U/I Artillery BDE	U/I Location	__°__'N	__°__'E
12th Infantry Division	Muzzafarabad	__°__'N	__°__'E
U/I BDE	U/I Location	__°__'N	__°__'E
U/I BDE	U/I Location	__°__'N	__°__'E
U/I BDE	U/I Location	__°__'N	__°__'E
U/I BDE	U/I Location	__°__'N	__°__'E
U/I BDE	U/I Location	__°__'N	__°__'E
U/I BDE	U/I Location	__°__'N	__°__'E
19th Infantry Division	Rawalkot [Jhelum ?]	34°47'N	73°30'E
U/I BDE	U/I Location	__°__'N	__°__'E
U/I BDE	U/I Location	__°__'N	__°__'E
U/I BDE	U/I Location	__°__'N	__°__'E
23rd Infantry Division	Mangla [Gujrat ?]	33°07'N	73°39'E
U/I BDE	U/I Location	__°__'N	__°__'E
U/I BDE	U/I Location	__°__'N	__°__'E
U/I BDE	U/I Location	__°__'N	__°__'E
U/I BDE	U/I Location	__°__'N	__°__'E

Following the 1999 military coup, Musharraf initially posted Lt.Gen. Mohammad Aziz [a Kashmiri], as the GOC, 10 Corps, but Qazi Hussain Ahmed of the Jamaat-e-Islami, and Maulana Fazlur Rahman of the Jamaat-ul-Ulema Pakistan criticised the proposed transfer of Lt.Gen. Aziz on the ground that this would weaken the so-called jehad in Kashmir. Gen. Musharraf, thereupon, cancelled his order and instead promoted Maj.Gen. Jamshaid Gulzar, the then head of the India Division in the ISI, as a Lt. Gen. and posted him as the GOC, 10 Corps.

During the five-year-long Taliban regime in Afghanistan, Pakistan had gained several advantages with a friendly neighbour at Kabul. It shifted large elements of its XI and XII Corps close to the Indian border in Jammu and Kashmir (J&K), Punjab and Rajasthan. The 9 Infantry Division of XI Corps had been deployed opposite Dras with Headquarters at Gulteri, under X Corps. In November 2001 it was reported that Pakistan had begun shifting elements of its forces from the Indian borders to its borders with Afghanistan. This was the first time in six years that troops had reverted to their original location under the XI Corps (Peshawar) and XII Corps (Quetta).

In December 2001 the Indian government ordered perhaps the largest post-Second World War military build-up, sending some three-quarters of India's 1.2 million soldiers on to offensive positions on the border with Pakstian. Pakistan responded by moving 10, 11 and 12 Corps from their Afghan frontier locations near Rawalpindi, Peshawar and Quetta to its eastern frontier with India.

XI Corps

The XI Corps, headquartered atn Peshawar in the North West Frontier Province bordering Afghanistan since it was raised in 1975, is sometimes referred to Army Reserve Center. It consists of two divisions, including one that replaced the division sent to FCNA. It reportedly also includes one independent brigade, though sources disagree as to whether this is an armor or artillery unit [most sources agree that it is an Independent Armored Brigade].

The XI Corps command was the primary support and logistic base for the Taliban. During the five-year-long Taliban regime in Afghanistan, Pakistan had gained several advantages with a friendly neighbour at Kabul. It shifted large elements of its XI and XII Corps close to the Indian border in Jammu and Kashmir (J&K), Punjab and Rajasthan. The 9 Infantry Division of XI Corps had been deployed opposite Dras with Headquarters at Gulteri, under X Corps.

By early July 1999, during the Kargil conflict, Pakistan had moved most of its strike corps to the eastern border, forcing India to heighten the vigil across the LoC and the international border. Pakistan's XI corps and XII corps, which had been stationed in Peshawar and Quetta, were believed to have moved east, reinforcing the V corps in Karachi, whose role had been to intercept any Indian attempt to cut the Karachi-Lahore road. The Pakistani concept of Riposte was neutralized, as the reserve formations were denuded of their forces, in that both XI Corps in Peshawar and XII Corps in Quetta were denuded of their divisions, with one in Afghanistan and the other in Jammu and Kashmir.

The X corps at Rawalpindi was in position across the Line of Control in Kashmir, and the four mountain divisions near the LoC had been reinforced with the three brigades that have moved into Skardu.

As of early 2001 it was reported that the 7 Infantry division from Mardan was moving under the command of Northern Areas Command [Force Command Northern Areas - FCNA], possibly to a location opposite Kargil in Kashmir. To make XI Corps viable after the move of 7 Infantry Division Pakistan would have to raise one more division.

In November 2001 it was reported that Pakistan had begun shifting elements of its forces from the Indian borders to its borders with Afghanistan. This was the first time in six years that troops had reverted to their original location under the XI Corps (Peshawar) and XII Corps (Quetta). As of late 2001 the 11 Corps was entrusted with the task of detecting the Al-Qaida activists who had fled Afghanistan in the wake of American airstrikes on Afghanistan.

In December 2001 the Indian government ordered perhaps the largest post-Second World War military build-up, sending some three-quarters of India's 1.2 million soldiers on to offensive positions on the border with Pakstian. Pakistan responded by moving 10, 11 and 12 Corps from their Afghan frontier locations near Rawalpindi, Peshawar and Quetta to its eastern frontier with India.

In mid-October 2001 Pakistani President General Pervaiz Musharraf re-shuffled several key security positions.

The new Inter Services Intelligence (ISI) chief was Lieutenant General Ehsanul Haq, former commander of the Peshawar-based 11 Corps. Although Gen Haq took charge of the Peshawar Corps only in May, he was familiar with Taliban bases, assets and secrets.

	City	Latitude	Longitude
XI Corps	Peshawar	34°00'N	71°33'E
U/I Armored BDE	U/I Location	__°__'N	__°__'E
7th Infantry Division	Mardan	34°12'N	72°02'E
9th Infantry Division	Rawalkot [Mardan ?]	34°47'N	73°30'E

XII Corps

XII Corps has been headquartered in Quetta since it was raised in 1984-85, and apparently consists of two infantry divisions. Unlike many other Corps, no independent brigades have been identified in association with 12 Corps, although one source suggests the possible presence of one Independent Armored or Independent Infantry Brigade. Differences between Nawaz Sharif and Ghulam Ishaq Khan started in the early 1990s due to Sharif's objection to Gen Abdul Wahid, Commander XII corps in Quetta who was appointed as the Army Chief, after Asif Nawaz passed away.

During the five-year-long Taliban regime in Afghanistan, Pakistan had gained several advantages with a friendly neighbour at Kabul. It shifted large elements of its XI and XII Corps close to the Indian border in Jammu and Kashmir (J&K), Punjab and Rajasthan.

By early July 1999, during the Kargil conflict, Pakistan had moved most of its strike corps to the eastern border, forcing India to heighten the vigil across the LoC and the international border.

Pakistan's XI corps and XII corps, which had been stationed in Peshawar and Quetta, were believed to have moved east, reinforcing the V corps in Karachi, whose role had been to intercept any Indian attempt to cut the Karachi-Lahore road. The X corps at Rawalpindi was in position across the Line of Control in Kashmir, and the four mountain divisions near the LoC had been reinforced with the three brigades that have moved into Skardu. The Pakistani concept of Riposte was neutralized, as the reserve formations were denuded of their forces, in that both XI Corps in Peshawar and XII Corps in Quetta were denuded of their divisions, with one in Afghanistan and the other in Jammu and Kashmir.

In the month preceding his coup, In the months before the coup, it had become clear to Gen. Musharraf that there was information being leaked to "the politicians" (particularly to Prime Minister Nawaz Sharif) from the monthly meetings of Corps Commanders. Gen. Musharraf told Prime Minister Nawaz Sharif that he wanted the suspect corps commander, Lt.-Gen. Tariq Pervaiz, of XII Corps, Quetta, removed. The Prime Minister said that this would be a lengthy process. Gen. Musharraf, as COAS, then moved within his jurisdiction to remove Lt.-Gen. Tariq Pervaiz from his post, and then retired him, without the Prime Minister's approval. Lt Gen. Tariq Parvez was sacked by Lt. Gen. Pervez Musharraf, Chief of Army Staff and Chairman of the Joint Chiefs of Staff Committee on 09 October 2001 for ill-discipline and disloyalty.

The composition of XII Corps appears to have undergone considerable evolution over time, reflecting the various deployments. As of early 2001 the Corps apparently consisted only of the 41 Infantry Division, and it was suggested that, to make this Corps a viable Corps, one more division will have to be raised, having lost 40 Infantry Division to IV Corps.

In November 2001 it was reported that Pakistan had begun shifting elements of its forces from the Indian borders to its borders with Afghanistan. This was the first time in six years that troops had reverted to their original location under the XI Corps (Peshawar) and XII Corps (Quetta). In December 2001 the Indian government ordered perhaps the largest post-Second World War military build-up, sending some three-quarters of India's 1.2 million soldiers on to offensive positions on the border with Pakstian. Pakistan responded by moving 10, 11 and 12 Corps from their Afghan frontier locations near Rawalpindi, Peshawar and Quetta to its eastern frontier with India.

	City	Latitude	Longitude
XII Corps	Quetta	__°__'N	__°__'E
U/I BDE	U/I Location	__°__'N	__°__'E
16th Infantry Division	U/I Location	__°__'N	__°__'E
33rd Infantry Division	U/I Location	__°__'N	__°__'E

XXX Corps

	City	Latitude	Longitude
XXX Corps	Sialkot	32°30'30"N	74°33'29"E
U/I Anti-tank BDE	U/I Location	__°__'N	__°__'E
2nd Ind Armored BDE	Rawalpindi	33°36'N	73°04'E
U/I Artillery BDE	U/I Location	__°__'N	__°__'E
8th Infantry Division	Sialkot	32°30'30"N	74°33'29"E
U/I BDE	U/I Location	__°__'N	__°__'E
U/I BDE	U/I Location	__°__'N	__°__'E
U/I BDE	U/I Location	__°__'N	__°__'E
15th Infantry Division	Sialkot	32°30'30"N	74°33'29"E
U/I BDE	U/I Location	__°__'N	__°__'E
U/I BDE	U/I Location	__°__'N	__°__'E
U/I BDE	U/I Location	__°__'N	__°__'E
U/I BDE	U/I Location	__°__'N	__°__'E

XXX Corps, headquartered at Sialkot, is reportedly responsible for the area between Jhelum and Narowal. It consists of two holding Infantry divisions with a total of at least seven brigades [versus the normal three for each division]. 15th Infantry Division is generally reported as having four brigades, while the 8th Infantry Division is various reported as having three or four. XXX Corps also includes at least one, and perhaps as many as three, independent brigades, certainly including one tank brigade, and with anti-tank and/or artillery independent brigades also reported.

XXX Corps was formed in 1986-87 from elements previously assigned to I Corps, which became a Reserve/Strike Corps, with the I Corps area of the front with India being transferred to the new XXX Corps.

XXXI Corps

XXXI Corps, headquartered at Bhawalpur [also reported as headquartered at Pannu Aquil], consists of two holding Infantry Divisions. One of these divisions is apparenty 37 Infantry Division, while the other is either 33 or [less probably] 40 Infantry Division. Sources generally agree that the Corps is supported by two independent brigades, but there is considerable divergence as to the composition of these two brigades.

Several sources suggest at least one Mechanised Infantry Heavy Anti Tank Brigade, as well as possibly one other Independent Brigade Group. At least one source claims an Independent Armored Brigade and an Artillery Brigade.

XXXI Corps was formed in 1986-87 from elements previously assigned to II Corps, which became a Reserve/Strike Corps, with the II Corps area of the front with India being transferred to the new XXXI Corps.

As of early 2001 it was reported that 37 Infantry Division had shifted from Bhawalpur to Sukkur. It had the responsibility for Sukkur-Rahim Yar Khan. This move threw open the area between Rahim Yar Khan and Fort Abbas, which would have to be covered by raising one more division. At that time, 33 Infantry Division was reported as likely to be moved from Bhawalpur, and could be employed for local offensive or provide depth to 37 Infantry division in the region of Sukkur-Rahim Yar Khan or along the Islamgarh-Kishengarh axis.

	City	Latitude	Longitude
XXXI Corps	Bhawalpur		
	[Pannu Aquil ?]	__°__'N	__°__'E
13th Ind Armored BDE	U/I Location	__°__'N	__°__'E
101st Ind BDE Group	U/I Location	__°__'N	__°__'E
33rd Infantry Division	Bhawalpur(?)	__°__'N	__°__'E
37th Infantry Division	Sukkur	__°__'N	__°__'E

Northern Area Command

The Northern Area Command, also known as Force Command Northern Areas [FCNA], is headquatered at Gilgit. After 1999 it has apparently functioned as the equivalent of a Corps command.

Some sources report that the Force Commander Northern Areas is the equivalent of a Division, and is subordinate to X Corps, while most sources agree that as of early 2002 it was an independent Corp-equivalent command reporting directly to the Army headquarters.

Sources differ as to the composition of the command, with some reporting one division and four independent brigades, while others sugges a total of five independent brigades. Apparently, as of early 2001 it was reported that the 7 Infantry division from Mardan was moving from the command of XI Corps in Peshawar to the command of Northern Areas Command, possibly to a location opposite Kargil in Kashmir.

	City	Latitude	Longitude
Northern Area Command	Gilgit, Kashmir	35°55'N	74°18'E
80th Inf BDE	Astor	35°22'N	74°51'E
150th Inf BDE	Gilgit	35°55'N	74°18'E
323rd Siachen Inf BDE	U/I Location	__°__'N	__°__'E
62nd Inf BDE	Skardu	35°18'N	75°37'E
61st Inf BDE	U/I Location	__°__'N	__°__'E
7th Infantry Division	U/I Location	34°12'N	72°02'E

Army Aviation Corps

Pakistan Army Aviation gained autonomy from Pakistan Air Force in 1958, and gained full corps status in 1977. Auster Mk 5 and Mk 6 were used at first. In 1957 60 O-1 Bird Dogs were delivered from US which mostly replaced the Austers, making two frontline Air Observation Post (AOP) squadrons possible. More O-1s were later assembled at Army's 503 Workshop at Dhaimal, eventualy producing 60 percent of the components locally.

The Army also started maintaining its own aircraft as well after the aquisition of these aircraft. Army Aviation School opened in 1959. Some 18 Bell 47/ OH-13s joined the Army in 1964 after the helicopter trained Pakistan pilots returned from the USA. These aircraft allowed the formation of several composite units. These units were used during the 1965 Indo-Pakistan war for spotting, liason, and FAC. The Bell 47 is a grand old helicopter but it went out of production in 1973 and they have all but disappeared in the commercial world.

After the war Pakistan aquired 24 Alouette IIIs from Aerospatiale of France, some of them were assembled by the Army itself. These Alouettes have been joined by several others from different sources, including sixSA 315B Lamas from Romania in 1987. The Lamas are used for high-altitute operations in Siachin and Karakoram.

Medium-lift capability came with the procurement of 12 Mil Mi-8s. These were used in rescue and disaster operations in East Pakistan along with Alouette IIIs. Both of the types also saw some action during the War of 1971 in East Pakistan and were withdrawn from the theatre through Burma (Myanmar).

The US supplied six UH-1Hs as a gift for future disaster relief operations in 1973. In 1974 Iran donated 10 AB 205As. The same year Saab MFI-17s were inducted for training and liason. The initial batch numbered 115, of them 23 were delivered as complete aircraft the rest in kit form to be assembled at Risalpur. These aircraft are locally called Mushshak. The production of this type was transferred from Sweden to Kamra, Pakistan. In 1975 12 Bell 206Bs were aquired from USA, and few JetRangers III joined them a few years later.

In 1976 the Army aquired 32 Aerospatiale SA 330J Pumas, which formed two new squadrons, and boosted the assault and medium-lift capability. Pakistan Army's requirement for armed attack helicopter was fulfilled in 1985. Two squadrons with ten AH-1S Cobras each were formed. These squadrons also operate a few Bell 206s as scouts. In 1997 Pakistan doubled its Mil Mi-8 inventory by aquiring 12 more in the form of Mil Mi-17 from CIS, half of these are seems to be located at Quetta. The location of the rest is unknown. The Army also operates Rockwell Turbo Commander 690s, a sigle Commander MA Jetprop 840 for surveys. And a single McDonnell Douglas MD-500E for Inter-Service Intelligence.

The force services of Pakistan made a choice of Mi-171 helicopter for a long time as a principal helicopter of middle / heavy class in its fleet. Pakistan purchased the first batch of Mi-171 helicopters from Ulan-Ude Aviation Plant in 2001 to fulfil the needs of its army aviation and air forces. The helicopters has proven to be adequate in operation and got a high valuation from Pakistani users. Pakistan Anti-Narcotics Force (ANF) enriched its fleet with two Mi-171 helicopters of Ulan-Ude Aviation Plant in 2008. The UK agreed to donate two Mi-17 helicopters and a spares packageto the value of up to £6 million to the Pakistan Anti-Narcotics Force (ANF) tobe used for counter narcotics activity on the Pakistan/ Afghan border. Funding for the gift was made available from Home Office capital budget for the Financial Year ending 31 March 2006. The helicopters provide the ANF with much needed independent aircapacity to help them conduct both operational and eradication related tasks. The UK had previously gifted Ml 17 helicopters to the Pakistan ANF in 1995. Both are out of service: one unfortunately crashed during the autumn 2005 earthquake, and the other was awaiting a major airframe overhaul. Without air assets, the ANF's ability to deploy effectively, and in a timely way is compromised.

On 24 September 2003, the Defense Security Cooperation Agency notified Congress of a possible Foreign Military Sale to Pakistan of Bell 407 Helicopters as well as associated equipment and services. The total value, if all options are exercised, could be as high as $97 million. The Government of Pakistan requested a possible sale of 40 Bell 407 helicopters with commercial avionics package, support equipment, spare/repair parts, publications/technical data, personnel training/equipment, and U.S. Government and contractor engineering and logistics support services, and other related elements of logistics support.

The proposed sale of Bell helicopters will have a significant impact on Pakistan's ability to secure its borders. At the same time, this technology poses no threat to the balance of power in the region. This proposed sale will have a dramatic impact on Pakistan's ability to support U.S. objectives in the Global War on Terror. The terrain along Pakistan's border is extremely rugged and difficult to secure. Its dense mountainous regions, rugged terrain and vast borders make it virtually impossible to secure without the mobility provided by aviation assets. Vehicle support is limited to utility trucks, and there is limited cross-country capability. The lack of mobility for observation, transportation and interdiction seriously limits Pakistan's ability to stop border-crossing violations. The addition of U.S. provided helicopters would add the following capabilities required for anti-terrorist and border security operations: (1) observation platforms to better patrol the mountainous border region, and (2) transportation platforms to move personnel to areas of suspected infiltrations.

In 2004, Pakistan and the US embarked on a long-term $235 million project to help build Army Aviation's capability. During the first phase of the project, Pakistan leased the helicopters while the US provided the resources, funding, training and support to help Pakistan establish a strong and reliable helicopter fleet. On 24 October 2007 the US formally handed over 26 Bell-412 helicopters and four completely refurbished Cobra helicopters to the Pakistan

Army. US Ambassador Anne Patterson handed the helicopters over to Defence Secretary Kamran Rasool. Rasool thanked the US government and said that the induction of these helicopters into the army would significantly enhance their operational capabilities. Speaking at the formalising ceremony of the final acceptance and transfer of 25 Bell-412 helicopters to the army at Qasim Airbase, Patterson praised Pakistan Army Aviation and said that the induction of these helicopters would strengthen their efforts to fight extremism and bring peace and stability to the region. She said the day marked a new chapter in Army Aviation's history. "This event demonstrates the continued commitment of the US to cooperation with Pakistan," Patterson said. "Our military assistance program are for the long term. They are the foundation for cooperation and engagement, and a way to strengthen our bonds as partners and allies."

On October 8, 2005, at about 8:35 am, worst ever earthquake in this region, measuring 7.6 on Richter scale, hit Islamabad, remote and mountainous areas of Kashmir and Pakistan's North West Frontier Province. It was estimated that more than 74,000 people died and about were 100,000 severely injured. All Aviation assets of the Pakistan Army Aviation were mobilized for relief and rescue operations. It was one of the biggest rescue operation which was undertaken by air due to badly damaged and almost non-existence of the road links. During the month of October 2005, Army Aviation and other Pilots flew over 4,000 hours to evacuate more than 1,00,000 victims of earthquake. More than 141 helicopters including those from allied friendly countries joined the rescue effort to shift more than 12,00,000 injured people to the hospitals. Till April, 2005, the entire Aviation fleet of helicopters had flown for 12,500 hours in affected areas for delivery of relief goods and rescue of injured persons.

On September 26, 2008 the Defense Security Cooperation Agency notified Congress of a possible Foreign Military Sale to Pakistan of AH-1F Cobra helicopter refurbishment as well as associated equipment and services. The total value, if all options are exercised, could be as high as $115 million. The Government of Pakistan requested a possible sale of refurbishment and maintenance of eight AH-1F Cobra Helicopters. The Government of Pakistan has also requested warranties, system integration, spare and repairs parts, including transportation for the parts, support equipment, personnel training and training equipment, publications and technical data, U.S. Government and contractor engineering and logistics support services, and other related elements of logistics support. The estimated cost is $115 million.

Army Aviation Corps.

VIP Flight Squadron, Rawalpindi - SA-330, KING-AIR 200, CITATION V, CESSNA 421, COMMANDER 690, COMMANDER 840, H-500 (special duties)

Aviation School and Centre, Rawalpindi (Qasim) - MUSHSHAK, ALOUETTE III, SCHWEIZER 300, BELL 206B, other on attachment.

2 Squadron, Lahore - MUSHSHAK, UH-1H.

3 Squadron, Multan - MUSHSHAK.

4 Squadron, HQ at Qasim (formerly known as Dhamial), - south of Rawalpindi. detachments at Rahwali, Gilget, Samugli (Quetta) - Mi-17.

5 Squadron, Qasim - ALOUETTE III.

6 Squadron, Qasim - UH-1H, Mi-17.

7 Squadron, Shahrae-Faisal - CESSNA O-1, MUSHSHAK.

8 Squadron, Qasim - SA 315/316 LAMA.

9 Squadron, Peshawar - CESSNA O-1(?), MUSHSHAK, ALOUETTE III

13 Squadron, Qasim - CESSNA O-1(?), MUSHSHAK, Y-12.

21 Squadron, Multan - PUMA, UH-IH.

24 Squadron, Multan - PUMA

25 Squadron, Dhamial (detachment at Gilget) - PUMA

31 Squadron, Multan - AH-1F COBRA ANTI-TANK.

32 Squadron, Multan - AH-1F COBRA ANTI-TANK.

Recent and Current Operations.

Internal Conflicts

The Pakistan Army maintains a high level of readiness in anticipation of any renewed conflict with India, but current military operations have focussed mainly on internal security and, more markedly, counter-insurgency operations.

Counter-terrorism/counter-insurgency operations are being carried out in the Federally Administered Tribal Areas (FATA) along the Afghan border, where over 100,000 army and Frontier Corps troops are deployed in North West Frontier Province (NWFP).

The low level insurgency in Balochistan, while primarily confronted by the paramilitary Frontier Corps, also involves the army's X Corps, HQ Quetta (temporary).

UN Contributions: As of August 2008, Pakistan has over 10,000 troops on UN peacekeeping service, contributing troops or military observers to 12 missions:

BINUB (Berundi) - one military observer.

UNOCI (Cote d/Ivoire) - ten military observers.

UNISOL (Sierra-Leone) - one military observer.

MINURSO (Western Sahara) - eight military observers and

MINUSTAH (Haiti) - one troop

MONUC (Democratic Republic of Congo) - 3,500 troops and 53 military observers.

UNMEE (Ethiopia/Eritrea) - two military observers.

UNMIK (Kosovo) - two military observers.

UNMIL (Liberia) - 16 military observers.

UNMIT (Timor-Leste) - four military observers.

UNOMIG (Georgia) - 11 military observers and

UNMIS (Sudan) - 18 milirary observers and 1,562 troops

Command and Control

Minister of Defence: Chaudhry Ahmad Mukhtar

Chief of Army Staff: General Ashfaq Pervez Kayani

Vice Chief of Army Staff: Vacant

The Pakistan Army is commanded by the Chief of Army Staff (CoAS). he is assisted by a Vice Chief (position vacant from November 2007) and six Principal Staff Officers (PSOs) who are all three-star generals:

Chief of the General Staff (CGS)

Adjutant General (AG)

Quartermaster General (QMG)

Master General of Ordanance (MGO)

Inspector General Training and Education (IG T&E)

Military Secretary (MS)

Within the army the most influential deliberative body is the Corps Commanders Conference chaired by the CoAS and also attended by the Vice and Deputy Chiefs and the three-star PSOs.

GHQ Pakistan Army, at present located in Rawalpindi, is reported to move to a new complex on the outskirts of Islamabad within the next two years.

Organization:

The army is structured in a conventional fashion, akin to that of the British Army before its series of reorganizations, and has not found it necessary to change for the sake of appearing modern. A drawback to the present system is that the span of higher command is too wide to effect continuous control by GHQ in Rawalpindi. There have been proposals create two intermediate HQ to command the corps on the eastern border, but the costs in funding and high-quality manpower would be prohibitive.

Some manpower savings have been effected by reducing the number of logistics and other support personnel, especially in officer's messes. but with the army heavily committed to operations in North West Frontier Province (NWFP) and Balochistan in addition to carrying out normal training, it is unlikely these savings will be translated into an actual reduction in overall strength.

Given the recently arisen imparitives of counter-terrorism and counter-insurgency and continuining dialouge and reduction of tensions on the eastern border, it is assessed that the army's basic organization will not alter, although they will continue to be rotational deployment of formations and units to the west.

Divisions and Brigades

The composition of fighting formations varies according to roles and tasks, with the aim of maintaining a balanced and flexible divisional groupings capable of accepting reinforcements of, for example, a further independent brigade under command for a particular operation.

Ongoing mechanization, following resumption of M-113 (variant) production, has resulted in both armoured divisions achieving greater mobility, and the mechanized infantry divisions having appropriate allocations of armour and tracked support, given the delivery of more SP-109s from the US infantry divisions in the two strike corps have re-equipped almost entirely with Armoured Personnel Carriers (APCs), but will not receive SP artillery in the short term.

Brigades are conventionally structured, as far as possible in square formation, and the independent armoured brigades in V Corps (HQ Karachi) are to all intents an armoured division. Force Command Northern Area (FCNA), a mountain division in all but name, is lightly equipped and has no armour. Within combat divisions, logistics brigades have been formed to command support elements.

This has resulted in promotion opportunities for officers of the support services that otherwise would not have been available.

Operational Concept

Of Pakistan's nine corps HQ, six are sited close to the indian border. Those in Peshawar (II Corps) and Quetta (XII Corps) are heavily involved in internal security and counter insurgency operations in North West Frontier Province (NWFP) and Balochistan. X Corps HQ, Rawalpindi commands formations along the Line of Control (LOC).

In Karachi, V Corps (with some elements at present involved in internal security operations in Sindh and Balochistan Provinces), has the role of countering a thrust by India intended to cut the main Karach-Lahore road. This important road is being complemented by the new indus highway leading up the center of the country, an initiative prompted by economic and strategic considerations. the corps is also responsible for countering possible landings by indian marines or special forces. The three heavy infantry formations, IV, XXX, and XXXI Corps are tasked with countering indian thrusts in their immediate areas.

Both I Corps (Mangla) and II Corps (Multan) are armour heavy "strike" corps, which would implement the doctrine of the riposte.

Army Strategic Forces Command is regarded as a corps and commanded by a lieutenant general with his HQ in Rawalpindi. it is responsible for training, deployment and activation of nuclear missile assets.

Order of Battle

The Pakistan Army does not make its Order of Battle public. the table below is based on a number of sources.

Corps and Sub-ordinate Formations with Locations.

Strategic Forces Command, Rawalpindi.

2 Missile Group, Probably Sargodha.

2 Missile Group, n/a.

I Corps, Mangla

6 Armoured Division, Kharian.

17 Mechanized Infantry Division, Kharian

37 Mechanized Infantry Division, Gujranwala.

II Corps, Multan

1 Armoured Division, Multan

14 Infantry Division, Okara (deployed to South Waziristan Agency 2007)

40 Infantry Division, Okara

IV Corps, Lahore

10 Infantry Division, Lahore

11 Infantry Division, Lahore

3 Independent Armoured Brigade

212 Independent Infantry Brigade

V Corps, Karachi

16 Infantry Division, Hyderabad

18 Infantry Division, Hyderabad

Three Independent Armoured Brigades, Malir (?), Pano Aqil (?), Hyderabad (?)

X Corps, Rawalpindi

Force Command Northern Area, Gilget (equivalent of a division, possibly five infantry divisions)

12 Infantry Division, Murree

19 Infantry Division, Jhelum

23 Infantry Division, Gujrat

111 Independent Infantry Brigade, Rawalpindi

XI Corps, Peshawar

7 Infantry Division, Mardan

9 Infantry Division, Kohat

XII Corps, Quetta

41 Infantry Division, Quetta

33 Infantry Division, Quetta

XXX Corps, Gujranwala

8 Infantry Division, Sialkot

15 Infantry Division, Sialkot

XXXI Corps, Bahawalpur

35 Infantry Division, Bahawalpur

34 Infantry Division, Pano Aqil

105 Independent Brigade Group, Bahawalpur(?)

Special Forces

The Special Services Group (SSG) is headquartered at Cherat and has a base at Attock. it is also responsible for the Airborne School at Peshawar. it consists of three battalions each of four companies.

Other SSG elements include:

Akbar Company (Combat Diver Unit)

Zarrar Company (Counter-terrorism)

Iqbal Company (Communications Unit)

Army Aviation Order of Battle

Unit, Base, Type and Role

1 Sqdn, Dhamial, JetRanger II/III, Liaison/Training

2 Sqdn, Lahore, UH-IH Iroquois, Mushshak, Liaison

3 Composite Sqdn, Multan, Mushshak, Liaison

4 Sqdn, Quetta, Mi-17, Support

Detachment of 4 Sqdn, Rahwali, Mi-17, Support

5 Sqdn, Dhamial, Alouette III, Observation/Liaison

6 Sqdn, Dhamial, Bell 412, Mi-17, Support

Emergency Relief Cell, Dhamial, AB-205A-1, Disaster Relief

7 Composite Sqdn, Faisal, O-1 Bird Dog, Mushshak, Liaison

8 Sqdn, Dhamial, SA-315B Lama, Observation/Liaison

Detachment 8 Sqdn, Skardu, Mushshak, Alouette III, Bell 412, Support

9 Composite Sqdn, Peshawar, Mushshak, Alouette III, Miscellaneous

13 Sqdn, Dhamial, Cessna 412, Commander 680/840, Y-12, VIP Transport

21 Sqdn, Multan, SA 330J Puma, UH-IH Iroquois, Support

24 Sqdn, Multan, SA 330J Puma, Support

25 Sqdn, Dhamial, SA 330J Puma, Helicopter Support

Detachment, Gilget, SA 330J Puma, Helicopter Support

31 Sqdn, Multan, AH-1F HueyCobra, Jet Ranger III, Attack/ Liaison (deployed to FATA)

32 Sqdn, Multan, AH-1F HueyCobra, Jet Ranger III, Attack/ Liaison (deployed to FATA)

Aviation School, Rahwali, Mushshak, Schweizer 300C, Alouette III, Bell 47G/OH-13S, JetRanger II/III.

Paramilitary Forces

Pakistan's paramilitary forces - in the main subordinate to the Ministry of the Interior in peacetime (but to GHQ in war)- number some 100,000 and free the army and navy from most of the responsibilities of policing borders and economic zones. their officers are provided by the regular forces. the army's already severe shortage of junior officers is exacerbated by this requirement and consideration should be given to creating an officer corps solely for paramilitary elements such as the Pakistan Rangers (who police the border with

India) and the Frontier Corps (responsible for the western border with Afghanistan and Iran). In war, some of the higher calibre units would provide reinforcement for the army, as formed body of troops of company or even battalion size.

The Frontier Corps consists of 14 units based in the North West Frontier Province (NWFP) and 13 units based in Baluchistan, with HQ based in Peshawar and Quetta.

The Pakistan Rangers HQ is in Sialkot with subordinate HQ in Sialkot, Bahawalpur and Rahim Yar Khan. The Rangers are responsible for low level border security but can be deployed elsewhere as required by the internal security situation.

Reserves

There is an army reserve of 500,000 whose members have a triennial attendance obligation to the age of 45. Refresher training is as adequate as can be expected of a three week period, but reserve service seems popular. The 180,000 strong National Guard would be useful in guarding vulnerable points. It consists of the Mujahid Force of 60,000, organized in battalions, some with light air defence capability. the Janbaz Force of 100,000, whose members are intended to serve close to their homes; and the National Cadet Corps in universities and colleges. these elements have some value in providing poorly trained but enthusiastic reinforcements for rear area units.

Operational Art and Tactical Doctrine

From the time of the 65 war, through that of 71 and until the Indian Army excercise Brass Tacks in 1987, emphasis was on static defence of the LOC and the border. Penetration of Indian territory would be undertaken only on an opportunity basis. the doctrine was flawed, mainly because of lack of strategic depth in Pakistan, but no alternative was given serious consideration until it was realised that a "stand and fight" doctrine would probably result in deep penetration by Indian forces without Pakistani forces being able to manoeuver effectively. the Indian army would have gained and retained the initiative, enabling it to destroy Pakistani formations piecemeal as they reacted to Indian thrusts.

The "Riposte" is simple in concept: it is intended that the two strike corps conduct a limited advance along narrow fronts with the objective of occupying indian territory near the border, probably to a depth of 40 to 50 km. Pakistan considers that international pressure would result in a ceasefire after a maximum of three weeks of conflict, enough time to gain some territory to be used in subsequent bargaining. there would be acceptance of Indian penetration, which would be inevitable given the comparitive lack of mobility within the Infantry heavy divisions. Independent Armoured and Mechanized Brigades are intended for quick counter attack and exploitation and would add considerable weight to advances by the strike corps.

The "Riposte" is practiced at all levels. Major excercises involve the crossing of water obstacles and minefields at night with emphasis on subsequent break-out and rapid advance. So far as has been seen, the concept has been adequately translated into workable plans which are continuously being refined. However, complete mechanization of the strike corps and other formations was slowed by the effects of US sanctions and it will take some time for them to achieve desired mobility, although US army surplus equipment is now being rapidly delivered, and local manufacture and rebuilding of US supplied AFV/APC has received considerable impetus, thus improving the mechanization process.

The army took great interest in the Indian army/airforce excercise Vajra Shakti (Thunder Power, conducted in Punjab from 1-10 May 2005). in view of its emphasis on maintaining mobility while operating closed down against nuclear attack. Pakistan's own counter - nuclear preparedness is patchy, and it is doubtful that even the strike corps could fight through a nuclear battlefield.

India's doctrine of "Cold Start" involving swift penetration of Pakistan with the aim of isolating, destroying or capturing vital points (such as nuclear stores and other installations has resulted in some modification to the Riposte, in that acceptability of penetration could be fatal to counter-penetration plans. in the event of an indian advance reaching or crossing the line of the main Lahore-Karachi highway, it is likely there would be consideration of employment of tactical nuclear missiles.

Bases

Major Army bases are located at:

Karachi

Mangla

Lahore

Multan

Peshawar

Quetta

Rawalpindi

Bahawalpur

Training

Training is the overall responsibility of the Inspector General, Training and Evaluation (IG T&E) in GHQ. The army relies largely on the efficient regimental system whereby each infantry regiment has its own training center, as have other arms and services.

Initial training of officers (now including females in other than the Medical Corps) is conducted mainly at the Pakistan Military Academy at Kakul, Abbotabad. Standards are adequate, although the course is too short, and emphasis has to be placed on instruction in the English language.

Regimental and special-to-arms and -services training is of a high standard but there is much learning by rote, which tends to reduce initiative. Instruction at army schools (such as the School of Infantry and Tactics at Quetta) is impressive and courses are conducted efficiently.

This also applies to the Command and Staff College. Directing staff are high quality and the syallabus is sound. However, the culture of chappa- an anxiety to conform, resulting in emphasis on obtaining "correct" solutions from former students - produces careful, but imitative papers. Despite this, topic discussion is energetic, and the product is generally good.

Advanced technical training and graduate/post-graduate studies are carried out under the aegis of the National University of Sciences and Technology (NUST), which involves the Colleges of Medicine, Signals, Military Engg and Electrical and Mechanical Engg. These are linked with civilian, naval and airforce institutions and with Michigan State (US) and Cranfield (UK) universities.

Advanced courses for officers are conducted at National Defence University in Islamabad, of which the two main courses (August to June) are the National Defence Course (brigadiers and equivalent) and the Armed Forces War Course (lieutenant colonels and equivalent). Instruction is world standard.

Individual and collective training in units is conducted in an annual cycle, usually dictated by the timing of higher-level excercises. Sub-unit and unit excercises generally held in summer, with brigade and divisional manoeuveres after the harvest and in winter.

There has been emphasis on computer-based war gaming, with consequent improvement in staff work, especially in logistics. In the 1965 and 1971 wars, few formations were far from base facilities and supply dumps and it is only comparitively recently that battlefield recovery and practice in forward supply have been alotted the importance they deserve. Much training focuses on obstacle crossing, as there are extensive natural and manmade water barriers on both sides of the border, especially in Punjab.

Since 2001, following the invasion of Afghanistan, there has been a gradual than accelerating requirement to counter terrorism and insurgency, especially in, but far from limited to, Baluchistan and

North West Frontier Province (NWFP). As the main task of the army was defence of the eastern border, and low level border control was almost exclusively the responsibility of the Pakistan Rangers and the Frontier Corps (the latter assisted by tribal irregulars), there was no particular emphasis on instruction in counter insurgency.

When it became necessary to deploy formation HQ and units to the western regions it became apparent that such instruction was essential, and unit and sub-unit training was undertaken concurrently with modification of syllabi in army schools such as the School of Infantry and Tactics. It is expected that this emphasis will be maintained, given the senstivity of the western border regions and the decreasing likelihood of conflict with India (?).

Army Procurement

Main Battle Tanks

Al-Khalid

Pakistan's efforts to develop its own indigenous tank, the Al-Khalid, suffered initially from difficulties over the supply of power/ transmission packs from a European source, As a result of co-operation with Ukraine over the T-80 Main Battle Tank (MBT), the Ukranian Malyshev Plant sold engine and gearbox units for the Al-Khalid to Pakistan in September 2000, and was contracted to provide a total of 315 packs. In November 2000 Pakistan announced that the Heavy Industries Taxila (HIT) facility would build a pre-production batch of Al-Khalids in co-operation with the China North Industries Corporation (NORINCO). The first 15 Al-Khalids appeared in July 2001. The production rate in 2004 was estimated by HIT to be 45-60 annually, dependent on budget allocation, and some 220 were in service as of May 2008. Development continues, with modifications in the fire control system and linkage.

Upgraded T-59

Though superseded by the Al-Khalid as the Pakistan Army's first line MBT, the Phase III Al-Zarrar version of the Type 59 has been upgraded and is adequate for training and emergency combat use. The program is centered on fitting a 125mm smoothbore main gun, an upgraded computerised fire control system and ATCOP TR3 laser range-finder, together with DNS 3 image intensifier.

Both Thales and Sagem night vision equipment is under trial. Improved armour protection has also been fitted in the shape of an external anti-mine plate on the chassis and Explosive Reactive Armour (ERA). Unlike the Al-Khalid MBT, the 125mm main gun is not fitted with an auto-loader, so the Al-Zarrar has a fourth crew member for this purpose.

The army has ordered 400 upgraded tanks of the holding od some 1,000, with the remainder being phased out as the Khalids enter service. The first batch of 80 was handed over in February 2004. it is unlikely Pakistan will seek to purchase MBTs from other sources in the forseeable future, and that it will concentrate on continuing close cooperation with China in this as in other aspects of military development.

Armoured Personnel Carriers

HIT has developed a number of M113A1 variants for the Pakistan Army. These include:

1. The Maaz is a modified M113A1 fitted with a Baktar Shikan anti-tank guided weapon (ATGW). The shape of the M113A1 has been modified, extending its nose slightly and adding additional diesel fuel tanks on the back.
2. Mouz - Modified M 113 fitted with RBS 70.
3. Talha - Modified M 113 APC.
4. Saad - Modified M 113 APC.
5. Al-Hamza - Infantry Fighting Vehicle (IFV) (25mm cannon).
6. Al-Qaswa - logistics vehicle.
7. Sakb - Command post vehicle.
8. Al-Hadeed - Recovery vehicle (modified Talha)

Artillery / Anti Tank

The country is developing its own MLRS system, the Azar (probably in conjuction with China), and it appears to be successful. The army urgently requires more self-propelled medium and heavy artillery pieces, and ageement with the US has been reached for supply of 115 M109A5 155mm SP guns at an estimated cost of US$ 56 million(deliveries underway). Its indigeneous anti-tank missile, the Baktar Shikan is in production but cannot be said to be a technological advance on existing systems. it is however cheap and easy to handle.

Pakistan is seeking to procure self-propelled mortar systems to equip mechanized infantry battalions with indigeneous firepower to complement the recent improvement in Pakistan's self-propelled artillery formations. This capability is seen as a requirement given the planned increase in the number of fully mechanized formations, but both the Artillery Directorate and Strike Corps are more concerned with the effectiveness of self-propelled howitzers and hence mortar procurement is likely to take second place and be based around converted M 113s or similar systems.

Army Aviation

The need to improve tactical mobility led to the induction of 10 additional Kazan/Mil Mi 17 medium transport helicopters and 26 Bell 412EP multirole medium helicopters. These have been supplemented by 20 refurbished AH 1F Huey Cobra close support/ attack helicopters from the US. The first 8 were handed over in Feburary 2007 and deliveries continue.

In October 2008, the Bush administration notified US Congress of its plans to provide as much as US$ 116 million in upgrades for eight of the Pakistan Army's AH 1F Cobra helicopters, which are being used in counter-insurgency operations in the country's tribal regions.

Since 2003, the US has provided Pakistan with upto 32 surplus Cobras, which are supposed to be used to provide surveillence, attack and close air support to ground forces engaging the Taliban and fighters linked to Al Qaeda based in Pakistan's federally administered tribal areas (FATA) and northwest frontier province (NWFP). The proposed Cobra refurbishment will include associated equipment and services as well as warranties, transportation and logistics support.

Prime contractor for the upgrades is US Helicopter in Ozark, Alabama, will send staff to join serving US personnel in Pakistan for three weeks to ensure delivery and operability of the upgraded equipment. A three person field office will also be established for three years to provide technical assistance for the upgrades to the Pakistan Army.

Unmanned Aerial Vehicles (UAVs)

In March 2006, the army finalised an order from Germant for the EMT Luna short-range battlefield reconnaissance, surveillance and target acquisition UAVs. Three or four systems are likely to be obtained but complete details are yet to be known.

In July 2006, Pakistan and Turkey signed a deal for the joint production of six to seven tactical UAVs, according to turkish and pakistani defence industry sources. During a visit to Turkey, Chief of the Air Staff, Pakistan Air Force, ACM Tanvir Mahmood Ahmad confirmed to Jane's that the two countries would co-operate on UAV production but declined to give further details. The decision to co-build UAVs came after months of study in the two countries. In May 2008, following a visit to Pakistan by Australia's Chief of Defence Force, that Pakistan had expressed interest in acquiring the Scan Eagle pilotless reconnaissance aircraft built by Boeing Australia.

Air Defence

Tactical air defence has been improved by the introduction of indigenously produced Anza MKI manportable surface to air missiles (SAMs)(based on the China Machinery and Export Corporation HN 5 series) and the Anza MK2 SAM based on the CPMIEC QW 1 Vanguard SAM).

Equipment in Service

Armour

Type: Al-Khalid

Manufacturer: HIT

Role:MBT

Original Total:220

Type: Type 59/59M (including Zarrar)

Manufacturer: HIT

Role:MBT

Original Total:600

Type: Type 69 (PRC improved version of Type 59. 100mm gun. Not battle survivable)

Manufacturer: Chinese State Factories

Role:MBT

Original Total:350

Type: Type 85 IIAP

Manufacturer: Chinese State Factories

Role:MBT

Original Total:300 (local assembly of kits and manufacture of some components. 125mm gun but fire-control system basic in early versions (upgrade in progress)) total planned production unknown. further acquisition unlikely.

Type: T 80UD

Manufacturer: Malayshev Plant, Ukraine.

Role:MBT

Original Total:320

Type: M 113A1/M 113A2

Manufacturer: HIT.

Role:APC

Original Total: 2,000

Type: UR 416

Manufacturer: Rheinmetall Landsystems GmbH.

Role:APC

Original Total: 35

Type: Type 531

Manufacturer: n/a.

Role:APC

Original Total: 100

Type: BTR 70/BTR-80 (UN Service)

Manufacturer: n/a.

Role:APC

Original Total: 120

Equipment in Service

Artillery

Type: 105mm M101

Manufacturer: Rock Island Arsenal

Role: Towed Howitzer

Original Total:300

Type: 105mm Model 56 Pack

Manufacturer: Oto Melera SpA

Role: Towed Howitzer

Original Total:110

Type: 122mm Type 54

Manufacturer: Norinco

Role: Towed Howitzer

Original Total:400

Type: 155mm M 198

Manufacturer: Rock Island Arsenal

Role: Towed Howitzer

Original Total: 124

Type: 155mm M 114

Manufacturer: n/a

Role: Towed Howitzer

Original Total: 144

Type: 155mm M 109A2

Manufacturer: BAE Systems, Ground Systems

Role: Towed Self-Propelled Howitzer

Original Total: 200

Type: 155mm M 109A5

Manufacturer: BAE Systems, Ground Systems

Role: Towed Self-Propelled Howitzer

Original Total: 115 (on 16 December 2005, DSCA notified Congress of a possible FMS of M109A5 155mm SP Howitzers plus associated equipment and services to Pakistan. This order was confirmed in May 2006 with deliveries expected during 2007/2008.)

Type: 203mm M 110A2
Manufacturer: n/a
Role: Towed Self-Propelled Howitzer
Original Total: 50

Type: 130mm Type 59-1
Manufacturer: Norinco
Role: Field Gun
Original Total: 400

Type: 130mm Type M46
Manufacturer: n/a
Role: Field Gun
Original Total: n/a

Type: 155mm M59
Manufacturer: n/a
Role: Medium Gun
Original Total: 30

Type: 107mm Type 81
Manufacturer: Norinco
Role: Multiple Rocket System
Original Total: n/a

Type: 122mm Type 83 (Azar)
Manufacturer: Institute of Industrial Control Systems
Role: Multiple Rocket System
Original Total: 45

Equipment in Service

Anti - Tank Weapons

Type: AT 11 Sniper / 9MM 119
Manufacturer: n/a
Role: Anti-Tank Guided Weapon
Original Total: 600 (part of the deal for T-80UD tanks)

Type: Green Arrow (PRC Red Arrow)
Manufacturer: n/a
Role: Anti-Tank Guided Weapon
Original Total: 700 (estimated)

Type: Baktar Shikan
Manufacturer: Institute of Industrial Control Systems (IICS)
Role: Anti-Tank Missile System
Original Total: 250

Type: TOW2A
Manufacturer: Raytheon
Role: Anti-Tank Missile System
Original Total: 100

Type: 75mm Type 52
Manufacturer: n/a
Role: Recoilless Rifle
Original Total: n/a

Type: 106mm M40A1
Manufacturer: Pakistan Machine Tool Factory Ltd
Role: Recoilless Rifle
Original Total: n/a

Type: RPG 7 40mm
Manufacturer: Pakistan Machine Tool Factory Ltd
Role: Portable Rocket Launcher
Original Total: n/a

Equipment in Service

Air Defence Weapons

Type: 40mm M1
Manufacturer: Bofors Weapons Systems
Role: Anti-Aircraft Gun
Original Total: 100

Type: 57mm Type 59
Manufacturer: Norinco
Role: Towed Anti-Aircraft Gun
Original Total: 100

Type: 37mm (Twin) Type 55/56
Manufacturer: n/a
Role: Towed Anti-Aircraft Gun
Original Total: 700

Type: Oerlikon Contraves Skyguard - Twin 35mm
Manufacturer: Oerlikon Contraves AG (Rheinmetall Defence)
Role: Towed Anti-Aircraft Gun
Original Total: 200

Type: Twin 23mm ZU 23-2
Manufacturer: n/a
Role: Towed Anti-Aircraft Gun
Original Total: n/a

Type: 14.5 mm ZPU-2

Manufacturer: Norinco

Role: Towed Anti-Aircraft Gun

Original Total: n/a

Type: 14.5 mm ZPU-4

Manufacturer: Norinco

Role: Towed Anti-Aircraft Gun

Original Total: n/a

Type: 12.7mm (Quadi) M55

Manufacturer: n/a

Role: Towed Anti-Aircraft Gun

Original Total: 45

Type: RBS 70 (Plus Giraffe Radars)

Manufacturer: Saab Bofors Dynamics AB

Role: Man Portable Surface to Air Missile System

Original Total: 200

Type: FIM 92A Stinger

Manufacturer: n/a

Role: Man Portable Surface to Air Missile System

Original Total: n/a

Type: HN 5A

Manufacturer: n/a

Role: Man Portable Surface to Air Missile System

Original Total: 30 (probably no longer in front-line service - either obsolete or in reserve)

Type: Anza Mk 1

Manufacturer: Institute of Industrial Control Systems (IICS)

Role: Man Portable Surface to Air Missile System

Original Total: n/a

Type: Anza Mk 11

Manufacturer: Institute of Industrial Control Systems (IICS)

Role: Man Portable Surface to Air Missile System

Original Total: n/a

Type: Anza Mk 111 (in development. probably based on the Chinese Qian Wei-2 man portable SAM)

Manufacturer: Institute of Industrial Control Systems (IICS)

Role: Man Portable Surface to Air Missile System

Original Total: n/a

Equipment in Service

Infantry Weapons

Type: 9mm Walther P38

Role: Pistol

Type: 9mm Sterling

Role: Sub-Machine Gun

Type: 9mm H&K MP5

Role: Sub-Machine Gun

Type: 7.62 mm G3

Role: Assault Rifle

Type: 7.62 mm Type 56

Role: Assault Rifle

Type: 7.62 mm AKM
Role: Rifle

Type: 7.62 mm RDP
Role: Light Machine Gun

Type: 7.62 mm MG1A3
Role: Machine Gun

Type: 0.5 in Browning M2 HB
Role: Heavy Machine Gun

Type: 12.7mm Type 54
Role: Heavy Machine Gun

Type: 60mm PMT
Role: Mortar

Type: 81mm PMT
Role: Mortar

Type: 120mm PMT
Role: Mortar

Army Aviation

Type: AH 1F/S Huey Cobra
Manufacturer: Bell
Role: Attack
Original Total: 28

Type: AH 1S Huey Cobra
Manufacturer: Bell
Role: Attack
Original Total: 6

Type: Y 12 (II)

Manufacturer: HAI

Role: Transport

Original Total: 4

Type: Y 12 (II)

Manufacturer: HAI

Role: Transport

Original Total: 4

Type: 206B Jetranger III

Manufacturer: Bell

Role: Observation

Original Total: 12

Type: O 1 Bird Dog

Manufacturer: Dhamial (Cessna)

Role: Utility

Original Total: n/a (10 surviving)

Type: Mushshak

Manufacturer: PAC

Role: Utility

Original Total: n/a (120 surviving)

Type: Super Mushshak

Manufacturer: PAC

Role: Utility

Original Total: 42 (stated requirement - none delivered so far)

Type: Mi 17 Hip H
Manufacturer: Mil
Role: Utility
Original Total: 37

Type: SA 330J Puma
Manufacturer: Aerospatiale
Role: Utility
Original Total: 32

Type: SA 315B Lama
Manufacturer: Aerospatiale
Role: Utility
Original Total: 24

Type: 412EP
Manufacturer: Bell
Role: Utility
Original Total: 26 (first delivered in 2004)

Type: 412EP
Manufacturer: Bell
Role: Utility
Original Total: 25 (delivered 2007)

Type: 407
Manufacturer: Bell
Role: Utility
Original Total: 40

Type: 205A-1

Manufacturer: Augusta Bell

Role: Utility

Original Total: 10

Type: 421 Golden Eagle

Manufacturer: Cessna

Role: Utility

Original Total: 1

Type: 690C Commander Jetprop 840

Manufacturer: Gulfstream Aerospace

Role: VIP Transport

Original Total: 2

Type: 206B Jetranger II

Manufacturer: Bell

Role: Trainer

Original Total: 15

Type: 300C

Manufacturer: Schwiezer (Hughes)

Role: Trainer

Original Total: 10

Type: 47G/OH-13 Sioux

Manufacturer: Bell

Role: Trainer

Original Total: n/a (10 surviving)

Notes: Locally developed Anza SAM may arm AH 1S in air-to-air missile role.

Chinese HJ-8 (built locally as Baktar Shikan) may arm other helicopters.

Unmanned Aerial Vehicles

Type: Luna (Germany)

Manufacturer: EMT

Role: Intelligence, Surveillance and Reconnaissance

Original Total: 4

Type: Falco (Italy)

Manufacturer: Finmeccanica

Role: Intelligence, Surveillance and Reconnaissance

Original Total: 4

Missiles

Type: BGM 71 TOW

Manufacturer: Raytheon

Role: Anti-Armour

Updated to May-2008

Jane's World Armies, 24th issue, Dec-08.

3

ORGANISATION AND FUNCTIONING OF INDIAN ARMY

The Indian Army is the largest branch of the armed forces of India and has the responsibility for land-based military operations. Its primary objectives include defending India from external aggression, maintaining peace and security within the country, patrolling borders and conducting counter-terrorist operations. It also conducts rescue and humanitarian operations during calamities and disturbances. Control and operation of the Army is administered by the Ministry of Defence.

With more than 1,130,000 soldiers in active service and about 1,200,000 reserve troops, the Indian Army is the world's second largest. It is a completely voluntary service and though there is a provision for military draft in the Indian constitution, it has never been imposed.

The Indian Army was formed soon after India gained independence in 1947 and retained most of the regiments of the British Indian Army. The Army is deployed in many of the world's conflict zones as a part of the United Nations Peacekeeping forces.

The force is currently headed by the Chief of Army Staff, General Deepak Kapoor. The Field Marshal is the highest attainable rank in the Indian Army and it is awarded by the President of India, on advise of the Union Government, only in exceptional circumstances. So far, only two officers have attained this rank.

OBJECTIVES

The Indian Army doctrine defines the role of the Indian Army as - "The Indian Army is the land component of the Indian Armed Forces which exist to uphold the ideals of the Constitution of India." As a major component of national power, along with the Indian Navy and the Indian Air Force, the roles of the Indian Army are as follows :

- Primary: Preserve national interests and safeguard sovereignty, territorial integrity and unity of India against any external threats by deterrence or by waging war.
- Secondary: Assist Government agencies to cope with 'proxy war' and other internal threats and provide aid to civil authority when requisitioned for the purpose."

HISTORY

Upon India gaining independence in 1947, the British Indian Army was divided into two parts to serve the newly created nations of Union of India and Islamic Republic of Pakistan. Most units went to India; four Gurkha regiments were transferred to the British Army while the rest went to India.

As the Indian Army derives from the British Indian Army, its structures, uniforms and traditions are essentially British in heritage. It is often said that the Indian Army is more British than the British.

FIRST KASHMIR WAR (1947)

Almost immediately after independence, tensions between India and Pakistan began to boil over, and the first of three full-scale wars between the two nations broke out over the then princely state of Kashmir. Upon the Maharaja of Kashmir's reluctance to accede to either India or Pakistan, an impatient Pakistan sponsored a 'tribal' invasion of parts of Kashmir. The men are alleged by India to have also included Pakistan army regulars. Soon after, Pakistan sent in its troops to annex the state. The Maharaja, Hari Singh, appealed to India, and to Lord Mountbatten — the Governor General — for help, but it was pointed out to him that India saw no reason to do so. He signed the Instrument of Accession and Kashmir unilaterally acceded to India (a decision ratified by Britain but never accepted by Pakistan).

Immediately after, Indian troops were airlifted into Srinagar and repelled the invaders. This contingent included General Thimayya who distinguished himself in the operation and in years that followed, became a Chief of the Indian Army. An intense war was waged across the state and former comrades found themselves fighting each other. Both sides made some territorial gains and also suffered significant losses. An uneasy UN sponsored peace returned by the end of 1948 with Indian and Pakistani soldiers facing each other directly on the Line of Control, which has since divided Indian from Pakistani-held Kashmir. Tensions between India and Pakistan, largely over Kashmir, have never since been entirely eliminated.

Participation in UN peace-keeping operations

Presently, the Indian army has dedicated one brigade of troops to the UN's standby arrangements. The large number of sustained troop commitments made by India has been praised for taking part in long and difficult operations. The Indian Army has participated in several UN peace-keeping operations, including the ones in Angola, Cambodia, Cyprus, Congo, El Salvador, Namibia, Lebanon, Liberia, Mozambique, Rwanda, Somalia, Srilanka & Vietnam. The army had also provided a paramedical unit to facilitate the withdrawal of the sick and wounded in Korea.

Inclusion of Hyderabad (1948)

After the partition of India, the State of Hyderabad, a princely-state under the rule of a Nizam, chose to remain independent. The Nizam, refused to accede his state to the Union of India. The following stand-off between the Government of India and the Nizam ended on 12 September 1948 when India's then deputy-Prime Minister Sardar Vallabhai Patel ordered Indian troops to secure the state. Within 5 days of intense fighting, the Indian Army, backed by the Indian Air Force, successfully defeated Hyderabad State forces. The following day, the State of Hyderabad was proclaimed as a part of the Union of India. Major General Joyanto Nath Chaudhuri, who led the Operation Polo was appointed the Military Governor of Hyderabad (1948-1949) to restore law and order.

Goa, Daman and Diu Operation (1961)

Even though the British and French vacated all their colonial possessions in the Indian subcontinent, Goa, Daman and Diu remained under Portuguese control. On 12th December, 1961, after repeated Portuguese refusals to negotiate their leaving, New Delhi launched Operation Vijay and ordered a small contingent of its troops to invade the Portuguese territories and secure them. Unable to withstand the assault that lasted twenty-six hours, Goa, along with Daman and Diu (enclaves lying to the north of Maharashtra) joined India.

Sino-Indian Conflict (1962)

Since 1959, India followed a "forward policy" under which Indian border patrol units continuously pushed their posts forward deep into territory claimed by the People's Republic of China (PRC). Small-scale clashes between the Indian and Chinese forces broke out as India insisted on the disputed McMahon Line being regarded as the international border between the two countries. Despite heavy casualties, Chinese troops did not retaliate the cross-border firing by Indian troops. China's misinterpretation of India's true intentions in Tibet created more rifts between the two countries.

Buoyed by the success of its military operations in Hyderabad and Goa, India took a more aggressive stance towards its border disputes with China. In 1962, the Indian Army was ordered to move to the Thag La ridge located near the border between Bhutan and Arunachal Pradesh and about three miles (5 km) north of the disputed McMahon Line. Meanwhile, Chinese troops too had made incursions into Indian-held territory and tensions between the two reached a new high when Indian forces discovered a road constructed by China in Aksai Chin.

After a series of failed negotiations, People's Liberation Army attacked Indian Army positions at the Thag La ridge. This move by China caught India by surprise and by October 12, Nehru gave orders for the Chinese to be expelled from Aksai Chin. However, poor coordination among various divisions of the Indian Army and the late decision to mobilize the Indian Air Force in vast numbers gave China a crucial tactical and strategic advantage over India. On October 20, Chinese soldiers attacked India in both the North-West and North-Eastern parts of the border and captured vast portions of Aksai Chin and Arunachal Pradesh.

As the fighting moved beyond disputed territories, China called on the Indian government to negotiate, however India remained determined to regain lost territory. With no peaceful agreement in sight, China unilaterally withdrew its forces from Arunachal Pradesh. The reasons for the withdrawal are disputed with India claiming various logistical problems for China and diplomatic support from the United States while China stated that it still held territory that it had staked diplomatic claim upon. The dividing line between the Indian and Chinese forces was christened as the Line of Actual Control.

The poor decisions made by India's military commanders raised several questions. The Henderson-Brooks committee was soon set up by the Government of India to determine the causes of the poor performance of the Indian Army. The report of committee apparently faulted much of the command of Indian Armed Forces and severely criticized the executive government for its failures on several fronts.

The committee found that the major reason for the defeat was low deployment of troops on India's border with China even after hostilities began and also criticized the decision to not allow the Indian Air Force to target Chinese transport lines out of fear of Chinese aerial counter-attack on Indian civilian areas. Much of the blame was also targeted at the incompetence of then Defense Minister, Krishna Menon who resigned from his post soon after the war ended. Despite frequent calls for its release, the Henderson-Brooks report still remains classified.

Second Kashmir War (1965)

A second confrontation with Pakistan took place in 1965, largely over Kashmir. Pakistani President Ayub Khan launched *Operation Gibraltar* in August 1965 during which several Pakistani paramilitary troops infiltrated into Indian-administered Kashmir and tried to spark an anti-India rebellion. Pakistani leaders believed that India, which was still recovering from the disastrous Sino-Indian War, would be unable to deal with a military thrust and rebellion. However, the operation was a major failure since the Kashmiri people showed little support for such a rebellion and India quickly moved forces to drive the infiltrators out. Within a fortnight of the launch of the Indian counter-attack, most of the infiltrators had retreated back to Pakistan.

Battered by the failure of Operation Gibraltar and expecting a major invasion by Indian forces across the border, Pakistan launched Operation Grand Slam on September 1, invading India's Chamb-Jaurian sector. In retaliation, the India's Army launched major offensive throughout its border with Pakistan, with Lahore as its prime target. Though the Indian Army's break through of the final phases of Pakistani defense was considerably delayed due to logistical issues, the conflict was largely seen as a debacle for the Pakistani Army.

Initially, the Indian Army met with considerable success in the northern sector. After launching prolonged artillery barrages against

Pakistan, India was able to capture three important mountain positions in Kashmir. By September 9, the Indian Army had made considerable in-roads into Pakistan. India had its largest haul of Pakistani tanks when the offensive of Pakistan's 1 Armoured Division was blunted at the Battle of Asal Uttar which took place on September 10th near Khemkaran.

Six Pakistani Armoured Regiments took part in the battle against three Indian Armoured Regiments with inferior tanks. By the time the battle had ended, the 4th Indian Division had captured about 97 Pakistani tanks in either destroyed, or damaged, or in intact condition. This included 72 Patton tanks and 25 Chafees and Shermans. 32 of the 97 tanks, including 28 Pattons, were in running condition. In comparison, the Indians lost only 32 tanks at Khemkaran-Bhikkiwind. About fifteen of them were captured by the Pakistan Army, mostly Sherman tanks. Pakistan's overwhelming defeat at the decisive battle of Assal Uttar hastened the end of the conflict.

At the time of ceasefire declaration, India reported 12,500 casualties of whom about 3,000 were killed, 8,400 were wounded and 1,100 were either taken as prisoners of war or were missing. On the other hand, it was estimated that about 3,800 Pakistani soldiers were killed in the battle, 9,000 were wounded and about 2,000 were taken as prisoners of war.

About 200 Pakistani tanks were either destroyed or captured by India and an additional 150 were permanently put out of service. India lost a total of 190 tanks during the conflict and about 200 more had to undergo repair. In all, India lost about half as many tanks as Pakistan lost during the war.

Given India's advantageous position at the end of the war, the decision to return back to pre-war positions, following the Tashkent Declaration, caused an outcry among the polity in New Delhi. It was widely believed that India's decision to accept the ceasefire was due to political, and not military, factors since it was facing considerable pressure from the United States and the UN to stop hostilities. According to one independent analyst, continuation of the war would have led further losses and ultimately defeat for Pakistan.

BANGLADESH LIBERATION WAR (1971)

An independence movement broke out in East Pakistan which was brutally crushed by Pakistani forces. Due to large-scale atrocities against them, thousands of Bengalis took refuge in neighboring India causing a major refugee crisis there. In early 1971, India declared its full-support for the Bengali rebels, known as Mukti Bahini, and Indian agents were extensively involved in covert operations to aid them.

On November 20, 1971, Indian Army moved the 14 Punjab Battalion and 45 Cavalry into Garibpur, a strategically important town near India's border with East Pakistan, and successfully captured it. The following day, more clashes took place between Indian and Pakistani forces. Wary of India's growing involvement in the Bengali rebellion, the Pakistan Air Force (PAF) launched a pre-emptive strike on Indian military positions near its border with East Pakistan on December 3.

The aerial operation, however, failed to accomplish its stated objectives and caused India to declare a full-scale war against Pakistan the same day. By midnight, the Indian Army, accompanied by Indian Air Force, launched major military thrust into East Pakistan. The Indian Army won several battles on the eastern front including the decisive of battle of Hilli, which was the only front where the Pakistani Army was able to buildup considerable resistance.[17] India's massive early gains was largely attributed to the speed and flexibility with which Indian armored divisions moved across East Pakistan.

Pakistan launched a counter-attack against India on the western front. On December 4, 1971, the A company of the 23rd Battalion of India's Punjab Regiment detected and intercepted the movement of the 51st Infantry Division of the Pakistani Army near Ramgarh, Rajasthan. The battle of Longewala ensued during which the A company, though being outnumbered, thwarted the Pakistani advance until the Indian Air Force directed its fighters to engage the Pakistani tanks. By the time the battle had ended, 34 Pakistani tanks and 50 armored vehicles were either destroyed or abandoned. About 200 Pakistani troops were killed in action during the battle while only 2 Indian soldiers lost their lives. Pakistan suffered another major defeat on the western front during the battle of Basantar which was fought from December 4th to 16th.

By the end of the battle, about 66 Pakistani tanks were destroyed and 40 more were captured. In return, Pakistani forces were able to destroy only 11 Indian tanks. None of the numerous Pakistani offensives on the Western front materialized. By December 16th, Pakistan had lost sizable territory on both eastern and western fronts.

Under the command of Lt. General J.S Aurora, the three corps of the Indian Army, who had invaded East Pakistan, entered Dhaka and forced Pakistani forces to surrender on 16th December, 1971, one day after the conclusion of the battle of Basantar. After Pakistan's Lt. General A.A.K. Niazi signed the Instrument of Surrender, India took more than 90,000 Pakistani prisoners of war, which included about 38,000 armed forces personnel and 52,000 militia and bureaucrats of West Pakistani origin. At the time of the signing of the Instrument of Surrender, 9,000 Pakistani soldiers were killed-in-action while India suffered only 2,500 battle-related deaths. In addition, Pakistan lost 200 tanks during the battle compared to India's 80.

In 1972, the Simla Agreement was signed between the two countries and tensions simmered. However, there were occasional spurts in diplomatic tensions which culminated into increased military vigilance on both sides.

Siachen Conflict (1984-)

The Siachen Glacier, though a part of the Kashmir region, is not officially demarcated. As a consequence, prior to the 1980s, neither India nor Pakistan maintained permanent military presence in the region. However, Pakistan started hosting a series of mountaineering expeditions to the glacier during the 1950s. By early 1980s, the government of Pakistan was granting special expedition permits to mountaineers and United States Army maps deliberately showed Siachen as a part of Pakistan. This practice gave rise to the contemporary meaning of the term *oropolitics*.

An irked India launched Operation Meghdoot in April 1984 during which the entire Kumaon Regiment of the Indian Army was airlifted to the glacier. Pakistani forces responded quickly and clashes between the two followed. Indian Army secured the strategic Sia La and Bilafond La mountain passes and by 1985, more than 1000 sq. miles of territory, claimed by Pakistan, was under Indian control.

The Indian Army continues to control more than 2/3rd of the glacier. Pakistan made several unsuccessful attempts to regain control over Siachen. In late 1987, Pakistan mobilized about 8,000 troops and garrisoned them near Khapalu, aiming to capture Bilafond La. However, they were thrown back after engaging the Indian Army personnel guarding Bilafond. During the battle, about 23 Indian soldiers lost their lives while more than 150 Pakistani troops perished. Further unsuccessful attempts to reclaim positions were launched by Pakistan in 1990, 1995, 1996 and 1999.

India continues to maintain a strong military presence in the region despite extremely inhospitable conditions and the conflict over Siachen is regularly cited as an example of mountain warfare. The highest peak in the Siachen glacier region, Siakangri, is strategically important for India because its immense altitude and proximity to the Karakoram Highway enables the Indian forces to keep check on any Pakistani or Chinese movement in the region.

Maintaining control over Siachen poses several logistical challenges for the Indian Army. Several infrastructure projects were constructed in the region, including a helipad 21,000 feet (6,400 m) above the sea level. In 2004, Indian Army was spending an estimated US$2 million a day to support its personnel stationed in the region.

Counter-insurgency Activities

The Indian Army has played a crucial role in the past, fighting insurgents and terrorists within the nation. The army launched Operation Bluestar and Operation Woodrose in the 1980s to combat Sikh insurgents. The army, along with some paramilitary forces, has the prime responsibility of maintaining law and order in the troubled Jammu and Kashmir region. The Indian Army also sent a contingent to Sri Lanka in 1987 as a part of the Indian Peace Keeping Force.

Kargil Conflict (1999)

In 1998, India carried out nuclear tests and a few days later, Pakistan responded by more nuclear tests giving both countries nuclear deterrence capability. Diplomatic tensions eased after the Lahore Summit was held in 1999. The sense of optimism was short-lived, however, since in mid-1999 Pakistani paramilitary forces and Kashmiri insurgents captured deserted, but strategic, Himalayan heights in the Kargil district of India.

These had been vacated by the Indian army during the onset of the inhospitable winter and were supposed to reoccupied in spring. The *mujahideen* who took control of these areas received important support, both in the form of arms and supplies, from Pakistan. Some of the heights under their control, which also included the *Tiger Hill*, overlooked the vital Srinagar-Leh Highway (NH 1A), Batalik and Dras.

Once the scale of the Pakistani incursion was realized, the Indian Army quickly mobilized about 200,000 troops and Operation Vijay was launched. However, since the heights were under Pakistani control, India was in a clear strategic disadvantage. From their observation posts, the Pakistani forces had a clear line-of-sight to lay down indirect artillery fire on NH 1A, inflicting heavy casualties on the Indians. This was a serious problem for the Indian Army as the highway was its main logistical and supply route. Thus, the Indian Army's first priority was to recapture peaks that were in the immediate vicinity of NH1a. This resulted in Indian troops first targeting the Tiger Hill and Tololing complex in Dras. This was soon followed by more attacks on the Batalik-Turtok sub-sector which provided access to Siachen Glacier. Point 4590, which had the nearest view of the NH1a, was successfully recaptured by Indian forces on June 14.

Though most of the posts in the vicinity of the highway were cleared by mid-June, some parts of the highway near Drass witnessed sporadic shelling until the end of the war. Once NH1a area was cleared, the Indian Army turned to driving the invading force back across the Line of Control.

The Battle of Tololing, among other assaults, slowly tilted the combat in India's favor. Nevertheless, some of the posts put up a stiff resistance, including Tiger Hill (Point 5140) that fell only later in the war. As the operation was fully underway, about 250 artillery guns were brought in to clear the infiltrators in the posts that were in the line-of-sight. In many vital points, neither artillery nor air power could dislodge the outposts manned by the Pakistan soldiers, who were out of visible range. The Indian Army mounted some direct frontal ground assaults which were slow and took a heavy toll given the steep ascent that had to be made on peaks as high as 18,000 feet (5,500 m). Two months into the conflict, Indian troops had slowly retaken most of the ridges they had lost; according to official count, an estimated 75%–80% of the intruded area and nearly all high ground was back under Indian control.

Following the Washington accord on July 4, where Sharif agreed to withdraw Pakistani troops, most of the fighting came to a gradual halt, but some Pakistani forces remained in positions on the Indian side of the LOC. In addition, the United Jihad Council (an umbrella for all extremist groups) rejected Pakistan's plan for a climb-down, instead deciding to fight on. The Indian Army launched its final attacks in the last week of July; as soon as the Drass subsector had been cleared of Pakistani forces, the fighting ceased on July 26. The day has since been marked as *Kargil Vijay Diwas* (Kargil Victory Day) in India. By the end of the war, India had resumed control of all territory south and east of the Line of Control, as was established in July 1972 per the Shimla Accord.

By the time all hostilities had ended, the number of Indian soldiers killed during the conflict stood at 527 while more than 700 regular members of the Pakistani army were killed. The number of Islamist fighters, also known as *Mujahideen*, killed by Indian Armed Forces during the conflict stood at about 3,000.

MAJOR EXERCISES

Operation Parakram

After the December 13, 2001 attack on the Indian Parliament, Operation Parakram was launched in which tens of thousands of Indian troops were deployed along the Indo-Pakistan border. India blamed Pakistan for backing the attack.

The operation was the largest military exercise carried out by any Asian country. Its prime objective is still unclear but appears to have been to prepare the army for any future nuclear conflict with Pakistan, which seemed increasingly possible after the December attack on the Indian parliament.

Operation Sanghe Shakti

It has since been stated that the main goal of this exercise was to validate mobilisation strategies of the Ambala-based *II Strike* Corps. Air support was a part of this exercise, and an entire battalion of paratroops was paradropped during the conduct of the war games, with allied equipment. Some 20,000 soldiers took part in the exercise.

Exercise Ashwamedha

Indian Army tested its network centric warfare capabilities in the exercise Ashwamedha. The exercise was held in the Thar desert, in which over 30,000 troops participated. Asymmetric warfare capability was also tested by the Indian Army during the exercise.

Structure of the Indian Army

Initially, the army's main objective was to defend the nation's frontiers. However, over the years, the army has also taken up the responsibility of providing internal security, especially in insurgent-hit Kashmir and north-east. The army has a strength of about a million troops and fields 34 divisions. Its headquarters is located in the Indian capital New Delhi and it is under the overall command of the Chief of Army Staff (COAS), currently General Deepak Kapoor.

Commands

The army operates 6 tactical commands . Each command is headed by General Officer Commanding-in-Chief with the rank of Lieutenant General. Each command is directly affiliated to the Army HQ in New Delhi. These commands are given below in their correct order of raising, location (city) and their commanders. There is also one training command known as ARTRAC.

Command	Command HQ	GOC-in-C
Southern Command	Pune	Lt Gen Pradeep Khanna, AVSM, VSM
Eastern Command	Kolkata	Lt. Gen. V K Singh,PVSM, AVSM, YSM
Central Command	Lucknow	Lt Gen. J K Mohanty, PVSM, UYSM, SM, VSM
Western Command	Chandimandir (Chandigarh)	Lt. Gen. TK Sapru, PVSM, YSM
Northern Command	Udhampur	Lt Gen P C Bhardwaj, PVSM, AVSM, VrC, SC, VSM
South Western Command	Jaipur	Lt Gen C K S Sabu, AVSM, VSM

Corps

Field Formation

A Corps is an army field formation responsible for a sector within a Command. There are 3 types of Corps in the Indian Army:

Strike, Holding & Mixed. A Command generally consists of 2 or more Corps. A corps has Army Divisions under its command. The Corps HQ is the highest field formation in the army.

Corps	Head Quarter	Command	General Officer Commanding (GOC)	Divisions
1 Corps	Mathura, Uttar Pradesh	Central Command	Lt. Gen.	4 Inf Div (Allahabad), 6 Mtn Div (Bareilly), 33 Armd Div (Hisar)
2 Corps	Ambala, Haryana	Western Command	Lt. Gen.	1 Armd Div (Ambala), 14 RAPID (Dehradun), 22 Inf Div (Meerut)
3 Corps	Rangapahar (Dimapur), Nagaland	Eastern Command	Lt. Gen. Rakesh Kumar Loomba, AVSM	23 Inf Div (Ranchi), 57 Mtn Div (Leimakhong)
4 Corps	Tezpur, Assam	Eastern Command	Lt. Gen. K T Parnaik, VSM	2 Mtn Div (Dibrugarh), 5 Mtn Div (Bomdila), 21 Mtn Div (Rangia)
9 Corps	Yol, Himachal Pradesh	Western Command	Lt. Gen. Vinay Sharma, AVSM, SM, VSM	26 Inf Div (Jammu), 29 Inf Div (Pathankot), 2,3,16 Ind Armd Bdes
10 Corps	Bhatinda, Punjab	Western Command	Lt. Gen. N S Brar, AVSM, VSM, ADC	16 Inf Div (Sri Ganganagar), 18 RAPID (Kota), 24 RAPID (Bikaner), 6 Ind Armd Bde, Engr Bde
11 Corps	Jalandhar, Punjab	Western Command	Lt. Gen. V S Tonk	7 Inf Div (Ferozpur), 9 Inf Div (Meerut), 15 Inf Div (Amritsar), 23 Armd Bde, 55 Mech Bde
12 Corps	Jodhpur, Rajasthan	South Western Command	Lt Gen	4 Arm . Bde, 340 Mech Bde, 11 Inf Div (Ahmedabad), 12 Inf Division (Jodhpur)

14 Corps	Leh, Ladakh	Northern Command	Lt Gen V K Ahluwalia, AVSM, YSM, VSM	3 Inf Div (Leh), 8 Mtn Div (Dras), artillery brigade
15 Corps	Srinagar, Jammu & Kashmir	Northern Command	Lt. Gen. Bikram Singh, AVSM, SM, VSM	19 Inf Div (Baramulla), 28 Inf Div (Gurez, Bandipora District), artillery brigade
16 Corps	Nagrota, Jammu & Kashmir	Northern Command	Lt Gen R K Swamy, AVSM, VSM	10 Inf Div (Akhnoor), 25 Inf Div (Rajauri), 39 Inf Div (Yol), artillery brigade, armoured brigade?
21 Corps(ex IPKF)	Bhopal, Madhya Pradesh	Southern Command	Lt. Gen. A S Lamba, AVSM	31 Armd Div (Jhansi), 36 RAPID (Sagar), 54 Inf Div (Sikandrabad), Arty Bde, AD Bde, Engr Bde
33 Corps	Siliguri, West Bengal	Eastern Command	Lt Gen P K Rath, AVSM	17 Mtn Div (Gangtok), 20 Mtn Div (Binnaguri, Jalpaiguri district), 27 Mtn Div (Kalimpong), arty bde

Regimental Organisation

In addition to this (not to be confused with the Field Corps mentioned above) are the Regiments or Corps or departments of the Indian Army. The corps mentioned below are the functional divisions entrusted with specific pan-Army tasks.

Arms

1. Indian Infantry Regiments
2. Armoured Corps Regiments - The Armoured Corps School and Centre is at Ahmednagar.
3. Regiment of Artillery - The School of Artillery is at Devlali near Nasik.
4. Corps of Engineers - The College of Military Engineering is at Dapodi, Pune. The Centers are located as follows-

Madras Engineer Group at Bangalore, Bengal Engineer Group at Roorkee and Bombay Engineer Group at Khadki, Pune.

5. Corps of Army Air Defence-Center at Gopalpur in Orissa State.
6. Mechanised Infantry - Regimental Center at Ahmednagar.
7. Corps of Signals
8. Army Aviation Corps

Services

1. Army Dental Corps
2. Army Education Corps - Center at Pachmarhi.
3. Army Medical Corps - Center at Lucknow.
4. Army Ordnance Corps - Centers at Jabalpur andSecunderabad.
5. Army Postal Service Corps
6. Army Service Corps - Center at Bangalore
7. Corps of Electrical and Mechanical Engineers- Centers at Bhopal and Secunderabad .
8. Corps of Military Police [2] - Center at Bangalore
9. Intelligence Corps - Center at Pune.
10. Judge Advocate General's Deptt. - Institute of Military Law kamptee,Nagpur.
11. Military Farms Service
12. Military Nursing Service
13. Remount and Veterinary Corps
14. Pioneer Corps

Other Field Formations

- Division: An Army Division is an intermediate between a Corps and a Brigade. It is the largest striking force in the army. Each Division is headed by [General Officer Commanding] (GOC) in the rank of Major General. It usually consists of 15,000 combat troops and 8,000 support elements. Currently, the Indian Army has 34 Divisions including 4 RAPID (Re-organised Army Plains Infantry Divisions) Action Divisions, 18 Infantry Divisions, 10 Mountain Divisions, 3 Armoured Divisions and 2 Artillery Divisions. Each Division composes of several Brigades.

- Brigade: The Brigade is smaller than the Division and generally consists of 3 Infantry Battalions along with elements of various Combat & Support Arms & Services. It is headed by a Brigadier equivalent to a Brigadier General. The Indian Army also has 5 Independent Armoured Brigades, 15 Independent Artillery Brigades, 7 Independent Infantry Brigades, 1 Independent Parachute Brigade,3 Independent Air Defence Brigades, 2 Independent Air Defence Groups and 4 Independent Engineer Brigades. These Independent Brigades operate directly under the Corps Commander (GOC Corps).
- Battalion: A Battalion is commanded by a Colonel and is the Infantry's main fighting unit. It consists of more than 900 personnel.
- Company: Headed by the Major, a Company comprises 120 soldiers.
- Platoon: An intermediate between a Company and Section, a Platoon is headed by a Lieutenant or depending on the availability of Commissioned Officers, a Junior Commissioned Officer, with the rank of Subedar or Naib-Subedar. It has a total strength of about 32 troops.
- Section: Smallest military outfit with a strength of 10 personnel. Commanded by a Non-commissioned officer of the rank of Havildar Major or Sergeant Major.

Regiments

Infantry Regiments: There are several battalions or units under the same formation in a Regiment. The Gurkha Regiment, for instance, has several battalions. All formations under a Regiment are battalions of the same arms or Corps (i.e., Infantry or Engineers). Regiments are not exactly field formations; they mostly do not make a formation. All Regiments of the Gurkha's for instance would not fight together as one formation, but can be dispersed over various Brigades or Corps or even Commands.

Artillery Regiments

The Regiment of Artillery constitutes a formidable operational arm of Indian Army. Historically it takes its lineage from Moghul Emperor Babur who is popularly credited with introduction of Artillery in India, in the Battle of Panipat in 1526. However evidence of earlier use of gun by Bahmani Kings in the Battle of Adoni in 1368 and King Mohammed Shah of Gujrat in fifteenth century have been recorded.

INDIAN ARMY STAFF

Strength

Indian Army statistics

Active Troops	1,300,000
Reserve Troops	1,200,000
Territorial Army	200,000**
Main Battle Tanks	4,500
Artillery	12,800
Ballistic missiles	100 (Agni-1,Agni-2)
Ballistic missiles	>500 (Prithvi-1)
Cruise missiles	BrahMos
Aircraft	10 squadrons of helicopters
Surface-to-air missiles	90000

* includes 300,000 1st line troops and 500,000 2nd line troops

** includes 40,000 1st line troops and 160,000 2nd line troops

Statistics

- 4 RAPID (Reorganised Army Plains Infantry Divisions)
- 18 Infantry Divisions
- 10 Mountain Divisions
- 3 Armoured Divisions
- 2 Artillery Divisions
- 13 Air Defence Brigades + 2 Surface-to-Air Missile Groups
- 5 Independent Armoured Brigades
- 15 Independent Artillery Brigades
- 7 Independent Infantry Brigades
- 1 Parachute Brigade
- 4 Engineer Brigades
- 14 Army Aviation Helicopter Units

Sub-Units

- 63 Tank Regiments
- 7 Airborne Battalions
- 200 Artillery Regiments
- 360 Infantry Battalions + 5 Para (SF) Battalions
- 40 Mechanised Infantry Battalions
- 20 Combat Helicopter Units
- 52 Air Defence Regiments

Rank Structure

The various rank of the Indian Army are listed below in descending order:

Commissioned Officers

- Field Marshal[1]
- General (the rank held by Chief of Army Staff)
- Lieutenant-General

- Major-General
- Brigadier
- Colonel
- Lieutenant-Colonel
- Major
- Captain
- Lieutenant

Junior Commissioned Officers (JCOs)

- Subedar Major/Honorary Captain[3]
- Subedar/Honorary Lieutenant[3]
- Subedar Major
- Subedar
- Naib Subedar

Non Commissioned Officers (NCOs)

- Regimental Havildar Major[2]
- Regimental Quarter Master Havildar[2]
- Company Havildar Major
- Company Quarter Master Havildar
- Havildar
- Naik
- Lance Naik
- Sepoy

Note:

1. Only two officers have been made Field Marshall so far: Field Marshal K M Cariappa – the first Indian Commander-in-Chief (a post since abolished) – and Field Marshal S H F J Manekshaw, the Chief of Army Staff during the Army in the 1971 war with Pakistan.

2. This has now been discontinued. Non-Commissioned Officers in the rank of Havildar are elible for Honorary JCO ranks.
3. Given to Outstanding JCO's Rank and pay of a Lieutenant, role continues to be of a JCO.

Combat Doctrine

The current combat doctrine of the Indian Army is based on effectively utilizing holding formations and strike formations. In the case of an attack, the holding formations would contain the enemy and strike formations would counterattack to neutralize enemy forces.

In the case of an Indian attack, the holding formations would pin enemy forces down whilst the strike formations attack at a point of Indian choosing. The Indian Army is large enough to devote several corps to the strike role. Currently, the army is also looking at enhancing its special forces capabilities.

Equipment

Most of the army equipment is imported, but efforts are being made to manufacture indigenous equipment. All Indian Military Firearms guns are manufactured under the umbrella administration of the Ordnance Factory Board, with principal Firearm manufacturing facilities in Ishapore, Cossipore, Kanpur, Jabalpur and Tiruchirapalli. Indian National Small Arms System (INSAS) rifle, which is successfully inducted by Indian Army since 1997 is a product of Rifle Factory, Ishapore. While ammunition is manufactured at Khadki and possibly at Bolangir.

Aircraft

The Indian Army operates more than 200 helicopters, plus additional unmanned aerial vehicles.

The Indian army had projected a requirement for a helicopter that can carry loads of up to 75 kg heights of 23,000 feet (7,000 m) on the Siachen Glacier in Jammu and Kashmir. Flying at these heights poses unique challenges due to the rarefied atmosphere. The Indian Army chose the Eurocopter AS 550 for a $550 million contract for 197 light helicopters to replace its ageing fleet of Chetaks and Cheetahs, some of which were inducted more than three decades ago. The deal has however been scrapped amidst allegations of corruption during the bidding process.

Aircraft	Origin	Type	Versions	In service[45]	Notes
HAL Dhruv	India	utility helicopter		36+	To acquire 73 more Dhruv in next 5 years.
Aérospatiale SA 316 Alouette III	France	utility helicopter	SA 316B Chetak	60	to be replaced by Dhruv
Aérospatiale SA 315 Lama	France	utility helicopter	SA 315B Cheetah	48	to be replaced by Dhruv
DRDO Nishant	India	reconnaissance UAV		12	Delivered 12 UAV's in 2008.
IAI Searcher II	Israel	reconnaissance UAV		100+	
IAI Heron II	Israel	reconnaissance UAV		50+	

Future Developments

India is currently reorganising their mechanised forces to achieve strategic mobility and high-volume firepower for rapid thrusts into enemy territory.

India has plans to progressively induct as many as 1,657 Russian-origin T-90S main-battle tanks (MBTs), apart from the ongoing upgradation of its T-72 fleet. the Indian Army has gone in for an urgent order of 4,100 French-origin Milan-2T anti-tank guided missiles (ATGMs). Defence ministry sources said the Rs 592-crore (USD 120 million approx.) order for 4,100 Milan-2T missiles was cleared after 26/11, with the government finally fast-tracking several military procurement plans.

Recipients of the Param Vir Chakra

Listed below are the most notable people to have received the Param Vir Chakra, the highest military decoration of the Indian Army.

Major Som Nath Sharma	4th Battalion, Kumaon Regiment	November 3, 1947	Badgam, Kashmir, India
Second Lieutenant Rama Raghoba Rane	Corps of Engineers	April 8, 1948	Naushera, Kashmir, India
Naik Jadu Nath Singh	1st Battalion, Rajput Regiment	February 1948	Naushera, Kashmir, India
Company Havildar Major Piru Singh	6th Battalion, Rajputana Rifles	July 17/18, 1948	Tithwal, Kashmir, India
Lance Naik Karam Singh	1st Battalion, Sikh Regiment	October 13, 1948	Tithwal, Kashmir, India
Captain Gurbachan Singh Salaria	3rd Battalion, 1st Gorkha Rifles (The Malaun Regiment)	December 5, 1961	Elizabethville, Katanga, Congo
Major Dhan Singh Thapa	1st Battalion, 8th Gorkha Rifles	October 20, 1962	Ladakh, India
Subedar Joginder Singh	1st Battalion, Sikh Regiment	October 23, 1962	Tongpen La, Northeast Frontier Agency, India
Major Shaitan Singh	13th Battalion, Kumaon Regiment	November 18, 1962	Rezang La
Company Quarter Master Havildar Abdul Hamid	4th Battalion, The Grenadiers	September 10, 1965	Chima, Khem Karan Sector
Lieutenant-Colonel Ardeshir Burzorji Tarapore	17th Poona Horse	October 15, 1965	Phillora, Sialkot Sector, Pakistan
Lance Naik Albert Ekka	14th Battalion, Brigade of the Guards	December 3, 1971	Gangasagar
2/Lieutenant Arun Khetarpal	17th Poona Horse	December 16, 1971	Jarpal, Shakargarh Sector
Major Hoshiar Singh	3rd Battalion, The Grenadiers	December 17, 1971	Basantar River, Shakargarh Sector
Naib Subedar Bana Singh	8th Battalion, Jammu and Kashmir Light Infantry	June 23, 1987	Siachen Glacier, Jammu and Kashmir
Major Ramaswamy Parmeshwaran	8th Battalion, Mahar Regiment	November 25, 1987	Sri Lanka
Captain Vikram Batra	13th Battalion, Jammu and Kashmir Rifles	July 6, 1999	Point 5140, Point 4875, Kargil Area
Lieutenant Manoj Kumar Pandey	1st Battalion, 11th Gorkha Rifles	July 3, 1999	Khaluber/Juber Top, Batalik sector, Kargil area, Jammu and Kashmir
Grenadier Yogendra Singh Yadav	18th Battalion, The Grenadiers	July 4, 1999	Tiger Hill, Kargil area
Rifleman Sanjay Kumar	13th Battalion, Jammu and Kashmir Rifles	July 5, 1999	Area Flat Top, Kargil Area

PAKISTAN ARMY

The Pakistan Army is the largest branch of the Pakistan military, and is mainly responsible for protection of the state borders, the security of administered territories and defending the national interests of Pakistan within the framework of its international obligations. The Pakistan Army, combined with the Navy and Air Force, makes Pakistan's armed forces the seventh largest military in the world. The Army is modelled on the United Kingdom armed forces and came into existence after the independence in 1947. It has an active force of 650,000 personnel and 528,000 men in reserve that continue to serve until the age of 45 and several other groups functioning under its many umbrella organisations. The Pakistani Army is a volunteer force and has been involved in many conflicts with India. Combined with this rich combat experience, the Army is also actively involved in contributing to United Nations peacekeeping efforts. Other foreign deployments have consisted of Pakistani Army personnel as advisers in many African, South Asian and Arab countries. The Pakistani Army maintained division and brigade strength presences in some of the Arab countries during the past Arab-Israeli Wars, and the first Gulf War to help the Coalition. The Pakistani Army is led by General Ashfaq Parvez Kayani

Combat Doctrine

Pakistan Army has a doctrine of limited "offensive-defense"which it has tried to refine consistently ever since 1989 when it was pushed out to the formations during "Exercise Zarb-e-Momin". The main purpose of this strategy is to launch a sizeable offensive into enemy territory rather than wait to be hit from the enemy's offensive attack. The doctrine is based on the premise that while on the offensive, the enemy can be kept off-balance while allowing Pakistani Army to be able to seize enemy territory of strategic importance which can be used as a bargaining chip on the negotiating table. In order to do this, currently Pakistani Army maintains two sizable Strike Corps which will be backed up by Defensive Corps forming the defensive tier behind the strike corps.

By pushing the offensive into enemy territory, the Pakistani Army hopes to consolidate its gains inside the enemy's territory. Pakistan will attempt to keep the enemy on its of the border rather than giving ground on the Pakistani side. In the 1990s, the Army created a strong centralized corps of reserves for its formations in the critical semi-desert and desert sectors in southern Punjab and Sindh provinces. These new formations were rapidly equipped with assets needed for mechanized capability. These reserve formations are dual-capable, meaning they can be used for offensive as well as defensive (holding) purposes.

Motto

The motto of the Pakistani Army reads: "Iman, Taqwa, Jihad fi Sabilillah". Translated into English, it means "Faith, Piety, to strive in the path of Allah putting aside all your physical needs]".

Organisation

The Chief of the Army Staff (COAS), formerly called the Commander in Chief (C in C), is challenged with the responsibility of commanding the Pakistani Army. The COAS operates from army headquarters in Rawalpindi, near Islamabad. The Principal Staff Officers (PSO's) assisting him in his duties at the Lieutenant General level include a Chief of General Staff (CGS), under whom the Military Operations and Intelligence Directorates function; the Chief of Logistics Staff (CLS); the Adjutant General (AG); the Quarter-Master General (QMG); the Inspector General of Training and Evaluation (IGT&E); and the Military Secretary (MS). A major reorganization in GHQ was done in September 2008 under General Ashfaq Parvez Kayani, when two new PSO positions were introduced: the Inspector General Arms and the Inspector General Communications and IT, thus raising the number of PSO's to eight. The headquarters function also includes the Judge Advocate General (JAG), and the Comptroller of Civilian Personnel, the Chief of the Corps of Engineers (E-in-C) who is also head of Military Engineering Service (MES), all of them also report to the Chief of the Army Staff.

Corps

There are 11 Corps including the newly formed strategic corps (2004) and Army Air Defence Command located at various garrisons all over Pakistan.

Corps	HQ Location	Major Formations under Corps	Commander
I Corps	Mangla,	6th Armoured Division (Kharian), 17th Infantry Division (Kharian), 37th Infantry Division (Gujranwala)	Lt Gen Nadeem Ahmad
II Corps	Multan, Punjab	1st Armoured Division (Multan), 40th Infantry Division (Okara)	Lt Gen Sikandar Afzal
IV Corps	Lahore, Punjab	10th Infantry Division (Lahore), 11th Infantry Division (Lahore)	Lt Gen Ijaz Ahmed Bakhshi
V Corps	Karachi, Sindh	16th Infantry Division (Pano Akil), 18th Infantry Division (Hyderabad), 25th Mechanized Division (Malir)	Lt Gen Shahid Iqbal
X Corps	Rawalpindi, Punjab	Force Command Northern Areas (Gilgit), 12th Infantry Division (Murree), 19th Infantry Division (Mangla), 23rd Infantry Division (Jhelum)	Lt Gen Tahir Mahmood
XI Corps	Peshawar, North West Frontier Province	7th Infantry Division (Peshawar), 9th Infantry Division (Kohat)	Lt Gen Muhammad Masood Aslam
XII Corps	Quetta, Balochistan	33rd Infantry Division (Quetta), 41st Infantry Division (Quetta)	Lt Gen Khalid Shameem Wynne
XXX Corps	Gujranwala, Punjab	8th Infantry Division (Sialkot), 15th Infantry Division (Sialkot)	Lt Gen Nadeem Taj
XXXI Corps	Bahawalpur, Punjab	26th Mechanized Division (Bahawalpur), 35th Infantry Division (Bahawalpur), 14th Infantry Division (Okara)	Lt Gen Muhammad Yousaf[2]
Strategic Corps	Rawalpindi, Punjab	47th Artillery Brigade (Sargodha), others	Lt Gen Syed Absar Hussain
Air Defence Command	Rawalpindi, Punjab	4th Air Defence Division (Karachi), 5th Air Defence Division (Sargodha),46th Independent Air Defence Brigade (Kahuta)	Lt Gen Muhammad Ashraf Saleem

List of Chiefs of Army Staff

Chief of Army Staff of the Pakistan Army

1. General Sir Frank Messervy (15 August 1947 - 10 February 1948)
2. General Sir Douglas Gracey (11 February 1948 - 16 January 1951)
3. Field Marshal Ayub Khan (16 January 1951 - 26 October 1958)
4. General Musa Khan (27 October 1958 - 17 June 1966)
5. General Yahya Khan (18 June 1966 – 20 December 1971)
6. General Gul Hassan (20 December 1971 - 3 March 1972)
7. General Tikka Khan (3 March 1972 – 1 March 1976)
8. General Muhammad Zia-ul-Haq (1 April 1976 - 17 August 1988)
9. General Mirza Aslam Beg (17 August 1988 - 16 August 1991)
10. General Asif Nawaz (16 August 1991 - 8 January 1993)
11. General Wahid Kakar (8 January 1993 - 12 January 1996)
12. General Jehangir Karamat (12 January 1996 - 6 October 1998)
13. General Pervez Musharraf (7 October 1998 - 28 November 2007)
14. General Ashfaq Parvez Kayani (28 November 2007 - present)

Structure of Army units

The Pakistani Army is divided into two main branches, which are Arms and Services. Arms include:

- Army Infantry Regiments
- Regiment of Artillery
- Armoured Corps Regiments

- Regiment of Air Defence
- Corps of Engineers
- Army Medical Corps
- Corps of Signals
- Army Aviation Corps
- Defence Security Group (DSG)

And Services include:

- Army Ordnance Corps
- Corps of Electrical & Mechanical Engineering (EME)
- Army Supply & Transport Corps (ASC)

Regiments

* The President's Bodyguard formed at independence from members of the Governor General's Bodyguard, itself successor to the Governor's Troop of Moghals raised in 1773
* 5th Horse is the successor to the 1st Sikh Irregular Cavalry (Wales's Horse), and the 2nd Sikh Irregular Cavalry, both raised in 1857
* 6th Lancers is the successor to The Rohilkhand Horse raised in 1857, and the 4th Sikh Irregular Cavalry raised in 1858
* Guides Cavalry (Frontier Force) is the successor to the Corps of Guides raised in 1846
* 11th Cavalry (Frontier Force) is the successor to 1st Regiment of Punjab Cavalry and 3rd Regiment of Punjab Cavalry, both raised in 1849
* 13th Lancers is the successor to the 1st Native Troop raised in 1804, and the 2nd Native Troop raised in 1816. It is also the senior most armour regiment of the Indian Sub-Continent.
* 15th Lancers is the successor to the Multani Regiment Of Cavalry raised in 14th January 1858.

- Infantry:
  - Frontier Force (FF)
  - Punjab
  - Sindh
  - Baloch
  - Azad Kashmir (AK)
  - Northern Light Infantry (NLI)
- The President's Bodyguard
- Armour
  - 4th Cavalry
  - 5th Horse
  - 6th Lancers
  - 7th Lancers
  - 8th Cavalry
  - 9th Lancers
  - Guides Cavalry (Frontier Force)
  - 11th Cavalry (Frontier Force)
  - 12th Cavalry (Frontier Force)
-
  - 13th Lancers
  - 14th Lancers
  - 15th Lancers (Baloch)
  - 16th Horse
  - 17th Lancer
  - 18th Horse
  - 19th Lancers
  - 20th Lancers
  - 22nd Cavalry
  - 23rd Cavalry (Frontier Force)
  - 24th Cavalry (Frontier Force)
  - 25th Cavalry (Frontier Force)
  - 26th Cavalry
  - 27th Cavalry
-
  - 28th Cavalry
  - 29th Cavalry
  - 30th Cavalry
  - 31st Cavalry
  - 32nd Cavalry
  - 33rd Cavalry
  - 34th Lancers
  - 37th Cavalry
  - 41st Horse (Frontier Force)
  - 52nd Cavalry
  - 53rd Cavalry
  - 54th Cavalry
  - 56th Cavalry
  - 57th Cavalry
  - 58th Cavalry

* 19th Lancers is the successor to the 2nd Mahratta Horse (Tiwana Horse) raised in 1858, and Fane's Horse raised in 1860

* 25th Cavalry (Frontier Force) is the famous unit which stopped Indian armour thrust in Chawinda in 1965

* The Punjab Regiment formed in 1956 from the 1st, 14th, 15th and 16th Punjab Regiments; can be traced back to the 3rd Battalion of Coast Sepoys raised in 1759
* The Baloch Regiment formed in 1956 from the 8th Punjab Regiment, The Baloch Regiment, and The Bahawalpur Regiment; can be traced back to the 3rd Extra Madras Battalion raised in 1798
* The Frontier Force Regiment is the successor to the Frontier Brigade raised in 1846
* The Azad Kashmir Regiment was raised in 1947, became part of the army in 1971
* The Sindh Regiment was raised in 1980 from battalions of the Punjab Regiment and Baloch Regiment
* The Northern Light Infantry was formed in 1977 from various paramilitary units of scouts, became part of the army in 1999 after the Kargil War
* The Special Service Group was formed in 1959 around a cadre from the Baloch Regiment

HISTORY OF THE PAKISTAN ARMY

1947 - 1958

The Pakistani Army was created on 30 June 1947 with the division of the British Indian Army and Pakistan received six armoured, eight artillery and eight infantry regiments compared to the forty armoured, forty artillery and twenty one infantry regiments that went to India. Fearing that India would take over the disputed region of Kashmir, the newly created Pakistani Army sent in irregulars and tribal groups in 1947 which lead to the Indo-Pakistani War of 1947.

Regular army units joined the invasion later on but were stopped on UK pressure but not before occupying the northwestern part of Kashmir. During the 1950s, the Pakistani Army received large amounts of economic and military aid from United States and Great

Britain after signing two Mutual Defense Treaties, Central Treaty Organization, (Cento) also known as the Baghdad Pact and SEATO, (South East Asian Treaty Organization) in 1954. This aid greatly expanded the Army from its modest beginnings.

The sole division HQ that went to Pakistan was the 7th. 8th and 9th Divisions were raised in 1947; 10, 12 and 14 Division were raised in 1948. 15 Div was raised in 1950. At some point before 1954, 6 Div was raised and 9 Div disbanded. 6 Div was disbanded at some point after 1954 as US assistance was available only for 1 armed and 6 infantry division. 1st Armoured Div was raised in 1956.

1958 - 1969

The Army seized control of Pakistan for the first time when General Ayub Khan came to power through a bloodless coup in 1958. Tensions with India continued in the 1960s and a brief border skirmish was fought near the Rann of Kutch area during April 1965, in which the Indian Army was repulsed with moderate casualties. Emboldened, the Pakistan Army leaders carried out Operation Gibraltar, an attempt to take Kashmir, that was launched later in the year, resulting in the Indo-Pakistani War of 1965, after the Pakistani infiltrators were discovered, India counter-attacked.

The 3-week war ended in a U.N. mandated ceasefire culminating in the Tashkent Declaration. However, the military generally considers the 1965 war as a victory over a rival that outnumbered it by almost 3 to 1 in all military aspects. In that regard, the valour of Major Raja Aziz Bhatti of thwarting an entire Indian Brigade planning to break into Lahore and the Battle Of Chawinda are considered to be one of the most courageous feats in the army.

At Chawinda the Pakistan Army was vastly outnumbered in terms of personnel and equipment but it is said that victory was achieved when Pakistani East Bengal Regiment soldiers tied bombs to their bellies in order to stop the advancing Indian tanks. An uprising against General Ayub Khan, during 1968 and 1969 resulted in Ayub Khan relinquishing his office as President and Chief of

Pakistan Army in favor of General Yahya Khan who assumed power in 1969.6 Armoured and 11 Infantry Divisions were raised in adhoc form 1964-65. 16, 18 and 23 Divisions were raised at some point between 1966-69; and 9 Division was re-raised in this period.

1969 - 1977

During the rule of General Yahya Khan, the Bengalis protested their poor conditions and civil unrest broke out in East Pakistan amidst incidents of massive human rights abuses carried out and genocide by the Pakistani Army and military.

India joined the war on the side of Bangladesh following seven months of civil war in November 1971, and on the 16th of December, 1971, over 50,000 Pakistani Armed forces personnel (army, air force and navy) around 40,000 government and civil employees surrendered to the Indian forces and Bangladesh became a republic. Consequently, the Pakistan army was modernized at a faster pace than ever before. After the war, General Yahya Khan resigned and Zulfikar Ali Bhutto took over the reins.

1977 - 1999

In 1977 the Pakistan Army took over the government of Pakistan after a coup by General Zia ul-Haq, which saw the end of another democratically elected government leading to the hanging of Zulfikar Ali Bhutto, after he was tried and found guilty of conspiracy of murdering a politician named Kasuri. General Zia ul-Haq ruled as a military dictator until his mysterious explosion aircraft death in 1988.

Pakistani army also helped the Saudi Arabian Government in regaining the control of the Kaaba with the help of French Commandos. Pakistani and French security forces retook the Kaaba in a battle which left approximately 250 dead, and 600 wounded. The Pakistanis and French were called in after poor results from assaults by the Saudi Arabian National Guard (SANG). 127 were reported to have been killed.

In the mid-1970s the Pakistani Army was involved in fighting an uprising in Balochistan. Various Balochi factions, some with the oblique support of the USSR, wanted independence or at least greater provincial rights. The rebellion was put down but the Army suffered heavy casualties.

With the Soviet invasion of Afghanistan, the United States began to provide large scale military and economic aid to Pakistan to modernize its conventional military capability and, ostensibly at least, prevent any Soviet attacks on it. This aid was also intended as an incentive for Pakistan to aid guerrilla forces (called "Army of GOD") in Afghanistan. The SSG created a unit called the Black Storks in which SSG commandos were dressed up as Afghan Mujahideen during the Soviet-Afghan war. They were then flown into Afghanistan and provided the Mujahideen with support. The United States allocated about 40% of its assistance package to non-reimbursable credits for military purchases, the fourth largest program after Israel, Egypt and Turkey. The remainder of the aid program was devoted to economic assistance.

After the Soviets withdrew by 1989 and the Pakistani Nuclear weapons program nearing maturity, Pakistan was placed under sanctions by USA in 1990. Various weapon systems ordered by Pakistan such as F-16 Jets were not delivered but various amendments have authorized return of spare parts and end items already paid for by Pakistan. There was a period of international sanctions due to Pakistan's nuclear tests. During 1999 the Pakistan Army for the fourth time overthrew a democratically elected government which resulted in additional sanctions being placed against Pakistan

The Army fought a brief border skirmish with India in Kargil 1999 after the Pakistan Army sent in their para-military NLI troops dressed as mujahiddin into Indian territory. There was a danger of the war spiraling out of control when Nawaz Sharif, under immense pressure from Washington, eventually ordered a withdrawal.

This decision and the resulting Pakistani casualties created great resentment in the Army against the Prime Minister and is rumored to have contributed to his eventual over throwing by the COAS. 40 and 41 Divs were raised in the 1980s; Two more divs have been raised under the rubric "Corps Reserves" for V and XXXI corps.

1999 - Present

In October 1999 the Pakistan Army for the fourth time, with popular support, overthrew a democratically elected government which resulted in additional sanctions being placed against Pakistan, resulting in General Pervez Musharraf coming to power in a bloodless coup. Musharraf stepped down as President in August 2008.

Since the 9/11 incident, Pakistan unrecognized the Taliban and has become a key ally of the United States in the fight against terrorism. As part of the U.S.'s War on Terrorism, the army has moved over 100,000 troops to the Pakistan-Afghan border to patrol against extreme elements cross border infiltration.

The Pakistan Army commenced operations in Balochistan during 2006, resulting in the killing of the leader of the Balochis, Nawab Akbar Bugti and has resulted in the crushing of a rebellion by the Balochistan Liberation Army.

PAKISTAN ARMY ROLE IN PEACEKEEPING

In the wake of the new world power equilibrium a more complex security environment has emerged. It is characterized by growing national power politics and state implosions which have necessitated involvement of the United Nations peace keeping forces for conflict resolution.

The United Nations has been undertaking peace keeping operations since its inception, but the need for employment of peace keeping forces has increased manifold since the Gulf War. In 1992 there were 11000 Blue Berets deployed around the world, by the end of the year the figure rose to 52000. Presently it exceeds a staggering figure of 80,000 troops.

Pakistan Contribution in UN Peace Keeping Missions

- UN Operation in Congo (ONUC) 1960-1964
- UN Security Force in New Guinea, West Irian (UNSF) 1962-1963
- UN Yemen Observer Mission Yemen (UNYOM) 1963-1964
- UN Transition Assistance Group in Namibia (UNTAG) 1989-1990
- UN Iraq-Kuwait Observer Mission (UNIKOM) 1991-2003
- UN Mission in Haiti (UNMIH) 1993-1996
- UN Transitional Authority in Cambodia (UNTAC) 1992-1993
- UN Operations in Somalia (UNOSOM) 1992-1995
- UN Protection Forces in Bosnia (UNPROFOR) 1992-1995
- UN Observer Mission for Rawanda (UNAMIR) 1993-1996
- UN Verification Mission in Angola (UNAVEM III) 1995-1997
- UN Transitional Administration for Eastern Slavonia (UNTAES) 1996-1997
- UN Mission of Observers in Prevlaka (UNMOP) 1996-2002
- UN Assistance Mission in Sierra Leone (UNAMSIL) 2001-2005
- UN Transitional Administration in East Timor (UNTAET) 1999-to-date
- UN Mission in Democratic Republic of the Congo (MONUC) 2003-to-date
- UN Mission in Liberia (UNMIL) 2003-to-date
- UN Mission in Ivory Coast (ONUCI) 2004-to-date
- UN Mission in Burundi (ONUB) 2004-to-date

- UN Mission in Sudan (UNMIS) 2005-to-date
- UN Mission in Kosovo (UNMIK) 1999-to-date

Currently, Pakistan has the most operational army in UN peace keeping missions. Notable are its achievements in DRC and Somalia

POLITICAL POWER OF THE ARMY

The Pakistani army has always played an integral part of the Pakistan government since its inception. It has virtually acted as a third party that has repeatedly seized power in the name of stabilizing Pakistan. General Ayub Khan came to power in 1956 due to political turmoil within the ruling party.

The situation was so dire that the speaker of the National Assembly was beaten to death right in front of the assembly hall. Ayub Khan reluctantly agreed to take power as a favour to the nation. Later on, General Yahya Khan would assume power in 1969. After the 1971 war, democracy was restored only to be cut short in 1977 after a coup which saw the hanging of Zulfikar Ali Bhutto, the Pakistani Premier. General Zia ul-Haq ruled as a dictator virtually unopposed until his death in 1988. Despite the exit of the army from mainstream politics, the political muscle of the military is everpresent. The former President, General (ret) Pervez Musharraf, came to power in a bloodless coup in October 1999 overthrowing the last democratically elected government led by Nawaz Sharif.

Fauji Foundation

Fauji Foundation (established in 1954) is a charitable trust, operating on a completely self sustaining basis, channeling approximately 80% of the profits from commercial ventures into social protection programmes that serve a beneficiary population representing approximately 7% of the country's population.

Spending more than Rs. 21 billion since inception on welfare, the Foundation provides services in the areas of healthcare, education, educational stipends, technical and vocational training.

Over 2.1 million patients treated per year through the FF Healthcare System

- Approximately 38,000 students enrolled in the FF Education System
- Approximately 70,000 educational stipends dispersed each year
- Over 6,000 individuals trained annually through the Vocational & Technical Training Centres

Considered the most sustainable social protection mechanism in the country, Fauji Foundation provides welfare services to approximately 10 million individuals on a completely sustainable basis. Running autonomously for over 50 years, the foundation has been providing healthcare, education, vocational and technical training to over 7% of the country's population through 294 welfare projects.

PERSONNEL TRAINING

Enlisted Ranks

Most enlisted personnel used to come from rural families, and many have only rudimentary literacy skills, but with the increase in the litracy level the requirements have been raised to Matriculate level (10th Grade). Recruits are processed gradually through a paternalistically run regimental training center, taught the official language, Urdu, if necessary, and given a period of elementary education before their military training actually starts. In the thirty-six-week training period, they develop an attachment to the regiment they will remain with through much of their careers and begin to develop a sense of being a Pakistani rather than primarily a member of a tribe or a village. Enlisted men usually serve for eighteen years, during which they participate in regular training cycles and have the opportunity to take academic courses to help them advance.

Officer Ranks

About 320 men enter the army bi-annually through the Pakistan Military Academy at Kakul in Abbottabad in the North West Frontier

Province; a small number—especially physicians and technical specialists—are directly recruited, and these persons are part of the heart of the officer corps. The product of a highly competitive selection process, members of the officer corps have completed twelve years of education and spend two years at the Pakistan Military Academy, with their time divided about equally between military training and academic work to bring them up to a baccalaureate education level, which includes English-language skills.

The army has twelve other training establishments, including schools concentrating on specific skills such as infantry, artillery, intelligence, or mountain warfare. A National University of Science and Technology (NUST) has been established which has absorbed the existing colleges of engineering, signals, electrical engineering and medicine. At the apex of the army training system is the Command and Staff College at Quetta, one of the few institutions inherited from the colonial period. The college offers a ten-month course in tactics, staff duties, administration, and command functions through the division level. Students from foreign countries, including the United States, have attended the school but reportedly have been critical of its narrow focus and failure to encourage speculative thinking or to give adequate attention to less glamorous subjects, such as logistics.

The senior training institution for all service branches is the National Defence University. Originally established in 1971 at Rawalpindi, to provide training in higher military strategy for senior officers, the school house was relocated to Islamabad in 1995. It also offers courses that allow civilians to explore the broader aspects of national security. In a program begun in the 1980s to upgrade the intellectual standards of the officer corps and increase awareness of the wider world, a small group of officers, has been detailed to academic training, achieving master's degrees and even doctorates at universities in Pakistan and abroad.

Pakistani officers were sent abroad during the 1950s and into the 1960s for training in Britain and other Commonwealth countries, and especially to the United States, where trainees numbering well in the hundreds attended a full range of institutions ranging from armored and infantry schools to the higher staff and command institutions.

After 1961 this training was coordinated under the International Military Education and Training (IMET) program, but numbers varied along with vicissitudes in the United States-Pakistan military relationship.

Of some 200 officers being sent abroad annually in the 1980s, over two-thirds went to the United States, but the cessation of United States aid in 1990 entailed suspension of the IMET program. In 1994 virtually all foreign training was in Commonwealth countries. However, after the 9/11 attacks, Pakistan again has begun sending officers to US Army schools. Today there are more than 400 officers serving in foreign countries.

Officers retire between the ages of fifty-two and sixty, depending on their rank.

RELIEF OPERATIONS AND ECONOMIC DEVELOPMENT

In times of natural disaster, such as the great floods of 1992 or the October 2005 devastating earthquake, army engineers, medical and logistics personnel, and the armed forces played a major role in bringing relief and supplies.

The army also engaged in extensive economic activities. Most of these enterprises, such as stud and dairy farms, were for the army's own use, but others performed functions beneficial to the local civilian economy. Army factories produced such goods as sugar, fertilizer, and brass castings and sold them to civilian consumers.

Several army organizations performed functions that were important to the civilian sector across the country. For example, the National Logistics Cell was responsible for trucking food and other goods across the country; the Frontier Works Organization built the

Karakoram Highway to China; and the Special Communication Organization maintained communications networks in remote parts of Pakistan.

Pakistan Army is involved in relief activities not only in Pakistan but also in many other countries of the world, like they went for relief activities after Bangladesh was recently hit by floods. Pak Army also went to Indonesia, Bangladesh and Sri Lanka after they were hit by tsunami.

Pakistan army and Navy sent ships and helicopters to the friendly nations for tsunami relief operation.

Women and Minorities in the Army

Women have served in the Pakistani Army since its foundation. Currently, there is a sizable number of Women serving in the army. Most women are recruited in the regular Army to perform medical and educational work.

There is also a Women's Guard section of Pakistan's National Guard where women are trained in nursing, welfare and clerical work and there are also women recruited in very limited numbers for the Janbaz Force.

Only recently has Pakistan began to recruit women for combat positions and the Elite Anti-Terrorist Force In 2007, several female graduates were nominated to be Sky Marshalls for Pakistan based airlines. In addition recently eight of the 41 cadets from the Pakistan Military Academy at Kakul became the first women guards of honour. Pakistan is the only country in the Islamic world to have women Major *Generals* in the Army.

Recruitment is nationwide and the army attempts to maintain an ethnic balance but most enlisted recruits, as in British times, come from a few districts in northern Punjab Province and the adjacent Azad Kashmir and the North West Frontier Province. Pakistan's Officer Corps are also mostly from Punjab and the North West Frontier Province and of middle-class, rural backgrounds.

Minorities in Pakistan are allowed to sit in all examinations, including the one conducted by Inter Services Selection Board however the proportion of religious minorities in the Pakistan army is still considerably very less. The army sees itself as a national institution although not many minorities have seen high ranks.

RANK STRUCTURE AND UNIFORM INSIGNIA

Awards for Valor

The Nishan-e-Haider (Sign of the Lion), is the highest military award given by Pakistan.

Recipients Nishan-e-Haider recipients receive an honorary title as a sign of respect: *Shaheed* meaning *martyr* for deceased recipients.

1. Captain Muhammad Sarwar Shaheed (1910–27 July 1948)
2. Major Tufail Muhammad Shaheed (1914–7 August 1958)
3. Major Raja Aziz Bhatti Shaheed (1928–10 September 1965)
4. Major Muhammad Akram Shaheed (1938–1971)
5. Major Shabbir Sharif Shaheed (1943–6 December 1971)
6. Jawan Sarwar Muhammad Hussain Shaheed (1949–10 December 1971)
7. Lance Naik Muhammad Mahfuz Shaheed (1944–17 December 1971)
8. Captain Karnal Sher Khan Shaheed (1970–5 July 1999)
9. Lalak Jan Shaheed (1967–7 July 1999)
10. Pilot Officer Rashid Minhas Shaheed (Day of martyrdom : 21 August 1971)

Two Pakistani pilots belonging to the army aviation branch of Pakistan army who carried out a daring rescue of a mountaineer are to be given Slovenia's top award for bravery.

Slovenian, Tomaz Humar got stranded on the western end of the 8,125m Nanga Parbat mountain were he remained for around a week on top of the world's ninth-highest peak. The helicopter pilots plucked the 38-year-old from an icy ledge 6,000m up the peak known as "killer mountain".

The Slovenian president has presented Lt Col Rashid Ullah Beg and Lt Col Khalid Amir Rana with the Golden Order for Services in the country's capital, Ljubljana, "for risking their lives during the rescue mission", a Pakistan army statement said.

Special Forces and Alliances

Special Service Group (SSG) is an independent commando division of the Pakistan Army.

It is an elite special operations force similar to the United States Army Special Forces (Green Berets) and the British Army's SAS.

Official numbers are put at 2,100 men, in 3 Battalions; however the actual strength is classified. It is estimated to have been increased to 4 Battalions, with the eventual formation of 2 Brigades of Special Forces (6 Battalions).

Weapons and Equipment

Small Arms

The light weapons include:

Al Khalid MBT

Al Zarrar MBT

M109 SP Howitzer

The M198 Howitzer

The M59 Howitzer

Two AVLBs. One with bridge, one without

Handguns

- M1911 pistol

Sub-machine guns and carbines

- Heckler & Koch MP5 9 mm Parabellum sub-machine gun

Assault rifles

- G3 Types A3 & P4 Assault Rifle*
- Type 81 Assault Rifle
- AK-101Assault Rifle
- AK-103 Assault Rifle
- Steyr AUG
- M4 Carbine

Grenades

- M67 grenade

Sniper rifles

- Anti Aircraft Machine Gun 12.7 mm, Type 54*
- Steyr SSG-4 and SSG-P2 sniper rifles*
- M82 Barrett rifle (US Semi-Automatic Sniper Rifle . 50 BMG)

Machine guns

- MG3 Machine Gun*
- M60 machine gun
- M249 Squad Automatic Weapon
- NSV (machine gun)
- FN MAG
- FN Minimi

Projectile launchers

- RPG-7
- Type 69 RPG
- RPG-29
- Mk 19 grenade launcher
- Carl Gustav recoilless rifle

Pakistan Army Inventory

Vehicle/System/Aircraft	Firm Number in Service	Status
Al Khalid Main Battle Tank	600	In Service, Under production. 600 planned
Type 85IIAP Main Battle Tank	500	In Service. Being phased out
Al-Zarar Tank Main Battle Tank	500	Currently under production
Type 79IIAP (Chinese T-81 Upgrade)	450	Being phased out by Al Khalid
T-80UD Main Battle Tank	320 + 250	Delivered by Ukraine between 1997 and early 2002. 250 more were ordered in early 2002.
Type 59	880	Being phased out by Al Zarrar & Al Khalid II
Hamza Infantry Fighting Vehicle	???	Being procured
Al-Fahd Infantry fighting vehicle	140	In Service
Talha Armoured Personnel Carrier	400+	Final number to be around 2,000
Sa'ad Armoured Personnel Carrier	???	Currently in production
M113 Armoured Personnel Carrier	1500+	In Service
BTR-70 Armoured Personnel Carrier	169	In Service
Mohafiz Light Armoured Personnel Carrier	???	In Service & Additional APCs being procured
Scorpion Light Jeep	260	In Service
Al Qaswa Logistical Vehicle	??	Being procured

M88 ARV Armoured Recovery Vehicle	???	In Service
M60A1 AVLB Armoured Vehicle Launched Bridge	???	In Service
M48 Armoured Vehicle Launched Bridge Armoured Vehicle Launched Bridge	???	In Service
Al-khalid II Main battle tank	3000 planned	under development
M109A5 155 mm Self-Propelled Howitzer	???	115 Ordered along with 150 A5 upgrade kits
M109A2 155 mm Self-Propelled Howitzer	150	In Service
M110A2 203 mm Self-Propelled Howitzer	40	In Service
Type 56 85 mm Towed Artillery	200	In Service
M-56 105 mm Towed Artillery	80	In Service
M101 105 mm Towed Artillery	300	In Service
T-60 122 mm Towed Artillery	200	In Service
Type 54 122 mm Towed Artillery	400	In Service
Type 59I 130 mm Towed Artillery	200	In Service
M-59 155 mm Towed Artillery	30	In Service
M114 155 mm Towed Artillery	60	In Service
M-198 155 mm Towed Artillery	120	In Service
M-115 203 mm Towed Artillery	40	In Service
Panther T-155 mm Towed Artillery	12	Produced and Delivered byTurkey
AH-1S Cobra Attack Helicopter	18	In Service,
AH-1F Cobra Attack Helicopter	20	In Service,
Bell 412 Huey Transport Helicopter	25	In Service

Bell 206 Jet Ranger Transport Helicopter	5	In Service
UH-1 Huey Transport Helicopter	10	In Service
Aérospatiale Puma Transport Helicopter	25	In Service
Mil Mi-17 Transport Helicopter	86	Additional helicopters planned
Bell 407 Light Transport Helicopter	45	
Eurocopter AS-550 Light Transport Helicopter	50	Replacing Alouette III & Lama
Aérospatiale Alouette III Light Transport Helicopter	40	Being phased out
Aérospatiale SA-315B Lama Light Transport Helicopter (variant of Aerospatiale Alouette II)	40	Being phased out

Mortarsy

- (Type) 81 mm
- AM-FFFF Series 120 mm
- Type 63-1

Anti-tank Guided Weapons

- TOW ATGM
- TOW II (recently procured)
- Bakter-Shikan ATGM
- FGM-148 Javelin

Army Air Defence

- Anti-aircraft guns: ZU-23/-33, -30, -36, -37, -57 mm
- Bofors RBS-23 BAMSE (source?)
- Bofors RBS-70

- SA-7 Grail
- General Dynamics FIM-92 Stinger
- General Dynamics FIM-43 Redeye
- Anza MKI, Anza MKII and Anza MKIII
- HQ-2B
- Oerlikon 35 mm twin cannon
- Bofors 40 mm gun

Future Plans

Throughout the International Defence Exhibition & Seminar (IDEAS) at Karachi in November 2006, Pakistani firms have signed joint development, production and marketing agreements with defence firms from South Korea, France and Ukraine. These agreements include new reactive armour bricks, 155 mm artillery shells, and other developments in armour and land weaponry. These agreements all relate to the Pakistan Army's AFFDP-2019 modernization program of its armour, artillery and infantry.

A few months prior to IDEAS 2006, the Pakistan Army and Heavy Industries Taxila (HIT) announced the development of the Al Khalid II Main Battle Tank (MBT). The Al Khalid II is poised to become the Pakistan Army's backbone main battle tank from 2012; thus replacing 1200 obsolete Chinese T-59 and 300 T-85IIAP. Not much is known about this tank, but it is reported that the Al Khalid II is a very extensive upgrade of the current Al Khalid.

Other reports suggest that it will be an entirely new tank based on Western designs. Turkish press reported that a Pakistani armour firm will participate in the Turkey's new generation tank project. Turkey and Pakistan have signed many memorandums of understanding in various defence-related fields. Given that many Pakistani firms have signed joint agreements with Western firms, it is possible that a considerable part of the Al Khalid II's design will be influenced from the Turkish tank design. Nonetheless, the new generation tank is expected to form the backbone of the Pakistan

Army's tank force; in the long-term. The Pakistan Army will standardize its artillery capability to 155 mm by 2019. This can be seen by the acquisition of 115 M109A5 self-propelled howitzers from the United States, and joint production deals of 155 mm shells with French and South Korean firms. It is expected that the army will procure a range of light, medium and heavy towed and self-propelled howitzer artillery from China, Europe and the United States. These will replace all non-155 mm and older systems. The Army reportedly ordered and procured an undisclosed number of WS-1B Multiple Launch Rocket Systems (MLRS). As part of the artillery modernization program, the Army will likely procure a fair number of new MLRS systems of various ranges and shell sizes.

Modernization of the Army Aviation is underway with the procurement of new transport and attack helicopters from the United States, Russia and Europe. Finalized acquisitions include 26 Bell 412EP and at least a dozen Mi-17 medium-lift transport helicopters from the U.S and Russia, respectively.

Forty Bell 407 and an unknown number of Fennec light helicopters from the U.S. and Eurocopter have also been ordered, respectively. Plans are underway to begin replacing the IAR 330 Puma, older Mil Mi-8/17, Bell Jet Rangers and older Huey helicopters; options include the Eurocopter NH-90 Tactical Transport Helicopter and UH-60M Blackhawk. The Pakistan Army has procured dozens of excess AH-1 Cobra attack helicopters since 2002; at least 20 have been brought into service to supplement the serving 18.

These gunships are expected to add muscle to current counterterrorist support operations in NWFP. The army reportedly has upgraded its entire fleet with AH-1Z King Cobra avionics and new weapon systems such as the TOW-2 and Hellfire missiles. Up to 30 new-generation attack helicopters will be procured to further enhance the Army's attack aviation arm; options include the Eurocopter Tiger, South African AH-2 Rooivalk and Boeing AH-64D Apache Longbow. It is likely that Pakistan ordered 6 AH-64D Apache Longbows.

Pakistan has no strategic depth; Indian tanks can drive from one side of the country to the other on one tank of gas. In military thought the concept referrs to a hard-to-reach place where a defeated army might safely cocoon. Pakistan's search for strategic depth against India had been a continuous one since its military rulers took power.

The attainment of 'strategic depth' has been a prime objective of Pakistan's Afghanistan policy since the days of General Ziaul Haq. The asymmetries of strategic depth and offensive military capability give India an operational advantage, and create a situation in which India's conventional ground forces could be defeated only by Pakistan's tactical nuclear forces.

Nation building remains a difficult process in Pakistan. But although the country has undergone a succession of traumatic sociopolitical experiences since achieving independence in 1947, it continues to demonstrate its resilience and its capacity to survive and adapt to changing circumstances. Joining the community of nations as a bifurcated state, with its two wings separated by 1,600 kilometers of foreign soil, Pakistan was faced with the immediate task of absorbing large numbers of refugees from India in the months immediately following partition. The new nation struggled with severe economic disadvantages made acutely painful by a shortage of both administrative personnel and the material assets necessary to establish and sustain its fledgling government.

With the death of Mohammad Ali Jinnah— the revered Quaid-i-Azam (Great Leader) — only thirteen months after independence, the nation was dealt another severe blow.

Created to provide a homeland for the Muslims of the Indian subcontinent, Pakistan was heir to a government structure and a political tradition that were essentially Western and secular. From its inception, Pakistan has worked to synthesize Islamic principles with the needs of a modern state. The young nation was immediately challenged by a host of other factors affecting national development, including ethnic and provincial tensions, political rivalries, and security considerations. The country subsequently survived civil war and the resultant loss of its East Wing, or East Pakistan, which became the independent nation of Bangladesh in December 1971, and has accommodated an influx of refugees resulting from the Soviet occupation of Afghanistan (December 1979-February 1989), which over the course of the conflict exceeded 3.2 million people.

India's relations with Pakistan are influenced by the centuries-old rivalry between Hindus and Muslims which led to partition of British India in 1947. The principal source of contention has been Kashmir, whose Hindu Maharaja chose in 1947 to join India, although a majority of his subjects were Muslim. India maintains that his decision and the subsequent elections in Kashmir have made it an integral part of India. Pakistan asserts Kashmiris' rights to self-determination through a plebiscite in accordance with an earlier Indian pledge and a UN resolution. This dispute triggered wars between the two countries in 1947 and 1965.

In December 1971, following a political crisis in what was then East Pakistan and the flight of millions of Bengali refugees to India, Pakistan and India again went to war. The brief conflict left the situation largely unchanged in the west, where the two armies reached an impasse, but a decisive Indian victory in the east resulted in the creation of Bangladesh.

Since the 1971 war, Pakistan and India have made only slow progress toward normalization of relations. In July 1972, Indian Prime Minister Indira Gandhi and Pakistani President Zulfikar Ali Bhutto met in the Indian hill station of Simla. They signed an agreement by which India would return all personnel and captured territory in the west and the two countries would "settle their differences by peaceful means through bilateral negotiations." Diplomatic and trade relations were re-established in 1976.

After the 1979 Soviet invasion of Afghanistan, new strains appeared in India-Pakistan relations; Pakistan supported the Afghan resistance, while India implicitly supported Soviet occupation. In the following eight years, India voiced increasing concern over Pakistani arms purchases, U.S. military aid to Pakistan, and Pakistan's nuclear weapons program. In an effort to curtail tensions, the two countries formed a joint commission. In December 1988, Prime Ministers Rajiv Gandhi and Benazir Bhutto concluded a pact not to attack each other's nuclear facilities. Agreements on cultural exchanges and civil aviation also were initiated.

Pakistan has had difficulty in establishing stable, effective political institutions. The country has experimented with a variety of political systems, has endured periods of martial law, and has had five constitutions, one inherited from the British and four indigenous creations since independence. Its political parties have suffered from regionalism, factionalism, and lack of vision. Power has shifted between the politicians and the civilmilitary establishment, and regional and ethnic forces have threatened national unity. However, the impulse toward cohesion has been stronger than the impetus toward division, and the process of nation building has continued. The return to democracy in 1988, and the peaceful, constitutional transfer of power to new governments in 1990 and 1993 testify to Pakistan's progress in the quest for political stability.

Pakistan's central government historically had difficult relations with the country's periphery, the areas least modernized and integrated by the the British. Bureaucrats in the new Pakistani government, largely of Punjabi and Urdu-speaking Muhajir background [ie, migrants from India], largely continued the patterns established by their British predecessors. They interacted with locals via traditional elites.

The government locked business wealth in the hands of a tiny number of families whose access to resources was tied to political loyalty. And to avoid alienating its support from big landowners, the government shunned effective land redistribution. Robert Looney, an economist at the Naval Postgraduate School in California, estimated that just 22 families owned 66 percent of industry, 97 percent of the insurance sector, and 80 percent of banking. Only one landlord in a thousand owned more than 500 acres, yet these large holders possessed fully 15 percent of the country's land. The form of government – democratic, nominated, directly or indirectly elected, dictatorial – did not matter. The professed ideology of the government in power – liberal, conservative, Islamic, left, right – made no significant difference. Politicians, military and civil bureaucrats, co-opted members of the religious oligarchy and professional and intellectual elites dominated every government. The capture of the institutions of the state and the market by this small elite is complete.

The military remains the country's most cohesive national institution. Since independence it has oscillated between indirect and direct political control, remaining a major power. The military's sense of mission in defending and preserving the Islamic state of Pakistan has always been strong. For Muslim members of the British Indian Army, the transfer of loyalties from the colonial to the ideological state was not difficult. Successors to the historical legacy of the Muslim armies of the once powerful Mughal Empire, Muslim soldiers could relate to a new role of protecting the faith and the state embodied in Pakistan. The military also provided alternative political leadership in times of crisis.

Politicians play one family enterprise against the other, diminishing the business community's potential to push for systemic reform. Dominant families concentrate on maintaining relationships with individual politicians who can ensure access to credit, foreign exchange and licenses. Populist pressures are rooted in the well-founded perception that industrial and commercial wealth has its origins in insider deals with government.

The armed forces of Pakistan have traditionally played a distinctive role in the life of the nation. As in many other developing countries, they are an important modernizing force in society and a key tool of national integration. As defenders of the nation's interests in Pakistan's troubled and volatile geopolitical neighborhood, the armed forces are accorded a particularly high status in public opinion. Less welcome, however, has been the repeated interference of the armed forces in the internal affairs and politics of the country. The military has frequently been called in to gain control of unrest that has gone beyond the ability of the police to cope; some of these intrusions have had a major impact and have been of fairly long duration. The military has assumed political as well as security control of the entire country three times under proclamations of martial law. Indeed, since it became an independent state in 1947, Pakistan has been under military control for much of its existence.

At the same time, however, democracy has always been seen as the "natural" state of the Pakistani polity, and the military has ultimately returned power to civilian hands. Thus, although the armed forces dominated the country to a certain extent, they have not perpetuated a military dictatorship. The military has been a permanent factor in the life of the country, but in a role that has ranged from complete control to vigilant observer. As political scientist Leonard Binder has observed, "Even [Pakistan's] dependence upon the military does not necessarily make of it a praetorian state, because there is little evidence that the state works in the sole interest of the military. Rather, it was the military which intervened in order to prevent the breakdown of the patrimonial system." Much of the political history of Pakistan has been set in this drama of contending influences, and the military in early 1994 was still searching for a role that would reconcile its interests and the broader needs of a country whose politicians were struggling to establish a credible authority of their own.

In 2007 "Talibanization" was spreading outward from the FATA across northern Pakistan. Lal Masjid [Red Mosque] clerics had been waging a campaign to impose a Taliban-style way of life in Pakistan and the radical students kidnapped several policemen, Chinese health workers and an alleged brothel owner. In July 2007 a shootout erupted after six months of tension over the activities of the hardline Red Mosque, which had kidnapped several Chinese and Pakistani civilians as part of a freelance anti-vice campaign. The military operation was launched after female students from Jamia Hafsa, a seminary attached to Red Mosque, occupied a children's library, snatched rifles from paramilitary rangers and shot dead one member of the force. The Red Mosque incident in the early part of July 2007 was followed by the restoration of Chief Justice of Pakistan and confusion about imposition of emergency rule in the country. Sectarian and extremist violence has resulted in fatal bomb attacks in Islamabad, Rawalpindi, Karachi, Peshawar, Quetta, Lahore, and other Pakistani cities since 2006. From 2007 through late 2008, over 1,000 bombings had killed more than 1,000 people throughout Pakistan and injured many more. Rallies, demonstrations, and processions occur from time to time throughout Pakistan on very short notice and have often taken on an anti-American or anti-Western character.

4

STRENGTHS OF THE ARMY

BACKGROUND

India achieved its independence from imperial Britain in 1947, after which it was divided into two countries - India and Pakistan, as per the *Mountbatten Plan*. After this partition, Pakistan chose to be an Islamic republic, aligned with United States while India chose to remain politically neutral, as a secular socialist democracy. These choices turned out to the turning points in the political and military future of both these countries.

Please note that what follows is not an evaluation of military power in combat situations, but a brief review of quantitative military balance, based on currently available manpower, equipments, infrastructure, command and strategy. Future military plans and projects are not discussed due to uncertain and volatile nature of such plans, often subject to cancellation, failure or modification.

MILITARY BUDGETS AND ECONOMIC IMPACT

Pakistan's defence budget for the year 2006-07 was $4.1 billion (~3% of GDP) in response to India's hike in defence budget of 2006-07 at $20.11 billion (~ 2.5% of GDP). Pakistan's hike in military budget would be partially funded by its government coffers and partially by borrowing whereas India's military spending would be entirely off its own funds. India's ambitious budget prompted Pakistan to up its own military budget, despite the country's widespread poverty and socio-political problems. Apart from its GDP, Pakistani military also gets a considerable funding from United States. Considering that India has a far larger economy overall, its military budget is also several times larger, despite being a smaller share of India's GDP.

MANPOWER AND GROUND FORCES

As of 2005, India has the second largest military manpower in the world - at 3,773,300 personell, next only to China. Pakistan's manpower of 1,449,000 personell, although smaller in numbers, is proportionally higher than India in terms of their population ratios. Pakistan's ground forces are equipped with American or Chinese weapons like *FIM 92 Stinger* SAMs, *BGM-71 TOW* anti-tank missiles, *T-82* tanks and other equipments. Indian ground forces are equipped with mostly home-made and Soviet technologies like IR guided *9K35 Strela-10* SAMs, 3rd Gen IR guided *Nag* anti-tank missiles, UAVs and a large inventory of tanks and support vehicles. In terms of both numbers and equipments, Indian military dominates the Pakistani ground forces.

COMPARISON OF AIR FORCES

As of 2006, Indian Air Force (IAF) has over 170,000 personnel and 3,382 aircrafts, of which 1,330 are combat aircrafts operating off 61 airbases - making it the fourth largest air force in the world. India's strike fighters consist of Russian and French aircrafts like *Mikoyan MiG-29*, *Dassault Mirage 2000*, *Sukhoi Su-30* - the last one developed under dual licensing by HAL, India's aerospace industry in Bangalore.

In addition to these, Indian Air Force also owns ground attack aircrafts, reconnaissance aircrafts, UAVs and support helicopters - a majority of them either of Soviet or French origin. Pakistan Air Force (PAF) has about 530 combat aircrafts and 65,000 active personnel, operating out of 9 airbases. Its strike fighters consist of US, Chinese and ageing French fighters like *F-16 Fighting Falcon*, *JF-*

17 Thunder and *Dassault Mirage ROSE-III*. It also has transport aircrafts like *Lockheed Martin C-130* and *Airbus A310*, however unlike India, there are no UAVs or reconnaissance aircrafts in the Pakistani Air Force.

NAVAL AND SEA BASED FORCES

After the overwhelming losses in the 1971 war against India, Pakistan rapidly increased the size of its naval fleet which doubled in the 1980s after a massive 3.2 billion dollar military and economic aid by US President *Ronald Reagan*. At present, Pakistan's navy owns over 45 vessels , most of them of US or European origin which include submarines, destroyers, frigates, patrol and mine warfare boats. It operates from its sole naval port in Karachi and sometimes from naval facilities in UK, USA and France.

It had recently been involved in various humanitarian operations during the 2005 Tsunami in South East Asia. Indian Navy on the other hand, is a three dimensional naval force consisting of missile-capable warships, an aircraft carrier, mine sweepers and a host of marine aircrafts. Most of the warships in the Indian navy are indigenously built in its own dockyards. The navy operates from its major naval bases in Visakhapatnam, Mumbai, Goa and the Andaman Islands. Indian Navy has significant capabilities of being a true blue water Navy and is experienced both in war and peacekeeping operations in the Indian Ocean.

THE NUCLEAR CLUB

India tested a nuclear bomb in 1974 using materials from Canada and technical help from Soviet Union. However, the embargo on heavy water export from Canada after the test stalled India's nuclear ambitions till 1998, when it shocked the world by conducting five nuclear detonations termed as *Shakti* tests. The highest yield was by a 48 kiloton staged fusion device, which India claimed was a thermonuclear bomb but seismic data on the tests proved otherwise. In the same year 1998, Pakistan conducted a series of six nuclear detonations in a test termed as *Chagai*. The highest yield was reported to be about 25 kiloton from a two stage boosted device. At present Pakistan's nuclear stockpile is slated to be around 30-40 warheads while India possesses 70-100 warheads. The nuclearisation of India and Pakistan became a turning point in the history of conflicts between these two countries with high tensions but no war, not very much unlike the US vs USSR Cold War.

BALLISTIC AND CRUISE MISSILE PROLIFERATION

In the nuclear delivery front, both India and Pakistan have a series of ballistic and cruise missiles in addition to ground attack aircrafts. The maximum range among India's operational ballistic missiles is 2000 km achieved by Agni-2. India's Agni ballistic missiles are indigenously developed by its own missile defence industry known as *IGMDP*. The maximum range among Pakistan's missiles is by *Hatf V Gauri* which is reported to do over 2200 kms. Pakistan's Hatf missiles are based on North Korean *No-Dong* series of IRBMs. Both Pakistan's *Hatf* and India's *Agni* ballistic missiles are nuclear capable. India has also developed a supersonic cruise missile *BrahMos* which is by far the fastest cruise missile at Mach 2.6 and maximum range of 290 km. It is reported to be nuclear capable but it is not confirmed yet. On the Pakistan side, its *Babur* cruise missile has a reported range of 700 km and a maximum speed of 880 km/h (Mach 0.7). As with India *BrahMos*, *Babur* is also reported to be nuclear capable but there is no confirmation yet.

The Final Verdict

Both Pakistan and India are almost evenly matched head to head in nuclear and missile fronts, however India has strategic and technological superiority over the conventional forces of Pakistan. Indian Navy is larger in fleet and personnel size with a more varied range of ships including an aircraft carrier while Pakistan's Navy is smaller and has no aircraft carriers. Indian's IAF is equipped with highly capable fighters like 4.5th generation *Su-30*s and 4th gen *Mirage 2000*s which are technologically superior to Pakistan PAF's

*F-16*s and *Mirage III*s. Additionally Indian pilots are better trained and more capable in air combat than Pakistani forces as was demonstrated by its various wars with Pakistan or joint exercises with US and UK. In the area of conventional ground forces both the Indian as well as Pakistani Army is well equipped and highly trained to survive in extremities of topography and climate in combat conditions, like wars in the high Himalayas.

If a purely conventional war were to take place between both these countries, India would most likely overpower Pakistan owing to its superior military technology and infrastructure, larger manpower, more territorial area and a strategic advantage in its sea and air forces. It must also be noted that a war between these two countries will matter more than India's conventional superiority as both these nations are nuclear powers on an equal deadlock. India has maintained a 'no first use' nuclear policy in the lines of a similar policy by China while Pakistan does not have any such policy, considering their only hope against India is in nuclear deterrance. It would be risky for India at the present scenario to go into any aggressive war against Pakistan as the repercussions would be serious a nuclear devastation for both countries.

Unfortunately India and Pakistan had adversarial relations since sixty years. After the Mumbai carnage Pakistan is under threat of pre-emptive strikes. Fourth Indo-Pakistan war could be triggered by another terrorist attack anywhere in India. This is a dangerous scenario. India and Pakistan have fought three wars, and war drums for the fourth war are getting louder.

It is in order therefore to comprehend Indian military capabilities, and Pakistan's ability to defend itself. Defense capability is an interplay of economic and military potential. Indian economy is booming, and its GDP growth is in double digits. The global recession has impacted Indian economy, but its defense capability remains intact. Military power and capabilities are sustained by economic and industrial potential. Geography, demography, population, oil resources and reserves, industrial capability including defense production, dollar reserves, self reliance, education, quality of manpower and leadership have a bearing on military power. Seven lakh Indian troops are tied down in Jammu and Kashmir. India has over one hundred billion dollar reserves. The West, Israel and Russia are India's weapon suppliers.

Indian Army has eighteen Corps with 34 Divisions including four Rapid Action Divisions, which would spear head ground offensives. Pakistan Army has ten Corps and twenty five divisions. Indian Army has eighteen Infantry, ten Mountain, three Armored, and two Artillery Divisions. Besides it has five Infantry, one parachute, thirteen Air Defense, and four Engineering Brigades, designated as independent formations. In addition there are two Air Defense Groups, and fourteen Army Aviation Helicopter units. This is a sizeable force, capable of launching major offensives from several fronts.

The decentralized command structure will be an advantage, as compared to Pakistan's centralized Army command organization. Pakistan Army has an active force of 620,000 well trained personnel, with 528000 reservists, and 150000 para-military troops. Pakistan armed forces are seventh largest in the world. Pakistan Army's doctrine of "Offensive Defense", evolved by General Mirza Aslam Beg was put to test in 1989 in Exercise Zarb-e Momin.

The doctrine is to launch a sizeable offensive into enemy territory, rather than wait for enemy strikes or attacks. In case of Indian land offensive Pakistan Army and Air Force will respond with land and air offensives to gain and hold enemy territory. Before embarking on further offensive, gains shall be consolidated. In 1990 the Central Corps of Reserves was created to fight in the desert sectors , where enemy land offensives are expected. These dual capable formations trained for offensive and holding actions are fully mechanized.

Pakistan Army has ten Corps including the newly formed Strategic Corps. The Army has twenty six divisions (eight less than India). Two more divisions were raised as Corps reserves for V and

XXXI Corps. Pakistan Army has two armored divisions, and ten independent armored brigades. Presently one hundred thousand troops are stationed on the Pak Afghan border to fight terror. Special Service Group-SSG comprises two airborne Brigades i.e. six battalions.

Pakistan Army has 360 helicopters, over two thousand heavy guns, and 3000 APC's. Its main anti-tank weapons are Tow, Tow Mk II, Bakter Shiken and FGM 148 ATGM. The Army Air Defence Command has S.A- 7 Grail, General Dynamics FIM-92 Stinger, GD FIM Red Eye, and ANZA Mk-I, Mk-II, Mk-III and HQ 2 B surface ti air missiles. Radar controlled Oerlikon is the standard Ack Ack weapon system.

The ballistic missile inventory of the Army is substantial. It comprises Ghauri III and Shaheen III IRB'S; medium range Ghauri I and II and Shaheen II, and short range Hatf I- B, Abdali, Ghaznavi, Shaheen I and M -11 missiles. All the ballistic missiles can carry nuclear war heads. Nuclear and conventional weapon capable Babur Cruise missile is the new addition to Pakistan's strategic weapon inventory. Number of ballistic missiles and war heads are almost the same as India has. So there is a parity in nuclear weapons, which is a deterrent.

Indian armor is of Russian origin. Out of 2295 Indian Army's Main Battle tanks, 2235 are of Russian origin. The main battle tanks are; 310 T-90-S Bishsma's (300 are on order), 1925 T-72M Ajeya's.. The T-90 and the T-72 have 125 mm smooth barrel guns. T-72 though old is the backbone of Indian Armor Corp's. 268 Ajeya's have been upgraded with Israeli Elbit thermal imaging systems. 1000 T-72 MBT's are awaiting up-gradation.

There have been several instances of T-72's gun barrel bursting. 124 Indian made Arjun (heavy 56 ton) MBT are on order. Sixty Arjun's are in operational service. Arjun's engine overheating problem has not been solved. Arjun has a 120 mm gun, but is unfit or desert operations. Pakistan Army is equally strong in armor, capable of giving a fitting response to any Indian military adventure.

Main Battle tanks Al-Khalid and Al-Zarrar are the backbone of Pakistan's armor Corp's. Both are Pakistan made. Pakistan's tank armory comprises :five hundred Al-Khalid MBT's; 320 Al-Zarrar type 85 II MBT's, 500 Al-Zarrar MBT's; 450 79II AP (Chinese type 81 upgrade, and 570 T-80 UD MBT of Ukranian make. In addition Pakistan has 880 Type 59, which were procured from China in 1970.This makes a total of three thousand six hundred and twenty tanks.

All Pakistani MBT's except T-59's have 125 mm smooth barrel guns. Indian armor offensives in Kashmir, Punjab, and Sind would be effectively challenged by Pakistani armor and mechanized formations, depending on PAF's ability to keep the skies over the battle areas clear of Indian Air Force. India's modern air defense system has Israeli Arrow anti-missile missiles, and 90,000 surface to air missiles-SAM's. India has one hundred nuclear armed ballistic missiles (Agni-1 and Agni II), and Brahmos the new supersonic cruise missile. Indian Army is well trained, equipped and highly professional, and so is Pakistan Army.

Air power is likely to play a key, if not a decisive role in any future major or minor India-Pakistan armed conflict. The aim of Indian pre-emptive strikes will be maximum destruction by surprise air attacks, combined with shock commando action. A possibe scenario is; intensive bombing of the target to be followed by attacks by armed helicopters and ground assault by heliborne Commandoes. An overview of Indian Air Force and Pakistan Air Force will help comprehension of IAF's offensive capabilities, and defensive capabilities of Pakistan Air Force.

Indian Air Force has 3000 aircraft including training, transport, helicopters and 800-1000 combat air craft, which operate from sixty air bases, including Farkhor airbase in Tajikistan.. Six hundred IAF's strike and air defense fighters are expected to be operational. Pakistan Air Force has 630 aircraft, which include 530 combat aircraft, with 400 operational at any time. In 1996 India signed an agreement with Russia for the purchase of 90 Su 30 Mk-1 multi-role fighter-bombers.

In 2004 a multi-billion licence was signed for building additional 140. 240 Su30-Mk-1's were ordered, 120 are already in service. With a maximum speed of Mach 2.3 and range of 8000 Km with refueling and ability to carry tons of conventional munitions and nuclear weapons, it is a lethal and menacing weapon system for the strike and interception role.

Other IAF's advanced strike and combat aircraft are: 51 Mirage-2000 (of Kargil fame), 60 Mig-29's (for air defense), 250 old Mig-21's (110 have been refurbished with Israeli help), 47 Jaguars and 70 Mig-27's for ground attack. 220 LCA Teja's under manufacture at HAL Bangalore will start entering service in 2010... IAF's fighter pilots are well trained and have out shone American pilots during joint exercises.

Pakistan Air Force has 200 rebuilt Mirage- 3's (for night air defense) and Mirage-5's for the strike role. They can carry nuclear weapons. They have been upgraded with new weapon systems, radars, and avionics. Additionally the PAF has 42 F-16's, 150 F-7's including 55 latest F-7 PG's. Manufacture of 150 JF 17 Thunder fighters (jointly designed) is underway at Pakistan Aeronautical Complex Kamra. The JF -17 Thunder is a 4th generation fly by wire multi-role fighter aircraft. Eight are already in PAF service. An order has been placed with China for the purchase of 36 JF-10, a Mach 2.3 -5th generation multi-role fighter, comparable in performance to the Su-30 Mk-1 with the Indian Air Force. PAF is on Red Alert, and is maintaining full vigil to intercept and destroy IAF intruders.

During the recent air space violation, the IAF intruders were in the sights of PAF's F-16's, but were allowed to escape unscathed to avoid a major diplomatic crisis. PAF pilots and technicians are well trained, high professionals, who will be able to prove their mettle in the future battle with India. A comparison of Indian Navy and Pakistan Navy reveals that Pakistan Navy could inflict substantial damage to the Indian Navy. Indian Navy has 16 submarines; Pakistan Navy has ten, some are brand new. Indian Navy has 27 war ships, Pakistan Navy has ten. Indian Aircraft Carrier Veerat, will be a menace, and must be sunk by submarine or air attacks, if it attempts to block Pakistan's sea lanes or ports. It is hoped that better sense prevails and India desists from invading and attacking Pakistan. If it does, the consequences will be horrible for both the countries.

Manpower and Ground Forces

India has the second largest manpower in its military globally - at 3,773,300 personell (2005), next only to China. Pakistan has a much smaller manpower of 1,449,000 personell which is proportionally higher than India in terms of their population ratios. Pakistan's ground forces are equipped with American or Chinese weapons like FIM 92 Stinger SAMs, BGM-71 TOW anti-tank missiles, T-82 tanks and other equipments. Indian ground forces are equipped mostly by home-made or Soviet technologies like IR guided 9K35 Strela-10 SAMs, 3rd Gen IR guided Nag anti-tank missiles, UAVs and a large inventory of tanks and support vehicles. In terms of numbers and equipments, both Indian and Pakistani ground forces are on an closely equal footing.

Comparison of Air Forces

As of 2006, Indian Air Force (IAF) has over 170,000 personnel and 3,382 aircrafts of which 1,330 are combat aircrafts operating off 61 airbases - making it the fourth largest air force in the world. India's strike fighters consist of Russian and French aircrafts like Mikoyan MiG-29, Dassault Mirage 2000, Sukhoi Su-30 - the last one developed under dual licensing by HAL, India's aerospace industry in Bangalore. In addition to these, India's air force owns ground attack aircrafts, reconnaissance aircrafts, UAVs and support helicopters - a majority of them either of Soviet or French origin. Pakistan Air Force (PAF) has about 530 combat aircrafts and over 65,000 active personnel, operating out of 9 airbases. Its strike fighters consist of US, Chinese and French fighters like F-16 Fighting Falcon, JF-17 Thunder and Dassault Mirage ROSE-III. It also has transport aircrafts like Lockheed Martin C-130 and Airbus A310, however there are no UAVs or reconnaissance aircrafts in the Pakistani Air Force.

Naval and Sea Based Forces

After the overwhelming losses in the 1971 war against India, Pakistan rapidly increased the size of its naval fleet which doubled in the 1980s after a massive 3.2 billion dollar military and economic aid by US President Ronald Reagan. At present, Pakistan's navy owns over 45 vessels , most of them of US or European origin which include submarines, destroyers, frigates, patrol and mine warfare boats. It operates from its sole naval port in Karachi and naval facilities in UK, USA and France.

It had recently been involved in various humanitarian operations during the 2005 Tsunami in South East Asia. Indian Navy on the other hand, is a three dimensional naval force consisting of missile-capable warships, an aircraft carrier, mine sweepers and a host of marine aircrafts; most of its warships indigenously built in its own dockyards. The navy operates from its major naval bases in Visakhapatnam, Mumbai, Goa and the Andaman Islands. Indian Navy has significant capabilities of being a true blue water Navy and is experienced both in war and peacekeeping operations in the Indian Ocean.

The Nuclear Club

India tested a nuclear bomb in 1974 using materials from Canada and technical help from Soviet Union. However the embargo in heavy water export from Canada after the test stalled India's nuclear ambitions till 1998, when it shocked the world by conducting five nuclear detonations termed as Shakti tests. The highest yield was by a 48 kiloton staged fusion device, which India claimed was a thermonuclear bomb but seismic data on the tests proved otherwise. In the same year 1998, Pakistan conducted a series of six nuclear detonations in a test termed as Chagai.

The highest yield was reported to be about 25 kiloton from a two stage boosted device. At present Pakistan's nuclear stockpile is slated to be around 30-40 warheads while India possesses 70-100 warheads. The nuclearisation of India and Pakistan became a turning point in the history of conflicts between these two countries with high tensions but no war, not very much unlike the US vs USSR Cold War.

Ballistic and Cruise Missile Proliferation

In the nuclear delivery front, both India and Pakistan have a series of ballistic and cruise missiles in addition to ground attack aircrafts. The maximum range among India's operational ballistic missiles is 2000 km achieved by Agni-2. India's Agni ballistic missiles are indigenously developed by its own missile defence industry known as IGMDP.

The maximum range among Pakistan's missiles is by Hatf V Gauri which is reported to do over 2200 kms. Pakistan's Hatf missiles are based on North Korean No-Dong series of IRBMs. Both Pakistan's Hatf and India's Agni ballistic missiles are nuclear capable. India has also developed a supersonic cruise missile BrahMos which is by far the fastest cruise missile at Mach 2.6 and maximum range of 290 km. It is reported to be nuclear capable but it is not confirmed yet. On the Pakistan side, its Babur cruise missile has a reported range of 700 km and a maximum speed of 880 km/h (Mach 0.7). As with India BrahMos, Babur is also reported to be nuclear capable but there is no confirmation yet.

The Final Verdict

Both Pakistan and India are almost evenly matched head to head in nuclear and missile fronts, however India has strategic and technological superiority over the conventional forces of Pakistan. Indian Navy is larger in fleet and personnel size with a more varied range of ships including an aircraft carrier while Pakistan's Navy is smaller and has no aircraft carriers. Indian's IAF is equipped with highly capable fighters like 4.5th generation Su-30s and 4th gen Mirage 2000s which are technologically superior to Pakistan PAF's F-16s and Mirage IIIs. Additionally Indian pilots are better trained and more capable in air combat than Pakistani forces as was demonstrated by its various wars with Pakistan or joint exercises with US and UK. In the area of conventional ground forces both the Indian as well as Pakistani Army is well equipped and highly trained to survive in extremities of topography and climate in combat conditions, like wars in the high Himalayas.

If a purely conventional war were to take place between both these countries, India would most likely overpower Pakistan owing to its superior military technology and infrastructure, larger manpower, more territorial area and a strategic advantage in its sea and air forces. It must also be noted that a war between these two countries will matter more than India's conventional superiority as both these nations are nuclear powers on an equal deadlock. India has maintained a 'no first use' nuclear policy on the lines of a similar policy by China while Pakistan does not have any such policy, considering their only hope against India is in nuclear deterrence. It would be risky for India at the present scenario to go into any aggressive war against Pakistan as the repercussions would be serious a nuclear devastation for both countries.

India's numerical and technical superiority in a conventional war is beyond question - therefore Pakistan's low nuclear threshold and maintenance of the first-use option.

However, in a surgical kind of strike being talked about in Indian and Pakistani circles, over Muridke or Muzaffarabad , cruise missiles are likely to be used. The Pakistani and Indian capability is evenly matched in these except for India's supersonic cruise missile with a speed of Mach 2.6 which is an obvious advantage in this kind of a strike, but it only has a range of 290 kms - enough to reach Muridke if launched from East Punjab but not much more. Pakistan's answer is the Babur cruise missile with a range of 700 km and a speed of Mach 0.7 - sub-sonic but pretty fast.

UAV's was the other Indian advantage which has recently been matched by Pakistan.

With the evenly matched air, missile and nuclear capability, a surgical strike doesn't seem to be the best option. If India is to win, it will have to be a full-scale conventional war with both sides avoiding breaching the other's nuclear threshold.

STRNGTH OF INDIAN MILITARY VS STRENGTH OF PAKISTAN MILITARY

Posted on December 27, 2008 by rajendra Parmanik

1.The Indian Army is the world's second largest army in terms of military personnel (after China).

Active Troops	1,300,000
Reserve Troops	1,200,000
Territorial Army	200,000
Main Battle Tanks	4500
Artillery	12,800
Ballistic missiles	100+
Cruise missiles	BrahMos
Aircraft	10 squadrons of helicopters
Surface-to-air missiles	90000+

The Pakistan Army, combined with the Navy and Air Force, makes Pakistan's armed forces the seventh largest military in the world.

Army	550,000
Navy	24,000
Air Force	45,000
Paramilitary Forces	302,000
Coast Guard	Classified
Total	921,000

2. Nuclear doctrine (INDIA)

The Indian military possesses nuclear weapons and sufficient means — by means of missiles and aircraft — to deliver anything over long distances. However, India has a nuclear no-first-use and no use against non-nuclear weapons state policy. It also maintains a non-nuclear doctrine based on credible minimum deterrence.

India is not a signatory to the Nuclear Non-proliferation Treaty (NPT), arguing that it unfairly favours the established nuclear powers: While the treaty places restrictions on the non-nuclear weapons states, it does little to curb the modernization and expansion of the nuclear arsenals of the nuclear weapons states; it provides no provision for complete nuclear disarmament.

Nuclear Doctrine (PAKISTAN)

The Pakistan military possesses nuclear weapons and sufficient means, through a range of missiles and aircraft — to deliver these over considerably long distances.

However, unlike India, Pakistan does not have no-first-use policy and maintains the use of nuclear weapons as a deterrent to India to offset the large conventional advantage India enjoys over Pakistan.

Pakistan is not a part of the Nuclear Non-proliferation Treaty (NPT), citing concerns that it unfairly favours the established nuclear powers, and provides no provision for complete nuclear disarmament. The Strategic Nuclear Command forms part of Pakistan's National Command Authority which is responsible for the management of the country's tactical and strategic nuclear weapons.

3.EQUIPMENTS OF INDIAN ARMY

Handguns

- FN Browning GP35 9mmx19 mm
- SAF (Small Arms Factory) Pistol 1A 9mmx19 mm, This is more or less a copy of the Canadian Inglis 9 mm
- Glock 17 9mmx19 mm, The Glock 19 along with the 17 is in use with the Special Protection Group (Prime Minister's Security)

Sub-machine guns and carbines

- Heckler & Koch MP5A3 9mmx19 mm SMG

- Heckler & Koch MP5K 9mmx19 mm SMG
- SAF Carbine 1A 9mmx19 mm, Indian made Sterling L2A1 SMG
- SAF Carbine 2A1 9mmx19 mm, Silenced Carbine
- UZI 9mmx19 mm SMG
- MINSAS carbine of the INSAS family; 5.56mm. Is in user trails.
- Kalantak rifle PDW that is in user trails.

Assault rifles

- RFI (Rifle Factory,Ishapore) SLR1A 7.62mmx51 mm NATO Assault Rifle, A modified FN FAL, This old work horse has now more or less been retired from IA service, most going to the police and paramilitary forces after reconditioning. Some however, remain in use.
- RFI SLR1C 7.62mmx51 mm, full Automatic variant of the SLR for use in APCs
- AK-7, clone of the AK-47
- INSAS 5.56mmx45 mm Assault Rifle
- Kalantak Rifle Under Trials
- Zittara Indian version of the IMI Tavor TAR-21 Israeli Micro-Tavor
- TAVOR TAR-21 5.56mmx45 mm, for special forces currently 3070 have been purchased from Israel [1]
- IMI Galil
- AK-101
- AK-103
- KBK AKMS 7.62mmx39 mm, Polish AKS47-3
- AK47M1 7.62mmx39 mm, all black Bulgarian AK. Most of these have been imported for police and paramilitary forces
- Soviet AKM AKMS 7.62mmx39 mm

- East German MPi-KM MPi-KMS72 7.62mmx39 mm (Second hand)
- Czech Vz.58 and Vz.58P 7.62mmx39 mm
- Colt M16A2 rifle for special forces

Anti-Tank Guided Missiles

- Nag- Third Generation fire and forget IIR Guided ATGM developed Indigenously. Its undergoing user trials. 443 missiles ordered.
- Milan 2- License Produced
- 9M113 Konkurs (AT-5 Spandrel)
- 9M111 Fagot (AT-4 Spigot)
- 9M14 Malyutka (AT-3 Sagger)- Being Phased out
- 9M119 Svir (AT-11 Sniper)- for T-90S.
- Lahat- fired from Arjun Tanks 120mm Cannon.

Machine guns

- MG 1B 7.62mmx51 mm, Indian made Bren- This is currently being retired. But may remain a while longer because of teething problems with its successor, the INSAS LMG
- MG 2A1 7.62mmx51 mm, Indian made MAG 58
- MG 5A 7.62mmx51 mm This is the Indian manufactured Co-axial MAG 58
- MG 6A 7.62mmx51 mm Another Indian version of the MAG58 specifically designed as a tank commanders gun.
- INSAS 5.56mmx45 mm LMG
- FN-Browning M1919 .30Cal, in very limited quantities
- Browning M2 machine gun .50cal, heavy machine gun in very limited numbers
- M607.62mm LMG

3.INDIAN AIRCRAFTS

COMBAT AIRCRAFTS

	Number
Su-30MKI Flanker-H	100
Mirage 2000H	39
MiG-29SMT	56
Jaguar IS	104(IS)
Jaguar IM	6
MiG-27	ML 120
MiG-21 Bison	109
MiG-21*bis*	48
MiG-21M/MF	72

PAK AIRCRAFTS

Chengdu JF-17 Thunder	10
General Dynamics F-16A Block-15 Fighting Falcon	28
General Dynamics F-16B Block-15 Fighting Falcon	16
Chengdu F-7PG Skybolt	46
Chengdu F-7MP Skybolt	90
Chengdu FT-7P Skybolt	15
Dassault Mirage ROSE-II (Mirage-VDF)	6
Dassault Mirage ROSE-II (Mirage-VDF)	14
Nanchang Q-5/A-5C Fantan	40

Both India And Pakistan Has many transport vehicles for the movement of man and machines. Both side has many Light Combat aircrafts but in this Sense India is much powerfull than Pakistan.

The Indian Air Force is the fourth largest air force in the world. In its history, it has generally relied on Soviet, British, Israeli and French technology to support its growth. However, in recent times, India has begun building its own original aircraft, including the HAL Tejas, which is a 4.5th generation fighter. Also, India and Russia are currently building a 5th generation stealth aircraft jointly. India has also developed an UAV called Nishant and an advanced light helicopter called the HAL Dhruv.

Recently, it completed a test of a long range BVR air to air missile named Astra and also conducted a successful test of its anti-ballistic missile defense system and hence became the 4th country after the US, Russia, and Israel to do so.

WEAPONS OF MASS DESTRUCTION INDIA

Ballistic Missiles

a. Prithvi I - Army Version (150 km range with a payload of 1,000kg)

   Prithvi II - Air Force Version (250 km range with a payload of 500kg)

   Prithvi III - Naval Version (350 km range with a payload of 500kg)

b. Dhanush is a System consisting of stabilization platform and missiles and can fire either the 250Km or the 350Km range missiles.

   Then the following year in December the missile's 350Km version was tested from the INS Rajput and hit the land based target

c. The Agni Missile system comprises of Agni I, Agni II and the Agni III 1500 Agni I uses the SLV-3 booster (from India's Space Program) for its first stage and a liquid-fueled Prithvi for its second stage.

d. On the other hand India's Agni II missiles have a range of the 1500 to 2500 kilometers. Unlike the Agni I, the Agni II has a solid-fueled second stage. India has also tested the Agni III IRBM with a range between 3000 and 5500km kilometres which has two stages. With a normal payload of 1000kg it can travel 5000km

e. The Surya-1 and -2 will be classified as strategic weapons, extending the Indian nuclear deterrent force to targets around the world. India currently is limited by the range of the Agni-3 missile.

The Surya-1 will have an expected range of 6000 - 10,000 km. It reportedly has a length of 40 m and a launch weight of 80,000 kg (some reports indicate as much as 275,000 kg. As the missile has yet to be developed, the payload and warhead are as yet unknown. It is believed to be a three-stage design, with the first two stages using solid propellants and the third-stage using liquid. The first test flight is expected in 2009, but there may be delays. The Surya- is a longer-ranged variant of the Surya-1. It has a reported range of over 20,000 km.

f. The Shaurya missile is a short-range surface-to-surface ballistic missile developed by DRDO of India for use by the Indian Army.It has a range of 600 km and is capable of carrying a payload of one-tonne conventional or nuclear warhead.The Shaurya missile provides India with a significant second strike capability.

g. Sagarika is a nuclear capable submarine-launched ballistic missile with a range of 750 km. This missile has a length of 8.5 meters, weighs seven tonnes and can carry a pay load of up to 500 kg

CRUISE MISSILES INDIA

a. Nirbhay is a long range, subsonic cruise missile being developed in India. The missile will have a range of 1000 km and will arm three services, the Indian Army, Indian Navy and the Indian Air Force.

b. India has acquired around 200 3M-54 Klub for arming Talwar class frigate, Shivalik class frigate, Kolkata class destroyer and Sindhughosh class submarine The Russian 3M-54 Klub is a multi-role missile system developed by the

Novator Design Bureau(OKB-8) with a range of 250Km-300Km and a average speed of .8 Mach with a maximum of 2.9 Mach

c. Popeye II, an air launched cruise missile capable of carrying nuclear warheads with a range of 80 Km can be launched from planes was given to India along with missile defence radars in a deal.

The exact number transferred to India is unknown, but possibly 20 missile to perhaps 50 missiles could have been given with possibly more being built in India.

d. India has Soviet P-70 Ametist submarine-launched cruise missiles.

The missiles can carry nuclear warheads and have a range of 50-65Km.

e. The P-270 Moskit is a Russian supersonic ramjet powered cruise missile capable of being launched from land and ships. India has most probably bought both land and ship variants which have a range of 120km.

f. Akash is India's medium range surface-to-air missile defense system The missile can target aircraft up to 30 km away, at altitudes up to 18,000 m.Akash is said to be capable of both conventional and nuclear warheads, with a reported payload of 60kg. Akash can be fired from both tracked and wheeled platforms.

NUCLEAR SUBMARINES

According to some accounts India plans to have as many as 20 nuclear submarines capable of carrying missiles with nuclear warheads.

The Advanced Technology Vessel (ATV) is a Nuclear Powered Ballistic Missile Submarine being constructed for the Indian Navy at Visakhapatnam, India The ATV is an SSBN and will be armed with the ballistic missiles.

Once it is completed, it can be equipped with 6-8 nuclear capable Dhanush,Sagarika or Agni SLBM ballistic missiles and upto 12 BrahMos cruise missiles. It is also to be fitted with an advanced sonar system. The second and third submarines of the class may incorporate the Nirbhay as well. As of July 2007, the Sagarika missile as well as Dhanush had undergone three successful tests each.

The ATV is to be unveiled on January 26, 2009 but trials will start later that year while induction is planned for 2010.

The INS Sindhuraj, INS Sindhuvir, INS Sindhuratna, INS Sindhushastra, INS Sindhukesari and INS Sindhuvijay are capable of launching 3M-54 Klub and BrahMos nuclear-capable cruise missiles.

India bought 10 Kilo class (in India known as Sindhughosh Class) submarine of which 6 have been refitted by the Russian Navy so that the they can launch cruise missiles such as nuclear capable BrahMos and 3M-54 Klub's 3M-14E variant.

The Submarine version of the BrahMos has been tested from static, underwater test stands in Russia and from the INS Sindhuvijay. As the Sinduvijay is similar to the other refitted submarines the test is considered a success.

PAKISTAN WEAPONS

- Hatf-I/IA/IB BRBM
- Abdali-I SRBM
- Ghaznavi-I SRBM
- Shaheen-I MRBM
- Ghauri-I MRBM
- Ghauri-II IRBM
- Shaheen-II IRBM
- Babur Cruise Missile
- Ra'ad Cruise Missile

- Ghauri-III IRBM
- Shaheen-III IRBM
- Tippu missile ICBM

AIRCRAFTS

- K-8 Karakorum
- JF-17 Thunder
- Shahbaz
- MFI-395 Super Mushaq
- MFI-17 Mushaq

SUBMARINES

- Agosta 90B class submarine
- Cosmos class MG110 Mini-Sub

STATISTICS

INDIAN ARMY

* 4 RAPID (Reorganised Army Plains Infantry Divisions)
* 18 Infantry Divisions
* 10 Mountain Divisions
* 3 Armoured Divisions
* 2 Artillery Divisions
* 6 Air Defence Brigades + 2 Surface-to-Air Missile Groups
* 5 Independent Armoured Brigades
* 15 Independent Artillery Brigades
* 7 Independent Infantry Brigades
* 1 Parachute Brigade
* 4 Engineer Brigades
* 14 Army Aviation Helicopter Units

Sub-Units

* 63 Tank Regiments
* 7 Airborne Battalions
* 200 Artillery Regiments
* 360 Infantry Battalions + 5 Para (SF) Battalions
* 40 Mechanised Infantry Battalions
* 20 Combat Helicopter Units
* 35+ Air Defence Regiments

Till now india and pakistan have fought four main wars and India Has defeated pakistan EveryTime.

5

ARMY WEAPONS AND ARMS

ARJUN

At the end of the 1971 war, the Indian army realized the limitations of their tank fleet in the harsh desert conditions of Rajasthan, a northwestern Indian state bordering Pakistan, so they initiated their own MBT design. The first "Arjun" (named after a mythical Hindu warrior prince) concept was laid out in 1974 by the Combat Vehicles Research and Development Establishment (CVRDE) of the Defence Research and Development Organization (DRDO). Based on 1971 battlefield experiences, the Arjun would have a locally-designed, rifled 120mm main gun, a German, MTU-based diesel powerplant (The Indians consider turbine engines fuel guzzlers), and a computerized fire control system with a laser rangefinder.

One of the early Arjun prototypes was unveiled in April 1985, with a number of prototypes undergoing technical testing while desert trials were scheduled for that summer.

At the time, it was reported to have a 120mm smooth-bore main gun and would use a 1400-hp MTU-based diesel until an indigenous one was ready. Weight would be about 50 tons, and the tank would cost about $1.6 million (U.S.). Development costs rose about 500 percent throughout the '80s, and through a development process plagued with delays, the end product visually resembles the

German Leopard II, however, unlike the German vehicle, its future remains in doubt. As of mid-2000 India planned to acquire T-90 tanks, based on field trials which had already been completed. Although orders had been placed for the supply of 124 Arjun tanks through the Defence Research Development Organisation, it would be difficult to predict when these orders would be fufilled. Until such time, T-90 tanks would serve to counter Pakistan's T-85 tanks.

Pakistan's announcment in 1995 of a deal with Ukraine to purchase T-84s caused a flurry of activity in the Indian tank development community. And on 9 January 1996, the Arjun was formally unveiled and cleared for mass production. Considered comparable to the M1A2 Abrams, Leopard 2, and Leclerc, the 59-ton "15th Variant" can achieve a maximum speed of 70 kph (55 mph) and cross-country speed of 40 kph with its 1400-hp powerplant. The 1,610-liter fuel tank allows for a cruising range of 200 km (120 miles). To ensure crew survivability, production versions will have the indigenously-researched and developed 'Kanchan' composite armor, an automatic fire detection and suppression system, and an NBC protection system designed and built by the Bhabha Atomic Research Center.

The rifled 120mm gun, which includes a muzzle reference system, is made of ESR steel and is fitted with a thermal sleeve and fume extractor. All main gun rounds use a semicombustible cartridge case with increased energy propellant for higher muzzle velocity and greater penetration characteristics. In addition to the usual suite of rounds, an antihelicopter round is under development as well.

The Arjun's fire control system includes a laser rangefinder, ballistic computer, thermal imaging night sight, stabilized panoramic sight for the tank commander, and a secondary telescopic sight. The LRF (integral to the gunner's sight) has a range of nearly 10 km and a thermal imager (which can "see"' at around 5.5 km, recognize a target at 3.1 km and identify targets at 2.5 km). The Arjun fire control system's ability to fire on the move during the night is a major step forward for Indian armored forces.

The Chassis and Automative System of MBT Arjun comprises main chassis, power pack (1400 HP engine coupled to hydromech transmission), running gear with hydropneumatic suspension, integrated fuel system, advanced electrical system and other dedicated special systems like integrated fire detection and suppression system. The chassis is fabricated from rolled homogenous armour plate using advanced welding technique. Frontal armour is of Kanchan composite sandwitched between armour plates.

This fully integrated Arjun chassis and Automative System having smooth riding characteristics can be used as a mobile platform for any advanced weapon system. An extremely effective hydropneumatic suspension system has been developed for MBT Arjun. The suspension is externally mounted and provides vehicle springing and damping. It consists of one bogey wheel pair for each suspension station. Gaseous medium in the hydropneumatic suspension is for all terrain maneuverability for exploiting the power available. Casing and hub of the hydropneumatic suspension are sealed for preventing dust ingression and water seepage into the casing during operation in marshy area or shallow/medium fording. The MBT Arjun is fitted with double-pin steel track with detachable rubber pads. It is made out of steel casting having two bores for insertion of rubberised pins. It is an integral piece incorporating guide horns and has got a provision for insertion of detachable pads. The end connectors are induction-hardened in the area which comes in contact with the sprocket teeth to prevent wear.

The integrated fire and explosion suppression system developed for MBT Arjun is based on state-of-the-art technology. The indigenous development of this system is considered to be a breakthrough in the field of fire protection engineering. It is capable of suppressing hydrocarbon fuel fire/explosion resulting from an enemy hit on the tank or due to any malfunctioning of the engine, transmission or any electrical short circuiting. The system is based on infra-red detectors for the detection of fire/explosion in the crew compartment of the battle tank and a continuous type of linear thermal detector popularly known as fire-wire for the engine compartment.

Halon-1301 has been employed as a fire extinguishing medium. The system is capable of detection and suppression of hydrocarbon fuel fire/explosion in the crew compartment within 200 milliseconds and in the engine compartment within 15 s thereby enhancing the chances of survivability of the crew and battle effectiveness of the tank. Further improvements were deemed necessary even after the Arjun design profile was accepted again in July 1996.

On 27 August 1996, the Defense Production and Supplies Secretary ordered 15 pre-production tanks from the Heavy Vehicles Factory, Avadi (at which point, estimates placed the project cost at $112 million). As of mid-1997 the list of faults after 20 years of development was not encouraging. In addition to numerous technical modifications to its fire and gun control systems, the fire control system in particular has been found unable to perform in temperatures above 42 degrees Celsius (108° F).

The DRDO has been considering scrapping the current Arjun fire control system in favor of whatever is accepted for the T-72M1 upgrade program. Defects noticed during the user trials of the Arjun Mk.1 MBT, including over-heating of the engine in Rajasthan desert areas, had supposedly been "by and large overcome" while other complaints were being addressed.

The first 120 tanks to be built would cost $4.2 million each, while other cost estimates places the figure at $5.6 million each per tank by 2001, given a purchase of 124 tanks to equip two regiments. Production of the first batch of tanks might take more than the planned five years, given the capacity at the Avadi factory. Planned Arjun variants include mobile assault guns, an observation post vehicle, an air defense (gun or missile) version, a recovery vehicle, an engineer vehicle, and bridgelayers. New bridgelayers and recovery vehicles were necessary, given the Arjun's substantial weight increase over the T-72M1 series.

Specifications

ARJUN Mk 1 (15th Preproduction Model)

Weight 59 tons (58.5 tonnes)

Length (gun forwards) 10.19m

Width (over tracks) 3.5m (w/ skirts) 3.85m

Height (w/o 12.7mm AAMG) 2.32m

Engine 1400 HP MTU 838 Ka 501Diesel

Transmission Semi-automatic with 4 forward and 2 reverse gears.(also reported as ZF automatic)

Fuel 1610 ltrs

Performance

Max Speed 72-70 kph (55 mph)

Cross Country Speed 40 kph

Cruising Range 200 km (120 miles)

Ground Pressure . 84 kg/cm Square

Ground Clearance .45m

Slide Slope: 60%

Climbing Gradient 35°

Trench 2.43 m (also given as 3m)

Vertical Obstacle .9m

Ford 1.4 m

Armament

Main Gun 120mm, stabalized w/ MRS (APFSDS, HE, HEAT, HESH and smoke)

12.7mm AA Gun (probably NVST)

7.62mm Coax (probably PK-T)

2 X 9 Smoke Grenade Launchers

LRF Range 10 km

Sights Thermal (Max Rng 5.5 km)

Active and Passive

Defensive Systems 'Arena' a possibilty, probable Laser Warning System

105 mm Indian and Light Field Guns

(IFG/LFG)

The 105 mm Indian and Light Field Guns (IFG/LFG) are high performance guns meeting the conflicting requirements of mountain, plain and desert warfare. The Indian Field Gun is the mainstay of the Field Artillery Branch of the Indian Army covering a maximum range of 17 km. The LFG is a close in weapon, designed to provide the necessary range, mobility and fire power required in the present day battlefield scenario. A unique feature of LFG is its light weight which makes it capaple of being helilifted for quick deployment in mountain terrain. This has been achieved by using high strength alloy steel. The optimised design provides a compact, robust and small profile ideally suited for cross-country mobility.

The Government has recently announced that there would be no further need to import ammunition. This indeed is a great tribute to the constant efforts made by the armament group of laboratories. It is noteworthy that of the total production value from the Indian Ordnance Factories, 70 per cent is based on the design provided by the armament group of laboratories which amounts to more than Rs 5000 crore.

Effective illumination of an area for night operations in the battlefield enhances operational capability of the Army. DRDO has perfected the technology of illuminating ammunition and has developed a veriety of illuminating ammunition for the Indian Army. These include 51 mm/81 mm/120 mm Mortar launched ammunition and 105 mm Indian Gun launched ammunition. The reliability and performance of indigenously developed illuminating ammunition is superior to the international standard.

PINAKA MULTIBARREL ROCKET LAUNCHER

The indigenously built Pinaka multi-barrel rocket launcher Weapon Area System can fire rockets with a range of 39-40 km, in a salvo of 12 rockets with 1.2 tons of high explosives within 40 seconds.

The complete system comprises a launch vehicle, a loader / replenishment vehicle, and a command post vehicle with a battery of six launchers. Pinaka can neutralise a target area of 350 square kilometres, and is meant as a supplement to the existing artillery system at a range beyond 30 km. It can be fitted with a variety of warheads ranging from blast-cum-pre-fragmented high explosives to anti-tank mines. This indigenously designed MLRS is far cheaper than the international competition, costing just Rs 23 million per system. By comparison the American M270 MLRS costs Rs 195 million, and the 9P140 URAGAN of Russia and the ASTROS-II of Brazil each cost Rs 38 million.

The Pune-based Armament Research and Development Establishment has successfully produced the 'Pinaka' Multi Barrel Rocket Launcher System for the Indian armed forces, to give it concentrated high volume firepower to destroy enemy targets as demanded by the top brass of the Indian army. The Pinaka system was tested at the interim test range (ITR) Chandipur-on-sea, and had undergone several tests since 1995. It has been subjected to user's trials by the Army, which was not entirely satisfied with the system, and additional tests were conducted in response to suggestions to improve its capability further.

In March 1999 the system was tested in the run-up to the country's largest ever air force exercise over the site of India's 1998 underground nuclear blasts, at the eastern Indian missile launch site of Balasore. Pinaka was finally put into field testing for assessing its capability during the Kargil conflict. Pinaka reportedly proved very successful during field testing in the high altitude conflict in Kargil. In mid-1998 it was reported that production is on at various ordnance factories, and four public sector undertakings would meet the December 1998 delivery deadline. But in May 1999 the Comptroller and Auditor General criticized the Defence Research and development Organisation (DRDO) for its failure to develop critical components of Pinaka, which led to a six-year delay in the induction of the system. Far from reaching the production stage, the DRDO has yet to develop various critical components of the system despite an expenditure of Rs 42.45 crore. The Defence Ministry in 1981 had planned to induct "Pinaka" into Indian Army regiments by 1994, and the project was originally given a Rs 26.47 crore budget. The expected date of completion of development is late 2000 at a cost of around Rs 80 crore.

The Armament Research and Development Establishment (ARDE) has also developed a high performance artillery rocket system which can fire within a range between 70 km to 100 km. This is a highly sophisticated "shoot-and-scoot" high mobility system capable of firing a salvo of 12 rockets, each with a payload of 100 kg within a time span of 30 seconds. This new artillery rocket system comprises of an advanced family of warheads including terminally guided submunitions with autonomous target search and engagement capability besides remotely delivered intelligent bomblets and minelets with self-neutralising capability.

Specifications

Range 7 km - 40 km

Rocket Diameter 214 mm

Warheads

- fragmentation high explosive
- incendiary
- anti-tank and anti-personnel minelettes
- anti-tank bomlettes

Rate of Fire

- 40 seconds [typically reported]
- 24-44 seconds [variously reported]

ALL WEATHER AIR DEFENCE GUN SYSTEM

A high performance family of All Weather Towed and Self Propelled Air Defence Gun System is under development to complement the Defence Research and Development Organisation (DRDO) surface-to-air missile systems such as Trishul and Akash.

The new gun will feature twin-gun cyclic rate of fire of 2000 rounds per minute aimed to engage and neutralise high speed aircraft, helicopters, remote-piloted combat air vehicles and stand-off weapons.

The integrated gun system is expected to have all weather day-night operations with on-mount passive suiteof electro-optic sensors like laser range finders, forward looking infra-red (FLIR), thermal imaging systems and low-light level TV, for tracking and engaging fast flying targets by means of a high precision computerised digital servo control system.

MBT-2000 / TYPE 2000 MAIN BATTLE TANK

Pakistan's development of the MBT-2000 *Al Khalid* began in 1988, and in January 1990 an agreement was reached with China to jointly design, develop and manufacture system. The design is an upgrade from the original T902M and work had been going on at China's NORINCO for some years, with initial prototypes produced in China were fielded for trials in August 1991. Pakistan's manufacturing plant at Taxila was completed in 1992. Since then development efforts have focused on improving the design for Pakistan's terrain and high temperatures.

The engine of the T90 2M is replaced by the Ukrainian 6TD 1200hp engine, and a newly developed thermal viewer system has been added to improve nocturnal fighting capability. Heavy Industries Taxila was expected to start production of Al-Khalid before the turn of this century. The Chinese ground army has not made any purchase orders and will not use the same tank when it does decide to buy a next-generation armored vehicle.

Specifications

Powerplant Ukrainian 6TD 1200hp

Maximum Speed 37 mph

Weight 48 tons

Armament

one 125mm smooth bore gun

one 12.7mm machine gun

one 7.62mm machine gun.

6

INDIAN ARMY IN THE WAR OF 1965

The Indo-Pakistani War of 1965 was a culmination of skirmishes that took place between April 1965 and September 1965 between India and Pakistan. This conflict became known as the Second Kashmir War fought by India and Pakistan over the disputed region of Kashmir, the first having been fought in 1947. The war began following the failure of Pakistan's Operation Gibraltar, which was designed to infiltrate forces into Jammu and Kashmir to precipitate an insurgency against rule by India. The five-week war caused thousands of casualties on both sides. It ended in a United Nations (UN) mandated ceasefire and the subsequent issuance of the Tashkent Declaration.

Much of the war was fought by the countries' land forces in Kashmir and along the International Border between India and Pakistan. This war saw the largest amassing of troops in Kashmir since the Partition of India in 1947, a number that was overshadowed only during the 2001-2002 military standoff between India and Pakistan.

Most of the battles were fought by opposing infantry and armored units, with substantial backing from air forces. Many details of this war, like those of other Indo-Pakistani Wars, remain unclear and many media reports have been riddled with media biases.

PRE-WAR ESCALATION

Since Partition of India in 1947, Pakistan and India remained in contention over several issues. Although the Kashmir conflict was the predominant issue dividing the nations, other border disputes existed, most notably over the Rann of Kutch, a barren region in the Indian state of Gujarat. When Junagadh, a former princely state, had been integrated into India, whose muslim prince wanted to join Pakistan.

On March 20, 1965, and again in April 1965, fighting broke out between India and Pakistan in the Rann of Kutch. Initially involving border police from both nations, the disputed area soon witnessed intermittent skirmishes between the countries' armed forces.

In June 1965, British Prime Minister Harold Wilson successfully persuaded both countries to end hostilities and set up a tribunal to resolve the dispute. The verdict, which came later in 1968, saw Pakistan awarded 350 square miles (900 km^2) of the Rann of Kutch, as against its original claim of 3500 square miles.

After its success in the Rann of Kutch, Pakistan, under the leadership of General Ayub Khan, believed the Indian Army would be unable to defend itself against a quick military campaign in the disputed territory of Kashmir as the Indian military had suffered a loss to China in 1962.

Pakistan believed that the population of Kashmir was generally discontented with Indian rule and that a resistance movement could be ignited by a few infiltrating saboteurs. Pakistan attempted to ignite the resistance movement by means of a covert infiltration, codenamed Operation Gibraltar. The Pakistani infiltrators were soon discovered, however, their presence reported by local Kashmiris, and the operation ended in a complete failure.

Pakistan claimed to have been concerned by attempts of India to absorb Kashmir - a state claimed by Pakistan as "disputed", into the Indian Union. The basis for this claim was the application of

Articles 356 and 357 of the Indian Constitution that allow the President of India to declare President's Rule in the State.

THE WAR

On August 15, 1965, Indian forces crossed the ceasefire line and launched an attack on the region referred to by the disputants as either "Azad Kashmir" or "Pakistan-occupied Kashmir". Pakistani reports cite this attack as unprovoked, while Indian reports cite the attack as a response to massive armed infiltrations of Kashmir by Pakistan.

Initially, the Indian Army met with considerable success, capturing three important mountain positions after a prolonged artillery barrage. By the end of August, however, both sides had experienced successes; Pakistan had made progress in areas such as Tithwal, Uri and Punch and India had captured the Haji Pir Pass, eight kilometers inside Pakistani-occuppied territory.

On September 1, 1965, Pakistan launched a counterattack, called "Operation Grand Slam", with the objective to capture the vital town of Akhnoor in Jammu, which would sever communications and cut off supply routes to Indian troops. Attacking with an overwhelming ratio of troops and technically superior tanks, Pakistan initially progressed against Indian forces, who were caught unprepared and suffered heavy losses. India responded by calling in its air force to blunt the Pakistani attack. The next day, Pakistan retaliated, its air force attacked Indian forces and air bases in both Kashmir and Punjab. Although Operation Grand Slam ultimately failed, as the Pakistan Army was unable to capture Akhnoor, it became one of the turning points in the war when India decided to relieve pressure on its troops in Kashmir by attacking Pakistan further south.

India crossed the International Border on the Western front on September 6, marking an official beginning of the war. On September 6, the 15th Infantry Division of the Indian Army, under World War II veteran Major General Prasad, battled a massive counterattack by Pakistan near the west bank of the Ichogil Canal

(BRB Canal), which was a *de facto* border of India and Pakistan. The General's entourage itself was ambushed and he was forced to flee his vehicle. A second, this time successful, attempt to cross the Ichhogil Canal was made over the bridge in the village of Barki, just east of Lahore.

These developments brought the Indian Army within the range of Lahore International Airport. As a result, the United States requested a temporary ceasefire to allow it to evacuate its citizens in Lahore.However,the Pakistani counter attack took Khem Karan from Indian forces which tried to divert the attention of Pakistanis from Khem Karan by an attack on Bedian and the adjacent villages.As said by Indian Lt. General Kaul,

"The C-in-C(Indian) got cold feet and decided, while the battle of Khem Karan was still in progress to take up an alternate position, several miles in the rear which would have meant giving up some well known and vital places and areas." (Kaul op. Cit. P478)

The thrust against Lahore consisted of the 1st Infantry Division supported by the three tank regiments of the 2nd Independent Armoured Brigade: they quickly advanced across the border, reaching the Ichhogil (BRB) Canal by 6 September.

The Pakistani Army held the bridges over the canal or blew up those it could not hold, effectively stalling any further advance by the Indians on Lahore.One unit of the Jat Regiment, 3 Jat, had also crossed the Ichogil canal and captured the town of Batapore (Jallo Mur to Pakistan) on the west side of the canal. The same day, a counter offensive consisting of an armored division and infantry division supported by Pakistan Air Force Sabres forced the Indian 15th Division to withdraw to its starting point.

Although 3 Jat suffered minimal casualties, the bulk of the damage being taken by ammunition and stores vehicles, the higher commanders had no information of 3 Jat's capture of Batapore and misleading information led to the command to withdraw from Batapore and Dograi to Ghosal-Dial. This move brought extreme disappointment to Lt-Col Desmond Hayde, CO of 3 Jat. Dograi was eventually recaptured by 3 Jat on 21 September, for the second time but after a much harder battle due to Pakistani reinforcements.

On the days following September 9, both nations' premiere formations were routed in unequal battles. India's 1st Armored Division, labelled the "pride of the Indian Army", launched an offensive towards Sialkot.

The Division divided itself into two prongs, was forced back by the 6th armoured division(an understrength formation of few armoured regiments) at Chawinda and was forced to withdraw after suffering heavy losses of nearly 100 tanks. Similarly, Pakistan's pride, the 1st Armored Division, pushed an offensive towards Khemkaran, with the intent to capture Amritsar (a major city in Punjab, India) and the bridge on River Beas to Jalandhar.

The Pakistani 1st Armored Division never made it past Khem Karan, however, and by the end of September 10 lay disintegrated by the defences of the Indian 4th Mountain Division at what is now known as the Battle of *Asal Uttar* (lit. meaning - "Real Answer", or more appropriate English equivalent - "Fitting Response"). The area became known as 'Patton Nagar' (Patton Town) as Pakistan lost or abandoned nearly 100 mostly US-made Patton tanks.The Pakistani 1st Armoured Division less 5th Armoured Brigade was next sent to Sialkot sector behind Pakistani 6th Armoured Division where it didnt see action as 6th Armoured Division was already in process of routing Indian 1st Armoured Division which was superior to it in strength.

The war was heading for a stalemate, with both nations holding territory of the other. The Indian army suffered 3,000 battlefield deaths, while Pakistan suffered no less than 3,800. The Indian army was in possession of 710 mile^2 (1,840 km^2) of Pakistani territory and the Pakistan army held 210 mile^2 (545 km^2) of Indian territory. The territory occupied by India was mainly in the fertile Sialkot, Lahore and Kashmir sectors, while Pakistani land gains were primarily in deserts opposite Sindh and in Chumb, in the northern sector.

Aerial Warfare

The war saw the Indian Air Force and the Pakistani Air Force engaged in full scale combat for the first time since independence. Though the two forces had previously faced off in the First Kashmir War during the late 1940s, that engagement was limited in scale compared to the 1965 conflict.

The two countries have made contradictory claims of combat losses during the war and hardly any neutral sources have verified the claims of either country. The Pakistan Air Force (PAF) claimed it shot down 104 IAF planes, losing only 19 in the process. The Indian Air Force (IAF) claimed it shot down 24 PAF planes, losing only 75 itself.[18] India also pointed out that, despite PAF claims of losing only a squadron of combat craft, Pakistan sought to acquire additional aircraft from Indonesia, Iraq, Iran, Turkey and China within 10 days of the beginning war.

Pakistan's strike force comprised the U.S. made F-86 Sabre jets, which claimed a fair share of Indian planes, though remaining vulnerable to the diminutive Folland Gnat, nicknamed "Sabre Slayer".[19] The F-104 Starfighter of the PAF was by far the fastest fighter plane operating in the subcontinent at that time. Unlike the PAF, whose planes largely consisted of American craft, the IAF flew an assortment of planes, from Vampires to Hawker Hunters, many of which were outdated in comparison to PAF planes.

Tank Battles

The 1965 war witnessed some of the largest tank battles since World War II. At the beginning of the war, the Pakistani Army had both a numerical advantage in tanks, as well as better equipment overall. Pakistani armour was largely American-made; it consisted mainly of Patton M-47 and M-48 tanks, but also included many M4 Sherman tanks, some M24 Chaffee light tanks and M36 Jackson tank destroyers, equipped with 90 mm guns. The bulk of India's tank fleet were older M4 Sherman tanks; some were up-gunned with the French high velocity CN 75 50 guns and could hold their own, whilst some older models were still equipped with the inferior 75 mm M3 L/40 gun. Besides the M4 tanks, India fielded the British-made Centurion Tank Mk 7, with the 105 mm Royal Ordnance L7 gun, and the AMX-13, PT-76, and M3 Stuart light tanks. Pakistan fielded a greater number and more modern artillery; its guns out-ranged those of the Indian artillery, according to Pakistan's Major General T.H. Malik.

At the outbreak of war in 1965, Pakistan had about 15 armoured cavalry regiments, each with about 45 tanks in three squadrons. Besides the Pattons, there were about 200 M4 Shermans re-armed with 76mm guns, 150 M24 Chaffee light tank and a few independent squadrons of M36B1 tank destroyers. Most of these regiments served in Pakistan's two armoured divisions, the 1st and 6th Armoured divisions - the latter being in the process of formation. The Indian Army of the time possessed 17 cavalry regiments, and in the 1950s had begun modernizing them by the acquisition of 164 AMX-13 light tanks and 188 Centurions. The remainder of the cavalry units were equipped with M4 Shermans and a small number of M3A3 Stuart light tanks. India had only a single armoured division, the 1st 'Black Elephant' Armoured Division, also called 'Fakhr I Hind' ('Pride of India'), which consisted of the 17th cavalry Poona Horse, the 4th Hodson's Horse, the 16th 'Black Elephant' Cavalry, the 7th Light Cavalry, the 2nd Royal Lancers, the 18th Cavalry and the 62nd Cavalry, the two first named being equipped with Centurions,. There was also the 2nd Independent Armoured Brigade, one of whose three regiments, the 3rd Cavalry, was also equipped with Centurions.

Despite the qualitative and numerical superiority of Pakistani armour, Pakistan was outfought on the battlefield by India, which made progress into the Lahore-Sialkot sector, whilst halting Pakistan's counteroffensive on Amritsar they were sometimes employed in a faulty manner, such as charging prepared defenses during the defeat of Pakistan's 1st Armored Division at Assal Uttar.

India's tank formations experienced same results. India's attack at the Battle of Chawinda, led by its 1st Armored Division and supporting units, was brought to a grinding halt by newly raised 6th Armoured Division(ex-100th indepedant brigade group) in the Chawinda sector. The Pakistanis pushed the Indians back farther after the Battle of Chawinda with Operation Windup. One true winner to emerge was India's Centurion battle tank, with its 105 mm gun and heavy armor, which proved superior to the overly complex Pattons and their exaggerated reputations..However, in the Sialkot sector outnumbered Pattons performed exceedingly well in the hands of the 25th Cavalry and other regiments of the 6th Armoured Division, which exacted a disproportionately heavy toll of Centurions from the Poona Horse and Hodson's Horse. The Indian Army has made much of the fact that some of its Centurions survived repeated hits; yet have failed to point out that the majority of tanks in the Sialkot sector were Shermans whose guns were inadequate even in 1944. Neither the Indian nor Pakistani Army showed any great facility in the use of armoured formations in offensive operations, whether the Pakistani 1st Armoured Division at Asal Uttar or the Indian 1st Armoured Division at Chawinda. In contrast, both proved adept with smaller forces in a defensive role such a the 2nd Armoured Brigade at Asal Uttar and the 25th Cavalry at Chawinda, where they defeated their better equipped but clumsier foes

Naval Hostilities

The navies of India and Pakistan did not play a prominent role in the war of 1965, although Pakistani accounts dispute this. On September 7, a flotilla of the Pakistani Navy carried out a small scale bombardment of the Indian coastal town and radar station of Dwarka, which was 200 miles (300 km) south of the Pakistani port of Karachi. Codenamed Operation Dwarka, it did not fulfill its primary objective of disabling the radar station and there was no immediate retaliatory response from India. Later, some of the Indian fleet sailed from Bombay to Dwarka to patrol the area and deter further bombardment. Foreign authors have noted that the "insignificant bombardment" of the town was a "limited engagement, with no strategic value."

According to some Pakistani sources, one submarine, PNS Ghazi, kept the Indian Navy's aircraft carrier INS Vikrant besieged in Bombay throughout the war. Indian sources claim that it was not their intention to get into a naval conflict with Pakistan, and wished to restrict the war to a land-based conflict. Moreover, they note that the Vikrant was in dry dock in the process of refitting. Some Pakistani defence writers have also discounted claims that the Indian Navy was bottled up in Bombay by a single submarine, instead stating that 75% of the Indian Navy was under maintenance in harbour. There were, however, unconfirmed reports of underwater attacks near Bombay by the Indian Navy against what they suspected were American-supplied Pakistani submarines.

Covert Operations

The Pakistan Army launched a number of covert operations to infiltrate and sabotage Indian airbases.[30] On September 7, 1965, the Special Services Group (SSG) commandos were parachuted into enemy territory. According to Chief of Army Staff General Musa Khan, about 135 commandos were airdropped at three Indian airfields(Halwara, Pathankot and Adampur). The daring attempt proved to be an "unmitigated disaster". Only 22 commandos returned to Pakistan as planned, 93 were taken prisoner (including one of the Commanders of the operations, Major Khalid Butt), and 20 were killed in encounters with the army, police or civilians The reason for the failure of the commando mission is attributed to the failure to provide maps, proper briefings and adequate planning or preparation.

Despite failing to sabotage the airfields, Pakistan sources claim that the commando mission affected some planned Indian operations. As the Indian 14th Division was diverted to hunt for paratroopers, the Pakistan Air Force found the road filled with transport, and destroyed many vehicles.

India responded to the covert activity by announcing rewards for captured Pakistani spies or paratroopers. Meanwhile, in Pakistan, rumors spread that India had retaliated with its own covert operations, sending commandos deep into Pakistan territory, but these rumors were later determined to be unfounded.

Losses

India and Pakistan make widely divergent claims about the damage they inflicted on each other and the amount of damage suffered by them. The following summarizes each nation's claims.

	Indian claims	Pakistani claims	Independent Sources
Casualties	-	-	3,000 Indian soldiers, 3,800 Pakistani soldiers
Combat flying effort	4,073+ combat sorties	2,279 combat sorties	
Aircraft lost	35 IAF (official), 73 PAF.Other sources based on the Official Indian Armed Forces History put actual IAF losses at 71 including 19 accidents (non combat sortie rate is not known) and PAF's combat losses alone at 43.	19 PAF, 104 IAF	20 PAF, Pakistan claims India rejected neutral arbitration. (Singh, Pushpindar (1991). *Fiza ya, Psyche of the Pakistan Air Force*. Himalayan Books. ISBN 81-7002-038-7.)
Aerial victories	17 + 3 (post war)	30	-
Tanks destroyed	128 Indian tanks,[42] 152 Pakistani tanks captured, 150 Pakistani tanks destroyed. Officially 471 Pakistani tanks destroyed and 38 captured	165 Pakistan tanks	200 Pakistani tanks
Land area won	1,500 mi² (3,885 km²) of Pakistani territory	2,000 mi² (5,180 km²) of Indian territory	India held 710 mi² (1,840 km²) of Pakistani territory and Pakistan held 210 mi² (545 km²) of Indian territory

There have been few neutral assessments of the damages of the war; some of the neutral assessments are mentioned below:-

- According to the United States Library of Congress Country Studies:

The war was militarily inconclusive; each side held prisoners and some territory belonging to the other. Losses were relatively heavy—on the Pakistani side, twenty aircraft, 200 tanks, and 3,800 troops. Pakistan's army had been able to withstand Indian pressure, but a continuation of the fighting would only have led to further losses and ultimate defeat for Pakistan. Most Pakistanis, schooled in the belief of their own martial prowess, refused to accept the possibility of their country's military defeat by "Hindu India" and were, instead, quick to blame their failure to attain their military aims on what they considered to be the ineptitude of Ayub Khan and his government.

- TIME magazine analyzing the conflict, reported that India held 690 Mi^2 of Pakistan territory while Pakistan held 250 Mi^2 of Indian territory in Kashmir and Rajasthan, Pakistan had lost almost half its armour temporarily. The same article stated that 'severely mauled by the larger Indian armed forces, Pakistan could continue the fight only by teaming up with Red China and turning its back on the U.N'.
- An excerpt from Stanley Wolpert's *India* summarizing the Indo-Pakistani War of 1965, is as follows:

In three weeks the second IndoPak War ended in what appeared to be a draw when the embargo placed by Washington on U.S. ammunition and replacements for both armies forced cessation of conflict before either side won a clear victory. India, however, was in a position to inflict grave damage to, if not capture, Pakistan's capital of the Punjab when the cease-fire was called, and controlled Kashmir's strategic Uri-Poonch bulge, much to Ayub's chagrin.

- Dennis Kux's *'India and the United States estranged democracies"* also provides a summary of the war.

Although both sides lost heavily in men and materiel, and neither gained a decisive military advantage, India had the better of the war. New Delhi achieved its basic goal of thwarting Pakistan's attempt to seize Kashmir by force. Pakistan gained nothing from a conflict which it had instigated.

- Newsweek magazine, however, praised the Pakistani military's ablility to hold of the much larger Indian Army.

"By just the end of the week, in fact, it was clear that the Pakistanis were more than holding their own."

Ceasefire

On September 22, the United Nations Security Council unanimously passed a resolution that called for an unconditional ceasefire from both nations. The war ended the following day.

The Soviet Union, led by Premier Alexey Kosygin, hosted ceasefire negotiations in Tashkent (now in Uzbekistan), where Indian Prime Minister Lal Bahadur Shastri and Pakistani President Ayub Khan signed the Tashkent Agreement, agreeing to withdraw to pre-August lines no later than February 25, 1966. The ceasefire was criticized by many Pakistanis who, relying on official reports and the controlled Pakistani press, believed that the leadership had surrendered military gains. The protests led to student riots. Pakistan State's reports had suggested that their military was performing admirably in the war - which they incorrectly blamed as being initiated by India - and thus the Tashkent Declaration was seen as having forfeited the gains. Some recent books written by Pakistani authors, including one by ex-ISI chief titled "The Myth of 1965 Victory", allegedly exposed Pakistani fabrications about the war, but all copies of the book were bought by Pakistan Army to prevent publication because the topic was "too sensitive".

India and Pakistan accused each other of ceasefire violations; India charged Pakistan with 585 violations in 34 days, while Pakistan countered with accusations of 450 incidents by India. In addition to the expected exchange of small arms and artillery fire, India reported that Pakistan utilized the ceasefire to capture the Indian village of Chananwalla in the Fazilka sector. This village was recaptured by Indian troops on 25 December. On October 10, a B-57 Canberra on loan to the PAF was damaged by 3 SA-2 missiles fired from the IAF base at Ambala A Pakistani Army Auster was shot down on 16 December, killing one Pakistani army captain and on 2 February 1967, an AOP was shot down by IAF Hunters.

The ceasefire remained in effect until the start of the Indo-Pakistani War of 1971.

Intelligence Failures

Strategic miscalculations by both India and Pakistan ensured that the war ended in a stalemate.

Indian Miscalculations

Indian military intelligence gave no warning of the impending Pakistan invasion. The Indian Army failed to recognize the presence of heavy Pakistani artillery and armaments in Chumb and suffered significant losses as a result.

The "Official History of the 1965 War", drafted by the Ministry of Defence of India in 1992, was a long suppressed document that revealed other miscalculations. According to the document, on September 22 when the Security Council was pressing for a ceasefire, the Indian Prime Minister asked commanding Gen. Chaudhuri if India could possibly win the war, were he to delay accepting the ceasefire. The general replied that most of India's frontline ammunition had been used up and the Indian Army had suffered considerable tank losses. It was determined later that only 14% of India's frontline ammunition had been fired and India held twice the number of tanks as Pakistan. By this time, the Pakistani Army had used close to 80% of its ammunition.

Air Chief Marshal (retd) P.C. Lal, who was the Vice Chief of Air Staff during the conflict, points to the lack of coordination between the IAF and the Indian army. Neither side revealed its battle plans to the other. The battle plans drafted by the Ministry of Defence and General Chaudhari, did not specify a role for the Indian Air Force in the order of battle. This attitude of Gen. Chaudhari was referred to by ACM Lal as the "Supremo Syndrome", a patronizing attitude sometimes held by the Indian army towards the other branches of the Indian Military.

Pakistani Miscalculations

The Pakistani Army's failures started with the supposition that a generally discontented Kashmiri people, given the opportunity provided by the Pakistani advance, would revolt against their Indian rulers, bringing about a swift and decisive surrender of Kashmir. The Kashmiri people, however, did not revolt. Instead, the Indian Army was provided with enough information to learn of Operation Gibraltar and the fact that the Army was battling not insurgents, as they had initially supposed, but Pakistani Army regulars.

The Pakistani Army also failed to recognize that the Indian policy makers would order an attack on the southern sector in order to open a second theater of conflict. Pakistan was forced to dedicate troops to the southern sector to protect Sialkot and Lahore instead using them to support penetrating into Kashmir.

"Operation Grand Slam", which was launched by Pakistan to capture Akhnoor, a town north-east of Jammu and a key region for communications between Kashmir and the rest of India, was also a failure. Many Pakistani commentators criticized the Ayub Khan administration for being indecisive during Operation Grand Slam. These critics claim that the operation failed because Ayub Khan knew the importance of Akhnur to India (having called it India's "jugular vein") and did not want to capture it and drive the two nations into an all-out war. Despite progress being made in Akhnur, General Ayub Khan relieved the commanding Major General Akhtar Hussain Malik and replaced him with Gen. Yahya Khan. A 24-hour lull ensued the replacement, which allowed the Indian army to regroup in Akhnur and successfully oppose a lackluster attack headed by General Yahya Khan. "The enemy came to our rescue", asserted the Indian Chief of Staff of the Western Command. Later, Akhtar Hussain Malik criticized Ayub Khan for planning Operation Gibraltar, which was doomed to fail, and for relieving him of his command at a crucial moment in the war. Malik threatened to expose the truth about the war and the army's failure, but later dropped the idea for fear of being banned.

Some authors have noted that Pakistan might have been emboldened by a war game - conducted in March 1965, at the Institute of Defence Analysis, USA. The exercise concluded that, in the event of a war with India, Pakistan would win. Other authors like Stephen Philip Cohen, have consistently commented that the Pakistan Army had "acquired an exaggerated view of the weakness of both India and the Indian military... the 1965 war was a shock".

Pakistani Air Marshal and Commander-in-Chief of PAF during the war, Nur Khan, later said that the Pakistan Army, and not India, should be blamed for starting the war. However propaganda in Pakistan about the war continued; the war was not rationally analyzed in Pakistan, with most of the blame being heaped on the leadership and little importance given to intelligence failures that persisted until the debacle of the 1971 war, when Pakistan suffered a decisive defeat at the hands of India, leading to the creation of Bangladesh.

Involvement of other Nations

The United States of America, which had previously supplied military equipment to India and Pakistan, imposed an embargo against further supplies to both countries once the war had started. The US was apprehensive that military equipment that it had provided to be used in a battle against communism, would instead be used by the countries to fight one another. The American embargo especially affected Pakistan since the majority of its equipment was provided by America. This would cause Pakistan to believe that it could not continue the war beyond September.

Following imposition of the American embargo, other NATO allies (including the UK) discontinued providing military equipment to the nations.

Both before and during the war, China had been a major military associate of Pakistan and had invariably admonished India, with whom it had fought a war in 1962. There were also reports of Chinese troop movements on the Indian border to support Pakistan. As such, India agreed to the UN mandate in order to avoid a war on both borders.

India's participation in the Non-Aligned Movement yielded little support from its members. Pakistan, however, gained assistance from countries of Asia with large Islamic populations, including Turkey, Iran and Indonesia. The USSR was more neutral than most other nations during the war and even invited both nations to talks that it would host in Tashkent.

CONSEQUENCES OF THE WAR

India

India continued to increase its defense spending after the war. The Indian Military, which was already undergoing rapid expansions, made improvements in command and control to address some shortcomings. Partly as a result of the inefficient information gathering preceding the war, India established the Research and Analysis Wing for external espionage and intelligence. India viewed the American policy during the war as biased, since Pakistan had started the war but the US did little to restrain Pakistan. After the war, India slowly started aligning with the Soviet Union, both politically and militarily. This would be cemented formally years later before the Indo-Pakistani War of 1971.

In light of the failures of the previous war against the Chinese, the performance in this war was viewed as a "politico-strategic" victory in India. The Indian premier, Shastri was hailed as a hero in India. However, India was criticized in some quarters for not being able to defeat the much smaller Pakistani military. In its October 1, 1965 issue TIME magazine quoted a Western ambassador as saying 'It used to be you could feed the word 'India' into the machine and it would spit out 'Maharajahs, snakes, too many babies, too many cows, spindly-legged Hindus.' Now it's apparent to everybody that India is going to emerge as an Asian power in its own right.'

Pakistan

At the conclusion of the war, many Pakistanis considered the performance of their military to be positive. September 6 is celebrated as 'Defence Day' in Pakistan, in commemoration of the successful defence of Lahore against the Indian army. The performance of the Pakistani Air Force, in particular, was praised.

The myth of a mobile, hard hitting Pakistan Army, however, was badly dented in the war, as critical breakthroughs were not made. Several Pakistani writers criticized the military's ill-founded belief that their "Martial Race" of soldiers could defeat India in the war. Moreover, Pakistan had lost more ground than it had gained during the war and, more importantly, failed to achieve its goal of occupying Kashmir; this result has been viewed by many impartial observers as a defeat for Pakistan.

Many high ranking Pakistani officials and military experts later criticized the faulty planning of Operation Gibraltar that ultimately led to the war. The Tashkent declaration was also criticized in Pakistan, though few citizens realised the gravity of the situation that existed at the end of the war.

Political leaders were also criticized. Following the advice of Zulfikar Ali Bhutto, Pakistan's foreign minister, Ayub Khan had raised very high expectations among the people of Pakistan about the superiority - if not invincibility - of its armed forces, but Pakistan's inability to attain its military aims during the war, created a political liability for Ayub. The defeat of its Kashmiri ambitions in the war led to the army's invincibility being challenged by an increasingly vocal opposition. And with the war creating a huge financial burden, Pakistan's economy, which had witnessed rapid progress in the early 60s, took a severe beating.

Pakistan was surprised by the lack of support by the United States, an ally with whom the country had signed an Agreement of Cooperation. USA declared its neutrality in the war by cutting off military supplies to both sides, leading Islamabad to believe that they were "betrayed" by the United States. After the war, Pakistan would increasingly look towards China as a major source of military hardware and political support.

Another negative consequence of the war was the growing resentment against the Pakistani government in East Pakistan(present day Bangladesh), particularly for West Pakistan's obsession with Kashmir. Bengali leaders accused the central government of not providing adequate security for East Pakistan during the conflict, even though large sums of money were taken from the east to finance the war for Kashmir. In fact, despite some Pakistan Air Force attacks being launched from bases in East Pakistan during the war, India did not retaliate in that sector, although East Pakistan was defended only by an understrenghted infantry division (14 Division), sixteen planes and no tanks.[88] Sheikh Mujibur Rahman was critical of the disparity in military resources deployed in East and West Pakistan, calling for greater autonomy for East Pakistan, which ultimately led to the Bangladesh Liberation war and another war between India and Pakistan in 1971.

7

INDIAN ARMY IN THE WAR 1971

On the 3rd of December 1971, the Pakistani Air Force (PAF) struck a number of Indian airfields in northern India. By midnight, India was officially at war with Pakistan. Two weeks later, the war was over. The Indian Army had overrun erstwhile East Pakistan (Bangladesh) and taken 93,000 POWs. It was one of the swiftest military campaigns in recent history.

The Setting

The partition of the Indian Subcontinent in 1947 created two independent countries: India and Pakistan. India, which became independent on 15 August 1947, stood for a secular, equitable polity based on the universally accepted idea that all men are created equal and should be treated as such. Pakistan, which officially came into existence a day earlier, was based on the premise that Hindus and Muslims of the Subcontinent constitute two different nationalities and cannot co-exist. The Partition created two different countries with most Muslim majority areas of undivided India going to the newly created nation, Pakistan (Land of the Pure). Pakistan was originally made up of two distinct and geographically unconnected parts termed West and East Pakistan. West Pakistan was made up of a number of races including the Punjabis (the most numerous), Sindhis, Pathans, Balochis, Mohajirs (Muslim refugees from India) and others. East Pakistan, on the other hand, was much more homogeneous and had an overwhelming Bengali-speaking population.

The Roots of Discord

Although the Eastern wing of Pakistan was more populous than than the Western one, political power since independence rested with the Western elite. This caused considerable resentment in East Pakistan and a charismatic Bengali leader called, Sheikh Mujibur Rehman, most forcefully articulated that resentment by forming an opposition political party called the Awami League and demanding more autonomy for East Pakistan within the Pakistani Federation. In the Pakistani general elections held in 1970, the Sheikh's party won the majority of seats, securing a complete majority in East Pakistan. In all fairness, the Sheikh should have been Prime Minister of Pakistan, or at least the ruler of his province. But West Pakistan's ruling elite were so dismayed by the turn of events and by the Sheikh's demands for autonomy that instead of allowing him to rule East Pakistan, they put him in jail.

ORIGINS OF THE CRISIS

The dawn of 1971 saw a great human tragedy unfolding in erstwhile East Pakistan. Entire East Pakistan was in revolt. In the West, General Yahya Khan, who had appointed himself President in 1969, had given the job of pacifying East Pakistan to his junior, General Tikka Khan. The crackdown of 25 March 1971 ordered by Tikka Khan, left thousands of Bengalis dead and Sheikh Mujibur Rehman was arrested the next day. The same day, the Pakistani Army began airlifting two of its divisions plus a brigade strength formation to its Eastern Wing. Attempts to dis-arm Bengali troops were not entirely successful and within weeks of the 25 March massacres, many former Bengali officers and troops of the Pakistani Army had joined Bengali resistance fighters in different parts of East Pakistan.

The Pakistani Army conducted several crackdowns in different parts of Bangladesh, leading to massive loss of civilian life. The details of those horrific massacres, in which defenceless people were trapped and machine-gunned, is part of Bangladeshi history. Survivors compare it to the Nazi extermination of Jews. At the same time, the Pakistani Administration in Dhaka thought it could pacify the Bengali peasantry by appropriating the land of the Hindu population and gifting it to Muslims. While this did not impress the peasantry, it led to the exodus of more than 8 million refugees (more than half of them Hindus) to neighbouring India. West Bengal was the worst affected by the refugee problem and the Indian government was left holding the enormous burden. Repeated appeals by the Indian government failed to elicit any response from the international community and by April 1971, the then Indian Prime Minister, Mrs. Indira Gandhi, decided that the only solution lay in helping Bengali freedom fighters, especially the Mukti Bahini, to liberate East Pakistan, which had already been re-christened Bangladesh by its people.

Pakistan felt it could dissuade India from helping the Mukti Bahini by being provocative. The Pakistan Air Force (PAF) in East Pakistan took to attacking suspected Mukti Bahini camps located inside Indian territory in the state of West Bengal. In the Western and Northern sectors too occasional clashes, some of them quite bloody, took place.

Pakistan was suggesting that should India continue with its plans it should expect total war as in 1965. Only this time, the Pakistanis would concentrate their forces in the West and thereby aim at capturing as much as Indian territory as possible. The Indians, on the other hand, would be fighting a war on two fronts (while at the same time keeping a fearful eye on the Chinese borders). Given this scenario, the Pakistanis felt that India at best would be able to capture some territory in East Pakistan and lose quite a bit in the West. In the end, the Pakistanis knew that the Western powers would intervene to stop the war and what would matter is who had the most of the other's territory.

Confident that another war would be as much of a stalemate as the 1965 Conflict, the Pakistanis got increasingly bold and finally on 3 December 1971 reacted with a massive co-ordinated air strike on several Indian Air Force stations in the West. At midnight, the Indian Prime Minister Mrs. Indira Gandhi in a broadcast to the nation declared that India was at war with Pakistan. As her words came on in million of Indian homes across the Subcontinent, the men at the front were already engaged in bitter combat...

PAF Strikes

For all practical purposes, the war started at about 5:40 pm on 3 December when Pakistan Air Force (PAF) combat aircraft struck nine Indian airfields along the Western borders. The air strikes were followed by a massive attack on the strategic Chhamb sector in the north. In the East, it was the Indian Army which went on the offensive. By late that night, artillery shells were raining down all along the Western and Eastern borders. India and Pakistan were locked in a two-front war.

In the West, the Indian Army had very limited offensive aims and was relegated more to a holding role. The initiative lay with Pakistan. In this theatre, Pakistan had near parity with India in armour and artillery while India had more infantry divisions. Pakistan's most successful thrust was in Chhamb where the 23rd Pakistani Division (along with two additional infantry brigades, one extra armoured brigade and Corps artillery units) under the able leadership of Major General Iftikhar Khan completely overwhelmed the forward defensive positions of the Indian 10 Division commanded by Major General Jaswant Singh.

Chhamb village was taken and the Pakistanis threatened to advance towards Jammu, the summer capital of the state of Jammu & Kashmir. Heavy fighting continued in this sector for a week until the indecisiveness of the Indian Divisional commander forced the Indian Corps Commander to intervene personally and launch heavy attacks to push the Pakistanis back to a non-threatening position. The Pakistanis surprisingly failed to take advantage of their initial successes in this sector and actually depleted the forces available to their commander, who was killed on 10 December in a helicopter crash.

Acting in accordance with its strategy to grab as much territory in the West as possible, Pakistan also launched a major attack on Punch in the state of Jammu & Kashmir. This attack, unlike the one on Chhamb, was completely repulsed, although here the Indian Army was at a locational disadvantage since the Pakistanis controlled the heights around the town. Smaller attacks were launched by Pakistan in Punjab at Fazilka and Hussainiwala. Here the forward Indian defences were breached but the Pakistani Army could not sustain its attacks. A more ambitious armoured thrust in the deserts of Rajasthan was similarly stopped in the famous Battle of Longewal. In all, it appeared that the Pakistani military high command could not make up its mind as to where it should deliver its main punch and kept pulling back until it was too late.

The Indian Army chief, General Sam Maneckshaw, had a completely different set of problems. His strategy had to take into account the Chinese, with whom the Indian Army had fought a full blown war only nine years earlier. The Chinese were now firm Pakistani allies and had been making threatening noises ever since India resolved to intervene in the East Pakistan issue. General Maneckshaw, despite the disappointment of his Corps and divisional commanders, had to hold back his Army in the West, keep a watchful eye on the long and difficult Chinese borders and, at the same time, ensure that his Eastern Army secured its objective of grabbing a good chunk of East Pakistani territory within 2 to 3 weeks. The Indian aim was to install a Bangladeshi interim government in East Pakistani territory before the cessation of hostilities. It was not all clear in the beginning whether things would work out quite the way as planned.

MODEST AIMS, AMBITIOUS ACTION

One of the less remarked upon aspects of the 1971 war was the varied character of the key men who planned and executed the operations. Best known was of course the flamboyant Indian Army Chief, General Sam Maneckshaw, a Parsee who had won the Military Cross in WW II. To the Indian public, it was General Maneckshaw with his twirled moustache, Gorkha cap and baton, who was the symbolic hero. Yet, there were below him, an equally varied and extra-ordinary set of men, who planned and executed their own battles. The Western Army was commanded by an Anglo-Indian Lt. Gen. K.P.Candeth and the Eastern Army, headquartered at Calcutta, by a Sikh, Lt. Gen. J.S.Aurora. General Aurora's a brilliant Chief of Staff was Major. Gen. J.F.R.Jacob, the scion of an old Jewish family of Calcutta. Together these men planned and executed the lightning operations of December 1971.

The 4th morning saw Indian forces and Mukti Bahini guerrillas ready for battle with the Pakistanis, who were by now well dug in and waiting for the Indian assault. The Indian forces easily outnumbered the Pakistanis by a ratio of about 2:1. However, according to conventional infantry wisdom, an attacking Army requires a three-is-to-one superiority in numbers to attack. India did not have that. Besides, the Pakistani Army commander in the East, General A.A.K.Niazi, was determined merely to delay the Indian advance. For, in this war, the real battle was against time. The longer it took the Indian to secure their limited objectives, the greater the probability of the United Nations intervening to stop the war and effect a stalemate. Pakistan was confident that a stalemate was all that the Indians could get. Towards this strategy, General Niazi, had fortified the towns and approaches to the East Pakistani heartland and had boasted before the war began that should hostilities begin, he would take the battle inside India.

The brief given by the Indian Army chief, General Maneckshaw, to the Eastern Command was very limited. The aim was to occupy only two areas of East Pakistan - Chittagong and Khulna - so that an interim Bangladeshi government could be established. The capture of the whole of East Pakistan was not even conceived. A major problem was the geography and terrain of East Pakistan. Three major rivers - the Brahmaputra, the Ganga and the Meghna - divided East Pakistan into four natural regions. Each of the rivers were major ones - all of them wider than any European river. Each sub-region was further divided into several pockets cut by smaller rivers and their tributaries. The idea that an attacking army could bridge these, fight the enemy and then take territory, all within a couple of weeks, was ludicrous.

Lt. General Aurora's Chief of Staff, Major General Jacob, however, did not entirely agree with the Indian Army top brass. "I think the aim of the government was to take as much territory as possible in East Pakistan so as to establish an Bangladeshi government in their own territory," he recalled in an interview with SAPRA INDIA. "Army Headquarters issued an operations instruction according to which our main objectives were to take Chittagong and Khulna ports, which were termed the entry ports. But we at Eastern Command felt differently. We felt that Dhaka was the geo-political centre of Bangladesh and therefore any campaign to be successful had to capture Dhaka."

The Eastern Command went ahead with its own plans, although Army Headquarters felt it was too ambitious and could not be achieved. Jacob's commander, Lt. Gen. Aurora, provided full support for his Army's own plans and allowed Jacob to pull down troops kept in reserve for a possible attack by the Chinese. Some of these troops had to be brought into battle so hurriedly that the only way was to paradrop them. This was accomplished with the help of the IAF and soon soldiers geared to fight the Chinese in the high mountains found themselves in the tropical riverine areas of Tangail in East Pakistan.

"We realised that any campaign to be successful had to be swift. The United Nations was putting great pressure on us and also the Russians had indicated that they did not want to exercise their veto any more," Jacob explained. "Therefore any campaign had to be quick. We realised that Niazi (the Pakistani Army commander in East Pakistan) was going to fortify the towns and defend them in strength.

We therefore decided not attack any towns but bypass them using subsidiary tracks to get to our objective: Dhaka."

The immense practical problem of moving thousands of troops and tonnes of equipment across rivers and marshes was accomplished largely due to the efforts of the Army Corps of Engineers, and with a lot of local help. The IAF chipped in by using helicopters to lift entire battalions across larger rivers that could not be quickly bridged by the Engineers. In most places, the swiftly moving contingents quickly overcame enemy resistance and moved forward. The Pakistanis for the most part, were completely taken by surprise.

Within 6 days of the war, Indian troops were deep inside East Pakistani territory and moving fast. The Mukti Bahini section of the advancing forces played a crucial role in guiding the Indian Army through the treacherous riverine areas and providing critical intelligence. It is doubtful whether the Indian Army could have moved so fast and decisively without the help of the Bangladeshis. At any rate, by the seventh day of the war, the Pakistani Army High Command, headquartered in Rawalpindi, was in a complete panic.

Using Sea Power

The 1971 war was the first, and only, occasion when the Indian political leadership exhibited a proper understanding of the use of military power for achieving a clear national aim. In past conflicts, Indian leaders either had no clear aim in mind and were merely reacting to events or they were confused about how best to use the military power available to them. During the 1962 India-China war, for instance, the Indian government ordered the Indian Air Force to withdraw its fighter bomber squadrons from the north east and not to hit the invading Chinese.

IAF bombers could have changed the course of the 1962 war had it been allowed to hit the thin and tenuous Chinese logistics lines. Similarly, in the 1965 India-Pakistan conflict, the Navy was ordered to keep its ships in port and not engage in any offensive action against Pakistan. The Pakistani Navy was given a free hand

and it managed to lob a few shells at one point in the Western Coast. The Indian Navy's chance to see some action came only in 1971 December.

Since East and West Pakistan were two separate geographical entities more than 1,600 miles apart, the only way Pakistani forces in East Pakistan could be sustained was through the sea. The Indian Prime Minister, Mrs. Indira Gandhi, decided that the Navy would be given the strategic task of denying both East and West Pakistan access to war supplies. The aim in short was a complete naval blockade of both parts of Pakistan. The bigger aim was of course to ensure that the conflict was not perpetuated beyond the time required to capture a chunk of East Pakistani territory.

The Indian Navy's best and biggest warship at that time was its sole aircraft carrier, INS Vikrant, a carefully preserved World War II vintage carrier built in Britain. Ideally, a task force centred around the Vikrant should have been used to block Karachi, which at that time was West Pakistan's sole deep water port. However, one of Vikrant's main boilers was out of operation and the ship could not maintain the kind of speed required for manoeuvring in a situation where the air threat would be considerable. It was decided that the Vikrant would be used to blockade the ports in East Pakistan, and destroy the riverine craft used by the Pakistanis there.

Vikrant in Action

The day war was declared, the Vikrant, which had been anchored off the northern-most tip of the Andaman & Nicobar chain of islands, moved towards the principal East Pakistani port, Chittagong. The Pakistanis, having learnt that Vikrant was positioned in the Bay of Bengal, despatched one of their submarines, PNS Ghazi, to the east. The Pakistani submarine thought it could sneak into Vizag harbour, the principal naval port in the Indian east coast. It was, however, detected and sunk before it could cause any damage. The Vikrant continued unhindered. Rear Admiral (retired) P.D.Sharma, who was then an aviator aboard the Vikrant, recalls what it was like:

"Fighter pilots practice for years and when they finally get an opportunity to see real action, it is thrilling - it is the moment one has been waiting for all one's life. And it was so for us aboard the Vikrant on 4th December 1971...

"The first sortie was mounted against Cox's Bazaar. Eight Sea Hawks went in led by the squadron commander. I was in the second sortie which attacked Chittagong. This was in the afternoon of the 4th because it took some time for the Vikrant to close in the range to Chittagong.

"We went in low level, pulled up and carried out repeated attacks on the airfield. In the first attack itself we inflicted considerable damage. We withdrew for the night and sailed towards the Mangla-Khulna area. Our next attacks were on those harbours. Then we came back to Chittagong. And by the time we were through with that area, especially Chittagong harbour, Chittagong airfield and the approaches to Chittagong, the scene was something to be seen. The place had been devastated. There were ships that had turned turtle, there were half-sunk ships by the quay side, the airfield was pockmarked with craters and no ship could even think of approaching the place."

THE ATTACK ON KARACHI

The most dramatic naval plan was drawn up by the Western Naval Command. It was decided that the main attack on Karachi harbour would be launched by tiny PT-15 missile boats instead of regular warships. There were several reasons for this decision. Regular ships without air cover would be vulnerable whereas the tiny missile boats would present difficult, fast-moving targets. Moreover, the Navy wanted to try out the missiles to see how effective they could be in real action, although this kind of use of missile boats, which were designed for coastal defence and not for long range offensive action of any kind, was highly unorthodox. At any rate, three missile boats were chosen for the mission and despatched in the dead of night from Bombay harbour.

Leading the missile boat squadron was Commodore (Retired) Babru Bahan Yadav:"The task given to us was not easy. Our ships were little more than boats and did not have the range to go all the way to Karachi on their own steam. So an oiler was placed about half-way to the target and we were able to refuel and carry on.

"As we neared their coast, we found some of their ships patrolling the area. The boat on my left was detailed to engage the contact. That boat was the first Indian warship to fire a missile in anger. Two missiles were fired and both were direct hits. It is interesting to recall that the radar contact which was on our screen slowly diminished and then suddenly disappeared. We were very jubilant at that time. Later, we found that this has been a Pakistani destroyer.

Very soon another ship was located right in front of my boat. We fired a couple of missiles as well but did not sink it. The boat on our right was ordered to attack the ship. It did so and managed to cripple it completely. We thought we had sunk it but later the Pakistanis claimed that the ship had been badly crippled and put out of action but not sunk. Anyway, as we continued, both the other boats could not keep up and had to turn back. Only Nipat, the boat I was on, could proceed towards Karachi harbour. We pressed on and fired missiles on Karachi which hit the oil installations there. The attack took place just 1 minute before midnight and we could see the flames from the oil installations lighting up the sea. It looked like Diwali (Indian festival of lights and firecrackers)."

It took a few more days for Commodore Yadav's boat to return to harbour as they had to take evasive action and ran out of fuel. In the meanwhile, the Pakistanis who were hunting for the boat put out a message that an Indian vessel had been sunk. Nipat, the only boat not accounted for at that time, was presumed sunk. But Nipat returned, thanks to the ingenuity of its engineers who managed to take out pump oil and use it to run the engines.

The Indian Navy accomplished the task assigned to it within the first few days of the war. No enemy shipping could move in or out of its harbours. Merchant ships did not dare approach Karachi. Control of the seas around both wings of Pakistan was with the Indian Navy.

BATTLE OF LONGEWAL

An Audacious Plan

The Battle of Longewal, fought in the deserts of the Indian state of Rajasthan, merits inclusion in any account of the 1971 India-Pakistan war because of the sheer audacity of the Pakistani generals who had planned it. Had it succeeded, India would have lost thousands of kilometres of a vast expanse of desert. But there is a fine line between the daring and the foolhardy. Did Pakistani generals cross that dividing line?

The Rajasthan sector was rather thinly held by both the Indians and by the Pakistanis for the simple reason that the Thar desert is not conducive to vehicular movement. Unlike in North Africa where the desert surface is relatively hard and the coastal areas allow for easy movement of traffic, the loose shifting sands of the Thar cannot be crossed by wheeled vehicles and even tracked vehicles are liable to get bogged down. The region also has very few dirt tracks and even fewer paved roads. On the Pakistani side, the principal town is Rahimiyar Khan which is also an important railway junction connecting prosperous Pakistani Punjab in the north with the barren province of Sindh and its capital, Karachi, in the south. On the Indian side, the four principal towns are Jaisalmir, Barmer, Bikaner and Jodhpur. The major portion of Indian forces in 1971 were concentrated near the border towns of Barmer and Jaisalmir, both of which are supported by a forward air force base. The original Indian plan was to attack Rahimiyar Khan from Jaisalmir with a view to cutting off the main railway artery in West Pakistan.

The Pakistani plan was no less ambitious and a surprise attack was launched along the Gabbar-Longewal axis. The main axis lay to the north, connecting the Indian town of Jaisalmir with the Pakistani town of Islamgarh and Rahimiyar Khan beyond it. The intruding Pakistani armoured column and accompanying towed artillery was spotted by an Indian patrol on 4th December after it had come 16 km into Indian territory. The first reports were dismissed, until the enemy took up position just 300 metres away from the isolated Indian Army company located at Longewal.

The unit had no anti-tank weapons or mines. The Pakistanis could have overrun the post within hours. But the Indian company commander, Major Kuldip Singh Chandpuri, showed presence of mind by bringing in the company's recoilless guns and heavy machine guns and directing concentrated and sustained fire at the enemy positions. The Pakistanis were taken aback by the extent of the fire and felt that the Indians must have a much larger force at Longewal than reported by their Intelligence. Instead of storming the post and carrying on to Jaisalmir as was the plan, the Pakistanis encircled the post and decided to set up their artillery to soften it up before attacking.

By this time, the GOC of 12 Indian Infantry Division based at Tanot north of Jaisalmir was fully in the picture and realised that the Pakistanis had launched a full-scale armoured thrust to take Jaisalmir by outflanking 12 Division's main forces concentrated in the Tanot-Kishengarh area. Later it was discovered that the commanding officer of 18 Pakistani Army Division had planned to breakfast at Ramgarh and have dinner at Jaisalmir before proceeding on to Jodhpur. In complete contrast to the Pakistani divisional commander's audacity was over-cautiousness of the Indian generals. Confronted by the surprise attack, both the Indian divisional commander and his senior in charge of Southern Command dithered. They neither continued with their planned attack on Rahimiyar Khan nor did they send a large enough force to engage the Pakistani intruders. The job of relieving pressure on the beleaguered Indian company was left to the Indian Air Force.

The IAF at that time had only two oldish Hawker Hunter aircraft positioned at Jaisalmir and that too mainly for reconnaissance purposes. Among the two pilots posted there was Squadron Leader

R.N.Bali:"It was on the 4/5th night that we learnt of a change in plans and that we had to take on the enemy tank thrust at Longewal. It was sometime after midnight when we received our orders and it took 2 to 3 hours to change the role of our aircraft from air defence to ground attack. But we had to wait till first light to launch our mission...

"We saw enemy tanks strewn around in an area in a radius of more than 30 kilometres since the enemy tanks had started taking evasive action. We had to split our basic two-level missions into one level so that each aircraft could go in turn by turn. We were lucky in the sense that there was no enemy air opposition in the first phase and we could afford to put in more time over the target and see what we were destroying."

Squadron Leader Bali and his colleague flew sortie after sortie all through 5th December and completely broke up the enemy formation. The second contingent of Pakistani armour following the spearhead too got bogged down and was shot up. On 6 December, the two Hunters were joined by another two Hunters and the air to ground battle continued. By 7 December the Pakistani column was in full retreat and the PAF had started flying sorties to cover them. The Indian Army should have pursued and destroyed the enemy force but it failed to do so because of the lack of initiative of the Indian generals.

But the Hunters had done their job well. Of the 54 or so Pakistani T-59 and Sherman tanks that had come in, as many as forty were destroyed or abandoned. Another 138 vehicles of all types were destroyed along with 5 field guns and three anti-aircraft guns. The desert around Longewal was a smouldering graveyard of tanks and vehicles. The Pakistanis replaced the commander of their 18 Division based at Rahimiyar Khan, well before the retreat probably because it was clear that he had not considered co-ordinating air support or even arranging for adequate air defence guns before launching his attack. The pity is that the Indian generals in that sector too failed to take advantage of the rout and in the end started the campaign far too late. 12 Division ultimately managed only to advance cautiously to the town of Islamgarh. In contrast, 11 Indian Army Division, operating from near Barmer about 240 km away towards the south, did a much better job and continued its advance across difficult terrain, which required the laying of duckboard before tanks or vehicles could advance. 11 Division was active throughout the war despite enemy air action, stiff enemy opposition and lack of water. At the cessation of hostilities, 11 Division was poised to take the town of Naya Chor about 50 kilometres inside Pakistan.

The lessons of Longewal are clear: success in any endeavour require^ balancing caution with courage. The Indian commander in the Jaisalmir sector lost out because he was too cautious while his Pakistani counterpart lost his job because he threw caution to the desert winds. And war can at times be brutally unforgiving..

The scene of action was in the eastern sector, a few minutes flying time away from Calcutta, the largest Indian metropolis in the east. The provocation was the repeated intrusion by groups of PAF F-86 Sabres into a salient inside Indian territory. This salient called Boyra was being used by Bangladeshi Mukti Bahini guerrillas to launch attacks inside East Pakistan. The Pakistani Army in the east had reacted angrily by launching a full scale attack in that sector but had had to beat a retreat after losing 13 tanks and many men. The job of messing up the Mukti Bahini was given to the PAF Sabres which began crossing into Indian territory, strafing the area and slipping back into Pakistani air space. The IAF had to get them while they were in Indian air space. The window was small: barely a couple of minutes wide, and the PAF fighters had to be intercepted over a 3 km wide corridor surrounded on three sides by Pakistani territory.

Four IAF Gnats were ordered to scramble at about 2:49 on 22 November afternoon to take on four Sabres strafing the Indian salient. The Gnats got three Sabres. The IAF formation leader, Flight Lieutenant R. Massey; Flight Lieutenant M. A. Ganapathy and Flying Officer D.Lazarus each got one Sabre. One Sabre crashed into a pond in Chaugacha on the East Pakistani side of the border, while the other two went down over Indian territory. Flt. Lt. Parvez Mehdi Qureshi and Fg Offr Khalil Ahmed, the two PAF pilots who ejected over India were captured and produced before a crowded press conference the next day. The action was splashed in newspaper front pages all over the country and the three pilots who scored hits became national heroes overnight. This encounter set the tone of the air battles that were to follow. News of the incident and the famous gun camera shots were splashed across newspaper headlines the world over and the tiny Gnat acquired a reputation of being the Sabre killer. Conversations picked up in the air suggested that PAF fighters were instructed not to engage with Gnats, although this small aircraft could easily be out flown by Sabres and Starfighters. The PAf also subsequently withdrew some its aircraft from East Pakistan leaving a sole squadron of Sabres to grapple with the eleven IAF squadrons positioned in the east.

Protecting the Skies

A major reason for India's rapid successes in the 1971 conflict was the excellent co-ordination effected between the Indian Air Force (IAF) and the Army. Air Chief Marshal P.C.Lal, the IAF's low profile chief, appreciated that the IAF's primary role would be to fly in support of the Army. Achieving complete air superiority was not the primary aim, especially on the western front where the Pakistani Air Force (PAF) had massed its squadrons, leaving only one squadron of F-86 Sabres for the defence of the east.

The Indians had more aircraft but most of them were generally much older than the aircraft in the PAF's inventory. The IAF's pride and the most advanced aircraft of the time was the MiG-21. But the MiG-21 required long runways not always available in many of the frontline air bases and required expert handling. The IAF's primary interceptor continued to be the Folland Gnat, a tiny but highly maneuverable aircraft that had been passed over by its British manufacturers. The Gnats flew the highest number of sorties during the war. The IAF's primary ground attack aircraft were the old

British built Hunters, the positively ancient Canberras and the spanking new Sukhoi-7s (acquired in 1968). The IAF also operated the indigenous Marut HF-24 fighters, which were somewhat under powered and difficult to manoeuvre, and a number of other obsolete types including the Harvard IIR's, the Vampires and Mysteres.

The PAF's mainstay was the F-86F Sabre, which was in service with many NATO countries although it belonged to a line that had been in production since the time of the Korean War. The Sabre was an excellent aircraft and had been substantially modified over the years to keep up with evolving Soviet combat aircraft. In 1971, the PAF Sabres included the ones upgraded to '40s' standards and newer Mk.6s from Canada. Pakistan also had the F-104 Starfighter, touted as the most sophisticated aircraft of the day. The rest of PAF's inventory was made up of Mirage-IIIs, newer Chinese variants of the MiG-19 (F-6s) and American B-57 bombers. A few IAF pilots had flown Sabres in the United States and knew the fine handling properties of their enemy's main combat fighter. The Indians rated the Mirage-III as the best PAF fighter but that aircraft was not seen as much as it was hoped. The IAF, despite its superiority in numbers, knew it would be a tough fight but was fully prepared for a no-holds barred contest.

Air Superiority in the East

The IAF's strength in the east was made up of 4 squadrons of Hunters, one of Su-7s, 3 of Gnats and 3 of the newer MiG-21s. The IAF also was prepared to hit any Chinese incursions into Indian territory in the eastern Himalayas. As it turned out, the Chinese did not stir and the IAF managed to knock out the PAF squadron within 2 days of the outbreak of war.

The IAF had gone into action within hours of Pakistan's pre-emptive strikes of 3/4 December 1971. Counter air sorties in the east were so successful that the PAF was neutralized within hours of the outbreak of war. In their first raid on the 4th of December a four ship formation of MiG-21FLs from the No.28 Squadron took out the runways at Tezgaon air base near Dhaka. Three Sabers attempting to intercept the MiGs were taken out by a combination of cannon fire and K-13 missiles. For the remainder of the war, round the clock attacks on the Kurmitola and Tezgaon air bases kept them, and the PAF non-operational.

Meanwhile, later that day Hunters from No.14 Squadron struck Chittagong Harbour as a prelude to strikes from the carrier INS Vikrant. The Hunters were to continue flying interdiction missions for the remainder of the war in, shooting up ammunition dumps and other fixed installations. Gnats and Sukhoi Su-7s flew many missions in support of army units as they moved swiftly towards Dhaka, delivering ordnance such as iron bombs to take out enemy bunkers which occasionally posed an obstacle to advancing infantry.

Canberras repeatedly struck Jessore forcing the enemy to abandon this strategic city. On the 11th of December three converted An-12s from the No.44 Squadron struck the Jaydebpur Ordnance factory in East Pakistan. Once Kurmitola and Tezgaon were put out of action the IAF had gained complete air superiority over East Pakistan.

The story of the old Caribou transporters speaks a lot about the mood of the times. Two of these old Canadian transporters were posted at Hashimara during the war and were used during the Tangail air drop and for minor missions. The Caribou air crew were getting restless. They wanted a piece of the action. Finally, Eastern Air Command agreed by allowing them to bomb Dhaka by night. The PAF had been knocked out by then but the Pakistanis still had plenty of Chinese made multi-barrel anti-aircraft guns, which could be pretty devastating.

The Caribous were fitted with old World War II bombs and told to circle Dhaka for as long as they could during the night. While the pilots droned over Dhaka along with the occasional AN-12 keeping the Pakistanis awake, an airman aboard the Caribou once in a while pushed out a bomb from the open back. None of the bombs caused significant damage but they kept the Pakistani generals getting much sleep. After the surrender, one Pakistani general was to angrily remark about the damned aircraft which did not allow any of them to sleep for a week or more.

The Western Air Situation

Pakistani military analysts writing after the War tried to make out that the Pakistani Air Force (PAF) was heavily outnumbered even in the West. One writer claims that Pakistan had just 10 squadrons against 44 fielded by India. Such absurd assertions notwithstanding, fact is in 1971 the Indian Air Force (IAF) had a total of about 34 effective combat squadrons plus three under strength Canberra bomber squadrons and one AN-12 transporter squadron, which as it turned out played a remarkable role as modified bombers during the War. Of these Indian squadrons, ten were in the East (plus one Canberra squadron) and four were kept as reserves for protecting the inner cities. This meant the IAf had about 20 front-line combat squadrons in the West. Some of the front-line Indian squadrons were broken up and posted at different stations. This could be one reason for confusion on the Pakistani air intelligence side - and considerable exaggeration.

The Pakistanis, according to the IISS (International Institute of Strategic Studies) Military Balance 1971, had 19 squadrons including two B-57B light bomber and one recce squadron. According to our studies, the Pakistanis had about 14 effective combat squadrons in the West excluding the B-57B bombers and recce aircraft. However, PAF squadrons tended to have more aircraft per squadron than the IAF. This was further bolstered by the acquisition of an unspecified number of F-86 Sabres, Mirage IIIs, Starfighters (from Jordan) and about 15 Chinese F-6s in the months prior to the war.

These aircraft were not accounted for the IISS in its 1971 Military balance or in any other report. Also, the serviceability of PAF Sabres was much higher - meaning more aircraft could be fielded. The Indians had 16 aircraft per combat squadron but the effective availability during the war was 12 per squadron. Bomber and transporter squadron had 10 aircraft each of which about 6 to 8 were serviceable at any given time. Many PAF squadrons, in contrast, had as many as 25 aircraft. Thus, while the PAf was outnumbered in the West, at no point was it ever fighting against overwhelming odds.

More important, the PAF on the whole was far better equipped to fight a modern air war than the IAF. The Pakistanis, for instance, had very effective air-to-air missiles which the Indians lacked. American made Sidewinder missiles were fitted on Chinese-made F-6 aircraft, on Sabres and on Starfighters. These were accurate missiles and accounted for at least three kills by PAF fighters in air-to-air combat. The Indians had only their guns and cannons to rely on. The Soviet-made MiG-21 was the only aircraft in the IAF's inventory fitted with missiles. But the missiles - the infamous K-13 - were a poor copy of the American Sidewinders and were so useless that they were scrapped after the war.

The other major advantage, and a critical one, the Pakistanis had was their radar and communication system built by the Americans. In most parts, particularly Punjab, the PAF had a real time radar surveillance system, the ability to track low flying aircraft coming over Pakistan and the means to guide their aircraft right to intruding enemy aircraft. India had nothing in comparison. Instead of low level radar, the IAF had to rely on men posted near the borders.

Every time a suspected enemy aircraft flew over, the observation post had to call in on their high frequency radio sets to warn the sector controllers. Even the medium and high level radar cover available to the IAF was poor with the result that each forward base had to earmark between one to two combat squadrons just for air defence. It was a primitive and wasteful system - and the Pakistanis knew it. The technologically inferior but numerically superior Indian Air Force could be tackled quite easily by a smaller but more modern force. This is what prompted the PAF to launch pre-emptive strikes against forward Indian air bases on 3 December 1971.

IAF Counter Strike

Within 30 minutes of the Pakistani President General Yahya Yahya Khan's declaration of war against India at 1630 hours on 3rd December 1971, Pakistani fighter bombers struck five Indian airfields - Srinagar, Avantipur, Pathankot, Amritsar and the advanced landing ground at Faridkot. More strikes by PAF B-57 bombers followed at night against Ambala, Agra, Halwara, Amritsar, Pathankot, Srinagar, Sirsa, Adampur, Nal, Jodhpur and Jamnagar. Not a single aircraft was destroyed in these raids and runways damaged were repaired within a matter of hours.

The IAF's counter strike in the west was mounted on much greater scale than in the east. Within hours of the first PAF strike, converted An-12s from No.44 Squadron (led by Wg Cmdr Vashist) struck ammunition dumps in the Changa Manga forests. In one of the first counter air sorties of the war, Sukhois from No.222 Squadron struck Risalwala air field, while aircraft from the No.101 attacked Pasrur.

The No.101 was to later become involved in providing support to the 10 Infantry Division in the Sialkot Sector, eventually destroying over 60 enemy tanks. Keamri oil installations near Karachi harbour were struck twice on the 4th by a three ship Hunter formations. And No.27 Squadron's Hunters continuously strafed enemy positions around Poonch and Chhamb. The four antiquated Harvard/Texans of the IAF also joined in ground support missions, their slow speed being particularly useful in hitting enemy gun emplacements in the valleys and gorges of Kashmir. Three counter air strikes were mounted on the 4th by Hunters of No.20 Squadron against PAF airfields at Peshawar, Chaklala and Kohat. The raids left 8 aircraft destroyed on the ground, including at least 1 Mirage III. Maruts from No.10 Squadron were heavily involved in counter air operations, hitting targets upto 200 miles inside Pakistani territory.

The second day of the war began with a Canberra strike against Masroor air base and other strategic installations around Karachi. A force of eight Canberras flying lo-lo over the Arabian sea set strategic and military installations around Karachi alight. A similar raid was mounted on the 6th. The success of these missions being confirmed by Photo Recon. Canberras reporting "the biggest blaze ever seen over South Asia".

On the 5th , one four-ship formation from No.20 struck Chaklala for a second time in as many days destroying a C-130 and an Twin Otter on the ground. A second four-ship formation went for radar installation around Lahore and Walton. And a third raid by No.20 was mounted against the radar site at Sakesar, unfortunately two Hunters were lost during this mission. Later that day Maruts from the Nos. 10 and 220 Squadrons, and their MiG escorts moved against rail heads at Sundra, Rohri and Mirpur Khas. Between the 5th and the 12th , two Sukhoi squadrons flying form Halwara and Adampur repeatedly struck railway marshalling yards around Lahore.

One of the most celebrated actions of the 5th and 6th December is contribution of four Hunters from the ATW in the defeat of a Pakistani armoured force at Longewala. A previous section covers this in great detail. The AN-12s were also quite busy on the 6th. A bombing raid by the AN-12s early in the day destroyed a Pakistani brigade in the Haji Pir salient. Later that day HQ 18 (Pakistan) Division at Fort Abbas was bombed, as were areas around Bhawalpur.

The 7th of December got off to a rather bizarre start; a Marut from the No.220 Squadron, on its way back from a bombing raid against Rohri, actually engaged and brought down with cannon fire an F-86 sent up to intercept it. Surprisingly no Maruts were ever lost to enemy aircraft, although four were downed by ground fire. Two days later an enemy Shenyang F-6 was to be brought down by a ground attack aircraft - this time a Su-7 from No.32 Squadron. Between the 7th and the 12th, Sukhoi and Mystere Squadrons were engaged in support of I and XI Corps in the Fazilka-Ferozepur sector. The Indian Army's efforts in the Fazilka area were also assisted by bombing raids by No.44 Squadron's AN-12s. A four-ship formation flying at 180 ft above sea level struck Pakistani installations across from Fazilka on the 9th. As fighting in the west intensified, the Pakistanis launched an offensive against Poonch on the 10th. To break up this offensive Canberras dropped 28,000 lbs. of ordnance on the enemy. On the 11th, in even larger interdiction sorties the Canberras delivered 36,000 lbs. of ordnance against enemy emplacements and tank farms. Despite the damage, the Canberras inflicted on the enemy, four of the force were lost to ground fire.

The war in 1971 revealed the true air-air combat capabilities of the MiG-21, altering perceptions held about it as an outcome of its disappointing performance in the Arab-Israeli war of 1967. The MiGs on both fronts had ample opportunity to engage the enemy in aerial combat.

The five squadrons that served on the western front conducted frequent armed reconnaissance missions deep into enemy territory to lure out PAF fighters. All Su-7 and Marut raids were given MiG-21 cover. Unfortunately for the Indian pilots who flew in the northern sector (Western Air Command) there was little by way of aerial engagements. On the 11th a Gnat of the No.23 Squadron engaged and severely damaged a Mirage over Pathankot. Those who flew with the South Western Air Command were luckier. On the 12th a Jordanian F-104A Starfighter, on loan to the PAF was shot down by cannon fire by a MiG-21FL of No.47 Squadron flying from Jamnagar.

A Marut strike against Naya Chor on the 16th was intercepted by three PAF Shenyang F-6s. In the ensuing dogfight one of the F-6's was brought down by cannon fire from one of the two MiG escorts from the No.29 Squadron. No Indian aircraft were lost in the engagement and the Maruts were able to hit their targets. The following morning a low flying Starfighter was destroyed by a MiG-21 scrambled from Utterlai. A few hours later MiG-21 escorts of a Marut mission near Umarkot destroyed a pair of Starfighters. While the hi performance MiGs were shooting down enemy fighters, the lumbering Antonovs were contributing more than their share to victory in the West. The Rohri railway yards which had remained under attack from day one of the war were hit by a pair of An-12s at dusk on the 13th. The following day the Antonovs delivered their coup-de-main against the enemy's fighting capabilities. On the evening of the 14th a three-ship formation of the Antonovs flying from Jodhpur struck the Sui Gas Plant. The damage caused by these aircraft was so extensive that it took six months to restore gas production at Sui to even 50% of capacity. Happily all three aircraft taking part in the mission were recovered safely, landing at Utterlai. Sadly however, that very night, Fg Offr N.S.Sekhon of the No.18 Squadron lost his life as he gallantly engaged 6 enemy Sabres over Srinagar by himself. Before being shot down Sekhon's Gnat managed to score hits on two of the enemy for which he was awarded the Param Vir Chakra posthumously.

The An-12s flew in the bombing role for the last time on the 17th. A mixed formation of Canberras and Antonovs commanded by Vashist sortied against Skardu air field in Pakistani occupied Kashmir. Of the thirty six bombs dropped on the runway by the Antonovs, twenty eight hit the target while two fell within yards of it (this was confirmed by a PR sortie later the same day). On the way back, Vashist's aircraft was chased by two Mirages. In order to evade them he climbed down into a valley and kept circling for twenty minutes until the Mirages gave up and left. The most astonishing thing about the An-12 bombing raids is that none of the eleven (ten bombers and one flying command post) converted aircraft were lost, although many were peppered by ack ack. The ease with which these rather slow aircraft could strike deep into enemy territory is testimony to the ineffectiveness of the Pakistani Air Force during the winter of 1971. Only the absence of modern weapons delivery systems for its air-to-surface weapons prevented the Indian Air Force from causing more damage than it did.

Who Won the Air War?

One of the last enduring debates on the 1971 War is the outcome of the air war. Both sides continue to claim that it won the air war. This debate continues because victory in the air is more difficult to quantify than victory on land or sea. In the land and sea wars, India emerged as the clear victor both in terms of objectives attained and losses/gains versus the enemy. In the air war, even estimates of losses on both sides are widely divergent. Immediately after the war, the official Indian Government figures given out were 86 Pakistan Air Force (PAF) aircraft destroyed as against 42 Indian Air Force (IAF) lost. The Pakistanis later claimed that they had actually won the air war by destroying over a 100 Indian aircraft while losing only 36 of their own. The truth, as usual, is somewhere in between.

Unlike in 1965, the Indian Air Force in 1971 handled claims of aerial victories by its pilots with great maturity. No "kills" were awarded until all claims could be verified, preferably by photo reconnaissance missions. Almost immediately after the War was over, the Air Chief asked the Halwara station commander, Air Marshal C.V.Gole, to visit every IAF station in the West to ascertain the performance of various squadrons. "Later, we had access to other information as well and we worked out a pretty accurate picture of losses on both sides", he explains. But discrepancies could well remain. For instance, Gole recalls that one SAM battery had fired missiles at a couple of attacking Pakistani B-57 bombers. One was hit and streaming smoke. A few hours later, some villagers called to say that they had found the debris of the Pakistani aircraft. On investigation it was found that what remained was not the debris of an aircraft but that of a missile. The hit was not taken into account. It was only much after the war that some Pakistani report spoke about a B-57 pilot who had become "Shaheed" after he tried to bail out his burning aircraft but could not make it.

Pakistani claims of their own losses are less than reliable. The main cause of this confusion has to do with various "Official" histories of the PAF quoting different figures. It has been estimated by some observers, based on signal intercepts from the PAF, that the PAF lost at least seventy-two aircraft (including at least fifty-five combat types). Pakistan itself admits to the loss of twenty-nine combat aircraft on the ground. Only 16 were claimed to have been shot down over India. Add to this the 13 Sabres destroyed by the PAF itself at Dhaka. Even then the figure comes to 58. However, a lot of this is inaccurate.

After almost a year's of research, we at SAPRA INDIA believe that the losses of combat aircraft on both sides were as follows:

Combat Aircraft Losses

Description	Pakistan	India
Air to Air	19	19
Ground Fire	15	35
On Ground	29	2
Total	63	56

* Combat aircraft and bomber losses only. Transporters and Recce PAF aircraft shot down or destroyed on the ground not included.

** PAF losses include 13 aircraft destroyed by PAF on the ground at Dhaka.

The PAF lost many more aircraft on the ground not only because the Indians launched many more counter air operations than the Pakistanis but also because the PAF itself destroyed 13 of its Sabres in Dhaka within a few days of the war. PAF's No. 14 squadron with about 18 aircraft felt it had been abandoned by its higher command and left to face the onslaught of ten full Indian squadrons. After a couple of gallant actions by Pakistani pilots, the PAF commanders in East Pakistan appear to have decided that the game was not worth the effort. The last aerial engagement in East Pakistan took place on 4 December.

Even if the Pakistani claim that the Indians lost more aircraft is accepted, does it suggest that the Pakistanis won the air war? The answer is a clear no. Because war, in the ultimate analysis, is not a numbers game. Winning a war has to do with achieving clear objectives. For the IAF, the aim was twofold: first, to prevent the

PAF from messing with the Indian Army's advances, logistics and launching points; and second, to seriously impair Pakistan's capacity to wage war. The PAF's job was to do the opposite. The pre-emptive air strikes on 3rd December were aimed at knocking out a good part of the IAF while it was on the ground. This failed for the simple reason that the Indians had learnt their lessons of the 1965 war and had constructed fortified pens and bunkers to store their aircraft. More important, young IAF fliers proved they had the grit to go out and fight, even if it meant losing one's life.

By the end of the first week of the war, PAF fighters in the West appeared to have lost their will to fight. By this time, the IAF was repeatedly hitting secondary targets including railway yards, cantonments, bridges and other installations as well as providing close air support to the Army wherever it was required. The most dangerous were the close air support missions which involved flying low and exposing aircraft to intense ground fire. The IAF lost the most aircraft on these missions as is proved by the high losses suffered by IAF Sukhoi-7 and Hunter squadrons. But their pilots flew sortie after sortie keeping up with the Army and disrupting enemy troop and tank concentrations.

Once it was known that the Indian Army was knocking at the gates of Dhaka, the PAF in the West virtually gave up flying. During the last few days of the war, the IAF brass ordered attacks on PAF airfields with the sole purpose of drawing out their aircraft. But that rarely succeeded as the PAF aircraft for the most part remained secured inside their pens, refusing to come out and fight. The strongest indictment of the Pakistani Air Force was made not by an Indian but by the Pakistani leader, Zulfiqar Ali Bhutto, who took over from General Yahya Yahya Khan after the 1971 defeat. On taking over, he made a speech in which he castigated the PAF chief Air Marshal Rahim Khan and several other officers by name.

A better analysis of effectiveness of the two air forces is provided by the losses per sortie figure. The IAF flew at least double the number of combat sorties per day than the PAF, thereby exposing itself to ground fire and enemy interdiction. Despite this, the IAF's attrition rate of 0.86 per 100 sorties during the 1971 War compares favourably with the Israeli rate of 1.1 in the Yom Kippur War. The PAF's overall attrition rate works out to 2.47 (including transporters and recce aircraft lost on the ground). If aircraft destroyed on the ground are not taken into account, the rate works out to 1.12, which is still very high given that PAF aircraft never really stood back to fight.

The question of loss is important but, in the ultimate analysis, secondary. Achieving air superiority cost the IAF dearly in 1971 but in the end it managed to achieve complete dominance over the skies in both East and West Pakistan.

DEFENDING THE WEST

Limited Plans

The Indian Army HQ's plans on the western front clearly demonstrate that India's aim was not the destruction of Pakistan. Operations instructions issued to commanders on the western front were quite limited and the larger aim was to ensure that the Indian Army took as much as territory from the Pakistanis and conceded as little of Indian territory as possible. India felt that whoever held the most territory would end up as the winner because the final word on the war would only be spelt out during the post-war negotiations that were expected to follow.

Pakistani commanders were aware of this basic dynamic and had concentrated virtually all their forces in the West. Their Air Force was equipped with Starfighters, new Chinese F-6s and newer versions of the F-86 Sabre. Their Army had a lot of fire power in the form of heavy artillery, new Chinese built T-59 tanks, and US-built Patton tanks. India had been preparing for war for some months but the Pakistanis were not perturbed. They felt that any Indian advance in the East could be held up for a while during which their concentrated forces in the West would seize strategically important Indian territory. In the end, India would be forced to negotiate and, the Pakistanis hoped, India's strategic designs would be frustrated. Bangladesh would never come into being.

The First Blow

Pakistan struck the first blow by attacking nine Indian air bases on 3 December 1971 and followed up by a massive attack on Chhamb (see "War is declared"). The Chhamb attack was stopped - but at a cost. Many of the major battle plans drawn up before the outbreak of war had to be hastily changed - even abandoned in some cases. One very disappointed soldier was Major. General. Z.C.Bakshi, commanding the 26 Indian Infantry Division. "I toured the front-lines in my jeep, flying my flag, and there was no problem," recalls the General. "At one or two places, Pakistani soldiers even saluted my jeep. And I knew we could break through these lines and threaten Sialkot town, which was the objective given to my Division."

Major. General. Bakshi had a reputation of being a fighter and had done brilliantly in the previous war. When he took over 26 Division, in the southern part of the state of Jammu & Kashmir, a major worry was a dagger-shaped strip of territory measuring 170 square kilometres under Pakistani control that protruded into the Indian side. This "dagger" threatened an important link town called Akhnur.

After studying the map a few times, Bakshi told his subordinates that this was no "dagger" but a chicken's neck:"We shall squeeze this part like a chicken's neck as soon as the war begins." And he did just that. Within two days of the outbreak of the war, the "chicken's neck" had been wrung by one brigade under 26 Division. But the more ambitious plan to move towards Sialkot was never effected. "After the Pakistani thrust at Chhamb, headquarters was in a in flap and they took away one of my brigades and told me to not to attack," says Bakshi. "All those brilliant plans prepared before the war went to waste all because people could not keep their cool in the heat of battle and let one temporary reverse cloud their judgement."

The Indians had prepared just two other offensive plans for the entire western sector, which stretches from Ladakh (Jammu & Kashmir) in the north to the salt water marshes of the Runn of Kutch (Gujarat) in the south. The terrain in this sector is highly varied and begins with tall snow covered mountains in the north, then turns into riverine flats before moving to scrub covered stretches and rich farmland further south in the plains of Indian Punjab. Below Punjab, is the state of Rajasthan, made up mostly of desert. The desert stops short of the state of Gujarat and gives way to vast dry flat lands ending with the marshes of Kutch, which eventually merge into the Arabian Sea. The western border is long - more than the distance between Paris and Moscow - and many an army has perished in the past in these areas. Taking territory here is a costly enterprise and the Indians knew it. This is why the overwhelming majority of its Army divisions were (and continue to be) termed as 'holding" formations as opposed to "strike" formations. The emphasis traditionally has been on defence rather than offense. The responsibility of defending the entire western sector was the responsibility of two Indian Army commands - the Western Command and the Southern Command. In 1971, India had just one strike formation, the 1 Corps. The other divisions under the Western and Southern commands were all designated holding formations. Though the holding corps also engaged in offensive action, these were all limited and not geared to carry the battle deep into enemy territory.

The three offensive missions drawn up by Indian Army Headquarters included the aborted 26 Division plan to move towards Sialkot, a major thrust by 1 Corps to capture the 30 km thick Shakargarh bulge which juts into the region between north Punjab and south Jammu & Kashmir, and a plan to move across the deserts to cut off the rail link between Pakistan's Punjab and Sindh provinces. The first two of these actions were to be carried out by Western Command, the largest of the two commands. The other command - Southern Command - was responsible for the borders south of

Anupgarh at the northernmost edge of Rajasthan right down to the Arabian Sea. Due to the difficult terrain in the south, only two Indian Army divisions from Southern Command took part in the fighting and their battles is part of the story of Longewala (see section on "Battle of Longewala").

All the battles that took place in the Western sector are two numerous to be recounted here but the fight for Shakargarh deserves mention. For, here the fighting was particularly bitter with the most lives lost on both sides. As for the Pakistanis, despite grandiose pre-war plans, their only notable success was in Chhamb. In other areas, Pakistani units fought tenaciously but got nowhere because of the failure of their higher command.

Attack by 1 Corps

The Shakargarh Bulge points to the north Punjab town of Pathankot, which is squeezed between the mountains rising in the east and the Pakistani border on the west. Pathankot is strategically important for the defence of Jammu & Kashmir and the northern parts of Himachal Pradesh. This was also the Headquarters of India's only strike corps, commanded at that time by Lt. General. K.K.Singh. His forces included three infantry divisions, two independent armoured brigades, two independent artillery brigades and the equivalent of about two engineers brigades. The corps was, however, tied down due to defensive commitments that took up more than a division's worth of troops. The Pakistanis too had a formation designated 1 Corps opposite its Indian counterpart. This too was a heavy formation possessing considerable strike force. It was made up of two infantry divisions and four independent armoured brigades, apart from artillery and other support units. The Pakistanis also had committed considerable reserves for this sector, which they were able to bring in with surprising agility.

The Indian corps commander decided to attack the bulge from three sides: one division (54 Div) was to attack from Samba, a town in the north of the bulge where he had shifted his HQ; another (39

Div) was deployed more towards the western tip of the bulge; and the other (36 Div) was to commence from the southern part of the bulge. All these divisions had far less than their full complement of units and in practice had to operate at the brigade level. The fighting showed that in the end it is not only plans but hard fighting that decides the course of battles.

The advances of 39 Division under Major General B.R. Prabhu was a series of disasters right from the beginning. Although his units crossed the enemy lines easily enough, they got bogged down in minefileds and could not secure their objectives. To be fair, the Div commander had none of his brigades and had to make do with one brigade and two independent armoured brigades less a regiment. This made him a little cautious and somewhat disinclined to rally his forces forward. This caused major problems for the other two depleted divisions which were pressing ahead only to find their flanks exposed because of 39 Div's lack of progress.

54 Div attacking from the north was the most active although during the initial days of the war two of its three brigades had been taken away for the protection of Chhamb. Nevertheless Major General W.A.G.Pinto, commanding the Div, and his able armoured brigade commander, Brigadier A.S.Vaidya (later General Vaidya, who became Chief of Army Staff), made tremendous progress. By 15 December 1971, the Div had control of all the points overlooking the Shakargarh-Zafarwal road. The big test was the crossing of the Basantar river, which had been mined by the Pakistanis and the minefield continued for 1,400 metres. The Pakistanis also had more than four independent armoured brigades worth of armour to throw at the Indians, which was far more than what the attackers had. The most formidable task was the river crossing.

By this time, the Pakistanis had got wind of the plan and had thrown in two infantry brigades and one armoured brigade to prevent the formation of a successful bridgehead. The Pakistani Air Force too was called in to fly relentless sorties against the Indian build-up. The Indian battalions and the brave engineers literally had to run through a wall of fire to establish crossing points and move across. The bridgehead was secured but the enemy was not dispersed. One Indian battalion had its commanding officer shot by Pakistanis infiltrating the bridgehead. Other units suffered horrendous losses in the concentrated artillery fire and aerial bombing. The Indian units pressed on regardless and by 15 December had established a bridgehead. The Pakistanis tried to destroy the bridgehead by launching a series of counter-attacks headed by tanks of Pakistan's 8 Independent Armoured Brigade. Indian tanks were rushed in to stop the Pakistanis from breaking through.

Two Indian tank regiments tried and were virtually decimated. Finally, the third Indian armoured regiment (17 Horse) held the Pakistanis with the help of three Indian infantry battalions. The fighting here was easily the most desperate in the war with the Pakistanis losing as many as 46 tanks in less than a days of fighting. The Pakistanis counter-attack was eventually stopped by nothing less than sheer grit. If anybody could tell the story best, it was Major Nisar, squadron commander of Pakistan's 13 Cavalry. The Pakistani armoured counter-attacks were stopped by 17 Horse and in the end it was just 3 tanks of a troop commanded by Captain V.Malhotra that ultimately took on one of the final Pakistani assaults from an entire squadron of tanks.

Leading the Pakistani squadron was Major Nisar. He was amazed to find his advance stopped by just three tanks. But before he could get over his surprise, he found most of his tanks hit. One of the Indian tanks, commanded by young Second Lieutenant Arun Khetarpal was responsible for most of the damage.

Even after both the other tanks or their commanders were put out of action, Khetarpal continued to fight until his tank was hit by Major Nisar's tank and caught fire. He was ordered to abandon his tank but he refused. He kept engaging the Pakistani tanks and stopped Major Nisar's tank with a hit. Although Nisar's tank ground to a halt it managed to fire one last shot at Khetarpal's stricken tank, killing the Second Lieutenant instantly. Major Nisar escaped by leaping out of his burning tank. The attack was stopped but out of the three squadron commanders only one lived to tell the tale-Captain Malhotra. After the cease fire, Major Nisar paid a courtesy calls across the lines to pay his complements.

He only found Captain Malhotra. Khetarpal was one of the few Indians in the country's 50 year history to have received the highest award for gallantry, the Param Vir Chakra. His posthumous citation read:"His calculated and deliberate decision to fight from a burning tank was an act of valour and self-sacrifice beyond the call of duty." But that is just what thousands of other soldiers did in the fighting in the Shakargarh bulge. The Pakistanis too fought to the man and in many areas, the fighting often ended up in hand-to-hand combat. From all accounts, this is the area where the Pakistanis fought for every inch of soil and the Indian shed blood for every yard they captured. The Indians clung on to every inch of territory they had conquered and the Indian Army's third Param Vir Chakra was won on these very killing fields. Major Hoshiar Singh led the forward company of the 3 Grenadiers into battle into the bridgehead and took a village called Jarpal. The Pakistanis counter-attacked later the same day.

Hoshiar Singh undaunted went from trench to trench to rally his men disregarding the bullets flying all around him. His behaviour so encouraged the men that they took on a battalion sized attack the next morning even after being pounded by artillery in which Hoshiar Singh was seriously wounded.

He continued to move amongst his men and kept up the fire against the enemy. When one of his machine gun crews was knocked out by a shell, he personally took over and shot a number of Pakistanis. At the end of the days fighting, over 85 Pakistani soldiers were found dead in front of their trenches.

That was the end of the Pakistani counter-attacks but the Indians could get no further as the cease-fire came into effect on the same evening. The Indians had halted their advance just 7 kilometres short of Zafarwal.

Some Indian military historians have been critical of 1 Corps' actions, arguing that much more could have been achieved had the corps commander not dispersed his resources and had not been forced to tie down a major chunk of his assets for defensive purposes.

But this is not quite fair considering that the actual offensive was late in starting and the Indians had actually less than a week to gain their objectives. Besides, this area was traversed by numerous rivers, ditches and defended embankments. The enemy had re-inforced the area in depth and laid extensive minefields all over the place. They also had significant artillery fire and were supported by the PAF. Making headway under such conditions in so limited a time was difficult.

Soldiers on both sides fought hard and if, in the end, the whole affair was a stalemate, it was justly so. Had the war dragged for even a week more, things would certainly have been very different. That is why the Pakistani high command despite having lost all its strategic objectives readily agreed to a cease-fire. The Indian Army in the west proved that the regimental colours its men carried were still a matter of honour. The stories of the 1971 War ensured that those traditions would be carried on by many generations of fighting men in the years to come. Most of all, Indian troops had learnt that after all was said and done, honour in battle meant standing one's ground and fighting - even to the last man or tank if necessary.

THE SURRENDER

Modest Aims, Ambitious Action

Dhaka's fall was imminent. Everybody concerned including the Pakistani generals holed up in that city knew it was only a matter of time before the Indian Army and the Mukti Bahaini would get in. General Tikka Khan after killing a few million East Pakistanis had fled to Rawalpindi, leaving a professional soldier Lt. General A.A.K. Niazi in charge. He wanted to avoid a carnage but could not disobey the orders from Rawalpindi asking him to hold on. For the

Indians, it was simply a question of how to speed up the surrender process.

The Indians got just the break they were looking for thanks to the Mukti Bahini intelligence. "Early on 14 December, the IAF got a message through the Mukti Bahini that an important meeting was scheduled in the Governor House (now 'Banga Bhaban') that morning.

Four MiG-21s of No. 28 Sqn from Gauhati were tasked to attack the Governor House. As Dr. Malek, the puppet Governor of the then East Pakistan, along with his cabinet and high officials were in session, the MiGs came screaming down and accurately fired salvos of rockets into the Darbar Hall.

The Governor was so traumatised that he resigned then and there, and rushed to the Hotel Intercontinental (now Sheraton), to seek shelter under the UN Flag. The Pakistani civil administration in the East ceased to exist. Of and on, between 12-14 December, the IAF transport planes came over Dhaka and dropped leaflets urging the Pak forces to surrender...By 15 December, at the request of the Pakistani Commander in the East, all air operations ceased and the negotiation for the surrender of the Pak forces started.

On 16 December morning, the IAF helicopter carrying the Indian negotiating team landed in Tejgaon", wrote Air Cdre Ishfaq Ilahi Choudhury (Retd).

On the morning of 16th December, Major General Jacob flew into Dhaka to persuade the East Pakistani Army commander, Lt. General A.A.K.Niazi, to accept an unconditional surrender.

The Pakistanis still had about 24,000 troops to defend Dhaka. He could have held on and some military eperts in Pakistan have criticsed him severely for accepting what is considered a "shameful surrender".

But Niazi needs to be applauded for saving the lives of thousands more and effectively rescuing the 94,000 Pakistani armed men who became POW and later returned unharmed to Pakistan. Had the

Pakistanis decided to fight on, they would have been massacred to the man.

For, General Niazi had been offered, and had accepted, fair treatment from the Indians. The Indians had promised to protect him and his soldiers.

The Mukti Bahini wanted the Indians to hand over the Pakistanis to them for trial and reprisals. If left to the Mukti Bahini and the general populace, the Pakistanis would have been butchered. Not surprisingly, General Niazi accepted the surrender terms and signed the unconditional surrender document at a public ceremony in Dhaka on 16 December 1971.

The act of surrender marked the birth of a new nation: Bangladesh. Sheikh Mujibur Rehman was released and returned triumphant to Dhaka after a brief stop-over at New Delhi where he was warmly embraced by Indian leaders.

In Dhaka, a grand ceremony was held with the Indian Eastern Army commander, Lt. General J.S.Aurora, in attendance with Sheikh Mujib. This was the Indian armed forces' finest hour. From a rag-tag, left over colonial remnaint, the three services had evolved into a new and formidable fighting force.

The East Pakistan campaign would always be remembered as a model in innovation and would serve to inspire generations of soldiers of the future.

The country's hero was Chief of Army Staff, General Sam Maneckshaw, who later went on to become the country's first Field Marshall. Indian had also won a great moral victory, for it had fought what was basically a liberation war. And as the Bangladeshi crowds and guerilla fighters rejoiced in the streets of Dhaka, it was clear that yet another round in the battle for liberty and justice had just been won.

8

INDIAN ARMY IN THE WAR OF KARGIL

Before the Partition of India in 1947, Kargil was part of the Baltistan district of Ladakh, a sparsely populated region with diverse linguistic, ethnic and religious groups, living in isolated valleys separated by some of the world's highest mountains. The First Kashmir War (1947–48) concluded with the Line of Control (LOC) bisecting the Baltistan district, with the town and district of Kargil lying on the Indian side in the Ladakh subdivision of the Indian state of Jammu and Kashmir. After Pakistan's defeat in the Indo-Pakistani War of 1971, the two nations signed the Simla Agreement promising not to engage in armed conflict with respect to that boundary. The town of Kargil is located 205 km (120 miles) from Srinagar, facing the Northern Areas across the LOC. Like other areas in the Himalayas, Kargil has a temperate climate. Summers are cool with frigid nights, while winters are long and chilly with temperatures often dropping to "48 °C ("54 °F).

An Indian national highway (NH 1) connecting Srinagar to Leh cuts through Kargil. The area that witnessed the infiltration and fighting is a 160 km long stretch of ridges overlooking this highway. The military outposts on the ridges above the highway were generally around 5,000 metres (16,000 ft) high, with a few as high as 5,485 metres (18,000 ft). Apart from the district capital, Kargil, the populated areas near the front line in the conflict included the Mushko Valley and the tiny town of Drass, southwest of Kargil, as well as the Batalik sector and other areas, northeast of Kargil.

One of the reasons why Kargil was targeted was that the terrain surrounding it, lent itself to pre-emptive seizure of unoccupied military positions. With tactically vital features and well-prepared defensive posts atop the peaks, a defender of the high ground would enjoy advantages akin to a fortress. Any attack to dislodge a defender from high ground in mountain warfare requires a far higher ratio of attackers to defenders, and the difficulties would be exacerbated by the high altitude and freezing temperatures.

Kargil was also just 173 km (108 mi) from the Pakistani-controlled town of Skardu, which was capable of providing logistical and artillery support to Pakistani combatants. In addition to these tactical advantages, the Kargil district had a Muslim majority, which may have led Pakistani forces to expect local support for the infiltration as it had been expected in Operation Gibraltar.

BACKGROUND

After the Indo-Pakistani War of 1971, there had been a long period with relatively few direct armed conflicts involving the military forces of the two neighbors - notwithstanding the efforts of both nations to control the Siachen Glacier by establishing military outposts on the surrounding mountains ridges and the resulting military skirmishes in the 1980s.

During the 1990s, however, escalating tensions and conflict due to separatist activities in Kashmir, some of which were supported by Pakistan, as well as the conducting of nuclear tests by both countries in 1998, led to an increasingly belligerent atmosphere. In an attempt to defuse the situation, both countries signed the Lahore Declaration in February 1999, promising to provide a peaceful and bilateral solution to the Kashmir conflict.

During the winter of 1998 -1999, some elements of the Military of Pakistan were covertly training and sending Pakistani troops and paramilitary forces, some allegedly in the guise of mujahideen, into territory on the Indian side of the LOC. The infiltration was code named "Operation Badr"; its aim was to sever the link between Kashmir and Ladakh, and cause Indian forces to withdraw from the Siachen Glacier, thus forcing India to negotiate a settlement of the broader Kashmir dispute. Pakistan also believed that any tension in the region would internationalise the Kashmir issue, helping it to secure a speedy resolution. Yet another goal may have been to boost the morale of the decade-long rebellion in Indian Administered Kashmir by taking a proactive role. Some writers have speculated that the operation's objective may also have been as a retaliation for India's Operation Meghdoot in 1984 that seized much of Siachen Glacier. According to India's then army chief Ved Prakash Malik, and many other scholars, much of the background planning, including construction of logistical supply routes, had been undertaken much earlier. On several occasions during the 1980s and 1990s, the army had given Pakistani leaders (namely Zia ul Haq and Benazir Bhutto) similar proposals for infiltration into the Kargil region, but the plans had been shelved for fear of drawing the nations into all-out war.

Some analysts believe that the blueprint of attack was reactivated soon after Pervez Musharraf was appointed chief of army staff in October 1998. After the war, Nawaz Sharif, Prime Minister of Pakistan during the Kargil conflict, claimed that he was unaware of the plans, and that he first learned about the situation when he received an urgent phone call from Atal Bihari Vajpayee, his counterpart in India. Sharif attributed the plan to Musharraf and "just two or three of his cronies", a view shared by some Pakistani writers who have stated that only four generals, including Musharraf, knew of the plan. Musharraf, however, asserted that Sharif had been briefed on the Kargil operation 15 days ahead of Vajpayee's journey to Lahore on February 20.

War Progress

There were three major phases to the Kargil War. First, Pakistan infiltrated forces into the Indian-controlled section of Kashmir and occupied strategic locations enabling it to control NH1. The next stage consisted of India discovering the infiltration and mobilizing forces to respond to it. The final stage involved major battles by Indian and Pakistani forces resulting in India capturing positions held by Pakistani forces and the withdrawal of Pakistani forces back across the Line of Control.

OCCUPATION BY PAKISTAN

During the winter season, due to extreme cold in the mountainous areas of Kashmir, it was a common practice for both the Indian and Pakistan Armies to abandon some forward posts on their respective sides of the LOC and to reduce patrolling of areas that may be avenues of infiltration. When weather conditions became less severe, forward posts would be reoccupied and patrolling resumed.

During February 1999, the Pakistan Army began to re-occupy the posts it had abandoned on its side of the LOC in the Kargil region, but also sent forces to occupy some posts on the Indian side of the LOC.

Troops from the elite Special Services Group as well as four to seven battalions of the Northern Light Infantry (a paramilitary regiment not part of the regular Pakistani army at that time) covertly and overtly set up bases on the vantage points of the Indian-controlled region. According to some reports, these Pakistani forces were backed by Kashmiri guerrillas and Afghan mercenaries.

Pakistani intrusions took place in the heights of the lower Mushkoh valley, along the Marpo La ridgeline in Dras, in Kaksar near Kargil, in the Batalik sector east of the Indus river, the heights above of the Chorbatla sector where the LC turns North as well in the Turtok sector south of the Siachen area.

INDIA DISCOVERS INFILTRATION AND MOBILIZES

Initially, these incursions were not detected for a number of reasons: Indian patrols were not sent into some of the areas infiltrated by the Pakistani forces and heavy artillery fire by Pakistan in some areas provided cover for the infiltrators. But by the second week of May, the ambushing of an Indian patrol team, acting on a tip-off by a local shepherd in the Batalik sector, led to the exposure of the infiltration.

Initially with little knowledge of the nature or extent of the encroachment, the Indian troops in the area assumed that the infiltrators were jihadis and claimed that they would evict them within a few days.

Subsequent discovery of infiltration elsewhere along the LoC, and the difference in tactics employed by the infiltrators, caused the Indian army to realize that the entire plan of attack was on a much bigger scale. The total area seized by the ingress is generally accepted to between 130 km^2 - 200 km^2; Musharraf however, stated that 500 square miles (1,300 km^2) of Indian territory was occupied.

The Government of India responded with Operation Vijay, a mobilisation of 200,000 Indian troops.

However, because of the nature of the terrain, division and corps operations could not be mounted; the scale of the subsequent fighting was mostly at the regimental or battalion level. In effect, two divisions of the Indian Army, numbering 20,000, plus several thousand from the Paramilitary forces of India and the air force were deployed in the conflict zone.

The total number of Indian soldiers that were involved in the military operation on the Kargil-Drass sector was thus close to 30,000. The number of infiltrators, including those providing logistical backup, has been put at approximately 5,000 at the height of the conflict. This figure includes troops from Pakistan-administered Kashmir that were involved in the war providing additional artillery support.

The Indian Air Force launched Operation Safed Sagar in support of the mobilization of Indian land forces, but its effectiveness during the war was limited by the high altitude, which in turn limited bomb loads and the number of airstrips that could be used.

The Indian Navy also readied itself for an attempted blockade of Pakistani ports (primarily Karachi port) to cut off supply routes. Later, the then-Prime Minister of Pakistan Nawaz Sharif disclosed that Pakistan was left with just six days of fuel to sustain itself if a full-fledged war had broken out.

INDIA ATTACKS PAKISTANI POSITIONS

The terrain of Kashmir is mountainous and at high altitudes; even the best roads, such as National Highway No. 1 (NH 1) from Leh to Srinagar, are only two lanes. The rough terrain and narrow roads slowed traffic, and the high altitude, which affected the ability of aircraft to carry loads, made control of NH 1A (the actual stretch of the highway which was under Pakistani fire) a priority for India.

From their observation posts, the Pakistani forces had a clear line-of-sight to lay down indirect artillery fire on NH 1A, inflicting heavy casualties on the Indians. This was a serious problem for the Indian Army as the highway was its main logistical and supply route. The Pakistani shelling of the arterial road posed the threat of Leh being cut off, though an alternative (and longer) road to Leh existed via Himachal Pradesh.

The infiltrators, apart from being equipped with small arms and grenade launchers, were also armed with mortars, artillery and anti-aircraft guns. Many posts were also heavily mined, with India later stating to having recovered more than 8,000 anti-personnel mines according to an ICBL report. Pakistan's reconnaissance was done through unmanned aerial vehicles and AN/TPQ-36 Firefinder radars supplied by the US.

The initial Indian attacks were aimed at controlling the hills overlooking NH 1A, with high priority being given to the stretches of the highway near the town of Kargil. The majority of posts along the Line of Control were adjacent to the highway, and therefore the recapture of nearly every infiltrated post increased both the territorial gains and the security of the highway. The protection of this route and the recapture of the forward posts were thus *ongoing objectives* throughout the war. The Indian Army's first priority was to recapture peaks that were in the immediate vicinity of NH1a. This resulted in Indian troops first targeting the Tiger Hill and Tololing complex in Dras, which dominated the Srinagar-Leh route. This was soon followed by the Batalik-Turtok sub-sector which provided access to Siachen Glacier.

Some of the peaks that was of vital strategic importance to the Pakistani defensive troops were Point 4590 and Point 5353. While 4590 was the nearest point that had a view of NH1a, point 5353 was the highest feature in the Dras sector, allowing the Pakistani troops to observe NH1A. The recapture of Point 4590 by Indian troops on June 14 was significant, notwithstanding the fact that Point 4590 resulting in the Indian Army suffering the most casualties in a single battle during the conflict. Though most of the posts in the vicinity of the highway were cleared by mid-June, some parts of the highway near Drass witnessed sporadic shelling until the end of the war.

Once India regained control of the hills overlooking NH 1A, the Indian Army turned to driving the invading force back across the Line of Control. The Battle of Tololing, among other assaults, slowly tilted the combat in India's favor. Nevertheless, some of the posts put up a stiff resistance, including Tiger Hill (Point 5140) that fell only later in the war. A few of the assaults occurred atop hitherto unheard of peaks – most of them unnamed with only Point numbers to differentiate them – which witnessed fierce hand to hand combat.

As the operation was fully underway, about 250 artillery guns were brought in to clear the infiltrators in the posts that were in the line-of-sight. The Bofors field howitzer (infamous in India due to the Bofors scandal) played a vital role, with Indian gunners making maximum use of the terrain that assisted such an attack. However, its success was limited elsewhere due to the lack of space and depth to deploy the Bofors gun.

It was in this type of terrain that aerial attacks were used with limited effectiveness. The IAF lost a MiG-27 strike aircraft which it attributed to an engine failure as well as a MiG-21 fighter which was shot down by Pakistan; Pakistan said it shot down both jets after they crossed into its territory and one Mi-8 helicopter to Stinger SAMs. During attacks the IAF used laser-guided bombs to destroy well-entrenched positions of the Pakistani forces.

In many vital points, neither artillery nor air power could dislodge the outposts manned by the Pakistan soldiers, who were out of visible range. The Indian Army mounted some direct frontal ground assaults which were slow and took a heavy toll given the steep ascent that had to be made on peaks as high as 18,000 feet (5,500 m). Since any daylight attack would be suicidal, all the advances had to be made under the cover of darkness, escalating the risk of freezing.

Accounting for the wind chill factor, the temperatures were often as low as "11 °C to "15 °C (12 °F to 5 °F) near the mountain tops. Based on military tactics, much of the costly frontal assaults by the Indians could have been avoided if the Indian Military had chosen to blockade the supply route of the opposing force, virtually creating a siege. Such a move would have involved the Indian troops crossing the LoC as well as initiating aerial attacks on Pakistan soil, a manoeuvre India was not willing to exercise fearing an expansion of the theatre of war and reducing international support for its cause.

Two months into the conflict, Indian troops had slowly retaken most of the ridges they had lost; according to official count, an estimated 75%–80% of the intruded area and nearly all high ground was back under Indian control.

WITHDRAWAL AND FINAL BATTLES

As Pakistan found itself struggling, the army had covertly planned a nuclear strike on India, the news of which alarmed U.S. President Bill Clinton, resulting in a stern warning to Nawaz Sharif. Following the Washington accord on July 4, where Sharif agreed to withdraw Pakistani troops, most of the fighting came to a gradual halt, but some Pakistani forces remained in positions on the Indian side of the LOC. In addition, the United Jihad Council (an umbrella for all extremist groups) rejected Pakistan's plan for a climb-down, instead deciding to fight on.

The Indian army launched its final attacks in the last week of July; as soon as the Drass subsector had been cleared of Pakistani forces, the fighting ceased on July 26. The day has since been marked as *Kargil Vijay Diwas* (Kargil Victory Day) in India. By the end of the war, India had resumed control of all territory south and east of the Line of Control, as was established in July 1972 as per the Shimla Accord.

World Opinion

Pakistan was criticised by other countries for allowing its paramilitary forces and insurgents to cross the Line of Control. Pakistan's primary diplomatic response, one of plausible deniability linking the incursion to what it officially termed as "Kashmiri freedom fighters", was in the end not successful. Veteran analysts argued that the battle was fought at heights where only seasoned troops could survive, so poorly equipped freedom fighters would neither have the ability nor the wherewithal to seize land and defend it.

Moreover, while the army had initially denied the involvement of its troops in the intrusion, two soldiers were awarded the Nishan-E-Haider (Pakistan's highest military honour). Another 90 soldiers were also given gallantry awards, most of them posthumously, confirming Pakistan's role in the episode.

India also released taped phone conversations between the Army Chief and a senior Pakistani general where the latter is recorded saying: "the scruff of the militants necks is in our hands," although Pakistan dismissed it as a "total fabrication". Concurrently, Pakistan made several contradicting statements, confirming its role in Kargil, when it defended the incursions saying that the LOC itself was disputed. Pakistan also attempted to internationalize the Kashmir issue, by linking the crisis in Kargil to the larger Kashmir conflict but, such a diplomatic stance found few backers on the world stage. As the Indian counter-attacks picked up momentum, Pakistani prime minister Nawaz Sharif flew to meet U.S. president Bill Clinton on July 4 to obtain support from the United States. Clinton rebuked Sharif, however, and asked him to use his contacts to rein in the militants and withdraw Pakistani soldiers from Indian territory.

Clinton would later reveal in his autobiography that "*Sharif's moves were perplexing*" since the Indian prime minister had travelled to Lahore to promote bilateral talks aimed at resolving the Kashmir problem and "*by crossing the Line of Control, Pakistan had wrecked the bilateral talks.*" On the other hand, he applauded Indian restraint for not crossing the LoC and escalating the conflict into an all-out war.

G8 nations supported India and condemned the Pakistani violation of the LOC at the Cologne summit. The European Union also opposed Pakistan's violation of the LOC. China, a long-time ally of Pakistan, did not intervene in Pakistan's favour, insisting on a pullout of forces to the LoC and settling border issues peacefully. Other organizations like the ASEAN Regional Forum too supported India's stand on the inviolability of the LOC.

Faced with growing international pressure, Sharif managed to pull back the remaining soldiers from Indian territory. The joint statement issued by Clinton and Sharif conveyed the need to respect the Line of Control and resume bilateral talks as the best forum to resolve all disputes.

Impact and Influence of Media

The Kargil War was significant for the impact and influence of the mass media on public opinion in both nations. Coming at a time of exploding growth in electronic journalism in India, the Kargil news stories and war footage were often telecast live on TV, and many websites provided in-depth analysis of the war. The conflict became the first "live" war in South Asia; it was given such detailed media coverage that one effect was the drumming up of jingoistic feelings.

The conflict soon turned into a news propaganda war. Press briefings by government officials of each nation produced such conflicting claims and counterclaims that an outside observer listening to both Indian and Pakistani coverage would wonder whether they were describing the same conflict.

The Indian government placed a temporary news embargo on information from Pakistan, banning the telecast of the state-run Pakistani channel PTV and blocking access to online editions of the *Dawn* newspaper.

The Pakistani media criticized this apparent curbing of freedom of the press in India, while India media claimed it was in the interest of national security.

The Indian government ran advertisements in foreign publications including *The Times* and *The Washington Post* detailing Pakistan's role in supporting extremists in Kashmir in an attempt to garner political support for its position.

As the war progressed, media coverage of the conflict was more intense in India than in Pakistan. Many Indian channels showed images from the battle zone in a style reminiscent of CNN's coverage of the Gulf War (one of the shells fired by Pakistan troops even hit a Doordarshan transmission centre in Kargil while coverage continued).

Reasons for India's increased coverage included the greater number of privately owned electronic media in India compared to Pakistan and relatively greater transparency in the Indian media.

At a seminar in Karachi, Pakistani journalists agreed that while the Indian government had taken the press and the people into its confidence, Pakistan had not.

The print media in India and abroad was largely sympathetic to the Indian cause, with editorials in newspapers based in the west and other neutral countries observing that Pakistan was largely responsible for the conflict. Some analysts believe that Indian media, which was both larger in number and more credible, may have acted as a force multiplier for the Indian military operation in Kargil and served as a morale booster. As the fighting intensified, the Pakistani version of events found little backing on the world stage.

This helped India gain valuable diplomatic recognition for its position.

WMDs and the Nuclear Factor

Since Pakistan and India each had weapons of mass destruction, many in the international community were concerned that if the Kargil conflict intensified, it could lead to nuclear war. Both countries had tested their nuclear capability in 1998 (India conducted its first test in 1974 while it was Pakistan's first-ever nuclear test).

Many pundits believed the tests to be an indication of the escalating stakes in the scenario in South Asia. When the Kargil conflict started just a year after the nuclear tests, many nations desired to end it before it intensified.

International concerns increased when Pakistani foreign secretary Shamshad Ahmad made a statement on May 31 warning that an escalation of the limited conflict could lead Pakistan to use "any weapon" in its arsenal.

This was immediately interpreted as a threat of nuclear retaliation by Pakistan in the event of an extended war, and the belief was reinforced when the leader of Pakistan's senate noted, "The purpose of developing weapons becomes meaningless if they are not used when they are needed."

Many such ambiguous statements from officials of both countries were viewed as warnings of an impending nuclear crisis where the combatants would consider use of their limited nuclear arsenals in 'tactical' nuclear warfare in the belief that it would not have ended in mutual assured destruction, as could have occurred in a nuclear conflict between the United States and the USSR.

Some experts believe that following nuclear tests in 1998, the Pakistani military was emboldened by its nuclear deterrent to markedly increase coercion against India.

The nature of the India-Pakistan conflict took a more sinister turn when the U.S. received intelligence that Pakistani nuclear warheads were being moved towards the border.

Bill Clinton tried to dissuade Pakistan prime minister Nawaz Sharif from nuclear brinkmanship, even threatening Pakistan of dire consequences. According to a White House official, Sharif seemed to be genuinely surprised by this supposed missile movement and responded that India was probably planning the same.

In an article in May 2000 Dr Sanjay Badri-Maharaj claimed that India too had readied at least five nuclear-tipped ballistic missiles, but could not back up this claim with any official proof.

Sensing a deteriorating military scenario, diplomatic isolation, and the risks of a larger conventional and nuclear war, Sharif ordered the Pakistani army to vacate the Kargil heights. He later claimed in his official biography that General Pervez Musharraf had moved nuclear warheads without informing him.

Recently however, Pervez Musharraf revealed in his memoirs that Pakistan's nuclear delivery system was not operational during the Kargil war; something that would have put Pakistan under serious disadvantage if the conflict went nuclear.

The threat of WMD included chemical and even biological weapons. Pakistan accused India of using chemical weapons and incendiary weapons such as napalm against the Kashmiri fighters.

India, on the other hand, showcased a cache of gas masks, among other firearms, as proof that Pakistan may have been prepared to use non-conventional weapons. US official and the OPCW determined that Pakistani allegations of India using banned chemicals in its bombs were unfounded.

AFTERMATH

India

From the end of the war until February 2000, the Indian stock market rose by over 30%. The next Indian national budget included major increases in military spending. There was a surge in patriotism, with many celebrities expressing their support for the Kargil cause. Indians were angered by media reports of the death of pilot Ajay Ahuja, especially after Indian authorities reported that Ahuja had been murdered and his body mutilated by Pakistani troops.

The war had produced higher than expected fatalities for the Indian military, with a sizeable percentage of them including newly commissioned officers. One month after conclusion of the Kargil war, the Atlantique Incident - where a Pakistan Navy plane was shot down by India - briefly reignited fears of a conflict between the two countries.

After the war, the Indian government severed ties with Pakistan and increased defence preparedness. India increased its defence budget as it sought to acquire more state of the art equipment.

Media reported about military procurement irregularities and criticism of intelligence agencies like RAW, which failed to predict the intrusions or the identity/number of infiltrators during the war.

An internal assessment report by the armed forces, published in an Indian magazine, showed several other failings, including "a sense of complacency" and being "unprepared for a conventional war" on the presumption that nuclearism would sustain peace. It also highlighted the lapses in command and control, the insufficient troop levels and the dearth of large-calibre guns like the Bofors.

In 2006, retired Air Chief Marshal, A.Y. Tipnis, alleged that the Indian Army did not fully inform the government about the intrusions, adding that the army chief Ved Prakash Malik, was initially reluctant to use the full strike capability of the Indian Air Force, instead requesting only helicopter gunship support. Soon after the conflict, India also decided to complete the project-previously stalled by Pakistan - to fence the entire LOC.

The end of the Kargil conflict was followed by the 13th Indian General Elections to the Lok Sabha, which gave a decisive mandate to the NDA government. It was re-elected to power in September–October 1999 with a majority of 303 seats out of 545 in the Lok

Sabha. On the diplomatic front, Indo-U.S. relations improved, as the United States appreciated Indian attempts to restrict the conflict to a limited geographic area. Relations with Israel – which had discreetly aided India with ordnance supply and matériel such as unmanned aerial vehicles and laser-guided bombs, as well as satellite imagery – also were bolstered.

Pakistan

Faced with the possibility of international isolation, the already fragile Pakistani economy was weakened further. The morale of Pakistani forces after the withdrawal declined as many units of the Northern Light Infantry suffered heavy casualties, and the government refused to acknowledge the dead bodies of its soldiers, an issue that provoked outrage and protests in the Northern Areas.

Pakistan initially did not acknowledge many of its casualties, but Sharif later said that over 4,000 Pakistani troops were killed in the operation and that Pakistan had lost the conflict. Responding to this, Pakistan President Pervez Musharraf said, "It hurts me when an ex-premier undermines his own forces," and claimed that Indian casualties were more than that of Pakistan.

Many in Pakistan had expected a victory over the Indian military based on Pakistani official reports on the war, but were dismayed by the turn of events and questioned the eventual retreat. The military leadership is believed to have felt let down by the prime minister's decision to withdraw the remaining fighters.

However, some authors, including ex-CENTCOM Commander Anthony Zinni, and ex-PM Nawaz Sharif, state that it was General Musharraf who requested Sharif to withdraw the Pakistani troops.

With Sharif placing the onus of the Kargil attacks squarely on the army chief Pervez Musharraf, there was an atmosphere of uneasiness between the two. On October 12, 1999, General Musharraf staged a bloodless *coup d'état*, ousting Nawaz Sharif.

Benazir Bhutto, an opposition leader and former prime minister, called the Kargil War "Pakistan's greatest blunder". Many ex-officials of the military and the ISI (Pakistan's principal intelligence agency) also believed that "Kargil was a waste of time" and "could not have resulted in any advantage" on the larger issue of Kashmir.

A retired Pakistani Army General, Lt Gen Ali Kuli Khan, lambasted the war as "a disaster bigger than the East Pakistan tragedy", adding that the plan was "flawed in terms of its conception, tactical planning and execution" that ended in "sacrificing so many soldiers."

The Pakistani media criticized the whole plan and the eventual climbdown from the Kargil heights since there were no gains to show for the loss of lives and it only resulted in international condemnation.

Despite calls by many, no public commission of inquiry was set up in Pakistan to investigate the people responsible for initiating the conflict. The PML(N) published a white paper in 2006, which stated that Nawaz Sharif constituted an inquiry committee that recommended a court martial for General Pervez Musharraf, but Musharraf "stole the report" after toppling the government, to save himself.

The report also claims that India knew about the plan 11 months before its launch, enabling a complete victory for India on military, diplomatic and economic fronts. A statement in June, 2008 by a former army corps commander of Pakistan that Sharif "was never briefed by the army" on the Kargil attack, reignited the demand for a probe of the episode by legal and political groups.

Though the Kargil conflict had brought the Kashmir dispute into international focus – which was one of the aims of Pakistan– it had done so in negative circumstances that eroded its credibility, since the infiltration came just after a peace process between the two countries was underway. The sanctity of the LOC too received international recognition.

President Clinton's move to ask Islamabad to withdraw hundreds of armed militants from Indian-administered Kashmir was viewed by many in Pakistan as indicative of a clear shift in US policy against

Pakistan. After the war, a few changes were made to the Pakistan army. In recognition of the Northern Light Infantry's performance in the war - which even drew praise from a retired Indian Lt.

General - the regiment was incorporated into the regular army. The war showed that despite a tactically sound plan that had the element of surprise, little groundwork had been done to gauge the politico-diplomatic ramifications.

And like previous unsuccessful infiltrations attempts, such as *Operation Gibraltar*, which sparked the 1965 war, there was little coordination or information sharing among the branches of the Pakistan military. One U.S. Intelligence study is reported to have stated that Kargil was yet another example of Pakistan's (lack of) grand strategy, repeating the follies of the previous wars.

Significant Notes

Note (I): Names for the conflict: There have been various names for the conflict. During the actual fighting in Kargil, the Indian Government was careful not to use the term "war", calling it a "war-like situation", even though both nations indicated that they were in a "state of war". Terms like Kargil "conflict", Kargil "incident" or the official military assault, "Operation Vijay", were thus preferred. After the end of the war however, the Indian Government increasingly called it the "Kargil War", even though there had been no official declaration of war. Other less popularly used names included "Third Kashmir War" and Pakistan's codename given to the infiltration: "Operation Badr".

Note (II): Casualties: Pakistan army losses have been difficult to determin, partly because Pakistan has not published an official casualties list. The US Department of State had made an early, partial estimate of close to 700 fatalities. According to numbers stated by Nawaz Sharif there were 4,000+ fatalities. His party Pakistan Muslim League (N) in its "white paper" on the war mentioned that more than 3,000 Mujahideens, officers and soldiers were killed. Another major Pakistani political party, the PPP, assesses the casualties to be three thousand soldiers and irregulars. Indian estimates, as stated by the country's Army Chief mention 1,042 Pakistani soldiers were killed Musharraf, in his hindi version of his memoirs, titled "Agnipath", differs from all the estimates stating that 357 troops were killed with a further 665 wounded. Apart from General Musharraf's figure on the number of Pakistanis wounded, the number of people injured in the Pakistan camp is not yet fully known. One Indian Pilot was officially captured during the fighting, while there were eight Pakistani soldiers who were captured during the fighting, and were repatriated on 13 August 1999.

CASUALITIES IN KARGIL WAR

"Battalions of Northern Light Infantry (NLI) were wiped out by the Indian Forces in Kargil", the deposed Prime Minister of Pakistan Nawaz Sharief told newsmen while in detention testifying to the ferocious counter attack launched by the Indian Army and Indian Air Force to evict the regular Pakistani intruders from Indian soil in the Drass, Batalik, Mushkoh sectors in June-July last year.

The nation gratefully commemorates the sacrifices made by 527 brave soldiers and airmen for the success of "Operation Vijay", which is being observed as *Kargil Vijay Diwas* on July 26, 2000.

Indian forces had thus foiled Pakistan's politico-strategic motives to internationalise Kashmir as a nuclear flash point requiring urgent third party intervention, to alter the Line of Control (LOC) and disrupt its sanctity by capturing unheld areas in Kargil and to achieve a better bargaining position for a possible trade off against the positions held by India in Siachen.

Another tactical move on the part of enemy, was to interdict the Srinagar-Leh road by disrupting the vital NH-1A and to give fillip to militancy in J&K. The Indian political leadership and the various Ministries of Government of India worked in perfect synergy to meet the challenge.

The media coverage on the Kargil war, especially the electronic media, served as a force multiplier leading to a national upsurge of giant proportions and a feeling of oneness with our courageous *jawans.* Significantly, as the *15 Corps* mobilised its forces for the counter attack and elements of the *18 Mountain Division* poured into the various sectors of Kargil, the people of Jammu & Kashmir were steadfast against the enemy forces.

The gallantry displayed by *'Ladakh Scouts'* and *'J&K Light Infantry'* is testimony to that. The rapid Indian deployment was not reckoned by the Pakistanis.

The use of the Indian Air Force in support of the Army in Kargil had a strong impact on the course of the tactical battle in terms of the interdiction of Pakistani supply lines within Indian territory, the damage inflicted on the Pakistani defences and the lowering of the morale of the intruders.

In a skilful use of naval power in the form of *'Operation Talwar'*, the *'Eastern Fleet'* joined the *'Western Naval Fleet'* and blocked the Arabian sea routes of Pakistan. Apart from a deterrent, the former Prime Minister Nawaz Sharief later disclosed that Pakistan was left with just six days of fuel (POL) to sustain itself if a full fledged war broke out.

At the end of the day, it was the courageous deeds of soldiers from the *Jat Regiment, Rajputana Rifles,* the *Grenadiers, Madras Regiment, Sikh Regiment* and *Mahar Regiment* at the icy heights of Kargil mountains that overwhelmed the enemy.

The *'Artillery Regiments'* performed a splendid job by destroying enemy positions and pinning them down by continuous barrage of fire from 155 mm Bofors howitzers and 130 mm field guns. When the strategic Tiger Hill fell on account of a brilliantly executed tactical plan, the Prime Minister of Pakistan Nawaz Sharief was blissfully unaware of the development. His wife Kulsoom Sharief heard the news on ZEE TV and rushed to inform Nawaz Sharief, who was then enjoying golf at his residence near Lahore.

Apart from sheer courage of forces fighting in very hostile and inclement weather conditions, the military leadership has to be given due credit for keeping up the great traditions of Indian Army namely, obedience to the civilian authority in letter and spirit. The situation was such and militarily so compelling that the Army Chief would have felt it absolutely necessary to violate the LOC and get behind the enemy and threaten its lines of withdrawal.

In doing so, the Indian side would have succeeded in driving out the enemy much earlier. While the Army considered this option, it also restrained itself to go by the Central Government decision, i.e. to avoid the escalation of the conflict. It is precisely because of this reason that the eviction of the enemy took a little over two months and resulted in heavy loss of life.

Strangely, a war limited to a small area like Kargil sector had gone to highlight the Indian Foreign Policy that is principally directed towards world peace.

By deciding not to take the war with Pakistan, by deciding not to violate the LOC, by deciding to wily-nily accept high rate of casualties on its side and thus limiting the conflict on its side and in determining that these are small sacrifices in the larger cause of world peace – all this reflects India's innate love for peace and good neighbourly relations even if it meant at some cost.

This exemplary demonstration of restraint, in the face of provocations, India was able to project itself to the international community that it stood for peace and not war. This peaceful assertion turned the tables on Pakistan to the extent that America, once Pakistan's most dependable ally, not only chose to condemn it as an aggressor but build up fresh solid relations between India and itself. The result is Pakistan's isolation and General Musharaaf's regime left in lurch. For, this is the first military regime in Pakistan that has been disapproved by America and P-5 countries. Kargil war brought into sharp focus India's commitment to peace. While remembering the martyrs of Kargil war, let us also imagine what these martyrs were saying while dying, "go back and tell them that we are giving up our today for their tomorrow."

9

INDIAN PEACE KEEPING FORCE

Indian Peace Keeping Force was the Indian military contingent performing a peacekeeping operation in Sri Lanka between 1987 and 1990. It was formed under the mandate of the Indo-Sri Lankan Accord signed between India and Sri Lanka in 1987 that aimed to end the Sri Lankan Civil War between militant Sri Lankan Tamil nationalists such as the Liberation Tigers of Tamil Eelam (LTTE) and the Sri Lankan military. Its task was to enforce the terms of the accord, and maintain peace. and was inducted into Sri Lanka on the request of then-Sri Lankan president J. R. Jayewardene under the terms of the Indo-Sri Lanka Accord. Currently LTTE is proscribed as a terrorist organization by the United States and European Union.

The force was initially not expected to be involved in any significant combat by the Indian High Command. However, within a few months, the IPKF became embroiled in battle with the LTTE to enforce peace. Then a couple months after that the IPKF began to engage the LTTE militarily. In the two years it was in northern Sri Lanka, the IPKF launched a number of combat operations aimed at destroying the LTTE-led insurgency. In the process, IPKF was also accused of number of Human Rights violations against the civilian population. The IPKF began withdrawing from Sri Lanka in 1989, following the election of the Vishwanath Pratap

Singh government in India and on the request of the newly-elected Sri Lankan President Ranasinghe Premadasa. The last IPKF contingents left Sri Lanka in March 1990.

BACKGROUND

Sri Lanka, from the early 1980s, was facing increasingly violent ethnic strife in the Sri Lankan Civil War. The origins of the Sri Lankan Civil War can be traced to the independence of Sri Lanka in 1948, after the end of British rule. At the time, a Sinhalese majority government was instituted. This government passed legislation deemed discriminatory against the substantial Tamil minority in Sri Lanka.

In the 1970s, two major Tamil parties united to form the Tamil United Liberation Front (TULF), a separatist Tamil nationalist group that agitated for a separate state of Tamil Eelam in north and eastern Sri Lanka that would grant the Tamils greater autonomy within the federal structure.

However, the Sixth Amendment to the Constitution of Sri Lanka, enacted in August 1983, classified all separatist movements as unconstitutional, Outside the TULF, Tamil factions advocating more militant courses of action soon emerged, and the ethnic divisions eventually led to violent civil war.

INDIAN INVOLVEMENT AND INTERVENTION

India had initially, under Indira Gandhiand later under Rajiv Gandhi, began to sympathize with the Tamil insurrection in Sri Lanka due to the strong support for the Tamil cause within the Indian state of Tamil Nadu. However, this emboldened the domestic support within Tamil Nadu to included providing sanctuary to the separatists, as well as help them smuggle arms and ammunition through which the LTTE emerged as the strongest force on the island. This activity was left unchecked as India's regional and domestic interests wanted to limit foreign intervention on what was deemed as a racial issue between the Tamils and the Sinhalese. To this end, the Indira Gandhi government sought to make it clear to Sri Lankan President Junius Richard Jayewardene that armed intervention in support of the Tamil movement was an option India would consider if diplomatic solutions should fail.

The first round of civil violence flared in 1983 when the killing of 13 soldiers of the Sri Lanka Army sparked anti-Tamil pogroms-the Black July riots-in which over 3000 Tamils were killed. The riots only aided in the deterioration of the ethnic relations. Militant factions, including the LTTE, at this time recruited in large numbers and continued building on popular Tamil dissent and stepped up the guerrilla war. By May 1985, the guerrillas were strong enough to launch an attack on Anuradhapura, attacking the Bodhi Tree shrine-a sacred site for Buddhist Sinhalese-followed by a rampage through the town. At least 150 civilians died in the hour long attack. However, after Gandhi's assassination, the Indian support for the militant movement waned at the very time the violence escalated. Rajiv Gandhi's government attempted to re-establish friendly relations with the various factions in Sri Lanka while maintaining diplomatic efforts to find a solution to the conflict as well as limiting overt aid to the Tamil fighters.

The Sri Lankan government, deducing a decline in support for the Tamil rebels from India, tried to rearming itself extensively for its anti-insurgent role with support from Pakistan, Israel, Singapore, and South Africa. In 1986, the campaign against the insurgency was stepped up. In 1987, retaliating against an increasingly bloody insurgent movement, the Vadamarachchi Operation (Operation Liberation) was launched against LTTE strongholds in Jaffna Peninsula. The operation involved nearly 4,000 troops, supported by helicopter gunships as well as ground-attack aircraft. In June 1987, the Sri Lankan Army laid siege on the town of Jaffna.

This resulted in large-scale civilian casualties and created a condition of humanitarian crisis. India, which had a substantial Tamil population in South India faced the prospect of a Tamil backlash at home, called on the Sri Lankan government to halt the offensive in an attempt to negotiate a political settlement. However, the Indian efforts were unheeded. Added to this, in the growing involvement of Pakistani advisers, it was necessary for Indian interest to mount a show of force. Failing to negotiate an end to the crisis with Sri Lanka, India announced on 2 June 1987 that it wound send a convoy of unarmed ships to northern Sri Lanka to provide humanitarian assistance but this was intercepted by the Sri Lankan Navy and forced to turned back.

Following the failure of the naval mission the decision was made by the Indian government to mount an airdrop of relief supplies in aid of the beleaguered civilians over the besieged city of Jaffna. On 4 June 1987, in a bid to provide relief, the Indian Air Force mounted Operation Poomalai. Five Antonov An-32s under fighter cover flew over Jaffna to airdrop 25 tons of supplies, all the time keeping well within the range of Sri Lankan radar coverage. At the same time the Sri Lankan Ambassador to New Delhi was summoned to the Foreign Office to be informed by the Minister of State, External Affairs, K. Natwar Singh, of the ongoing operation and also indicated that the operation was expected not to be hindered by the Sri Lankan Air Force. The ultimate aim of the operation was both to demonstrate the seriousness of the domestic Tamil concern for the civilian Tamil population and reaffirming the Indian option of active intervention to the Sri Lankan government.

THE INDO-SRI LANKA ACCORD

Following Operation Poomalai, faced with the possibility of an active Indian intervention and lacking any possible ally, the President, J. R. Jayewardene, offered to hold talks with the Rajiv Gandhi government on future moves. The siege of Jaffna was soon lifted, followed by a round of negotiations that led to the signing of the Indo-Sri Lankan Accord on July 29, 1987 that brought a temporary truce. Crucially however, the negotiations did not include the LTTE as a party to the talks.

The signing of the Indo-Sri Lankan Accord on 29 July 1987 brought a temporary truce to the Sri Lankan Civil War. Under the terms of the agreement, Colombo agreed to a devolution of power to the provinces the Sri Lankan troops were withdrawn to their barracks in the north, the Tamil rebels were to disarm.

THE MANDATE FOR THE IPKF

Among the provisions undersigned by the Indo-Sri Lanka Accord was the commitment of Indian military assistance should this be requested for by the Sri Lankan Government, as well as the provision of an Indian Peace Keeping Force that would "guarantee and enforce the cessation of hostilities".

It was on these grounds, and on the request of President J. R. Jayewardene, that Indian troops were inducted to Northern Sri Lanka. J N Dixit, the then Indian ambassador to Colombo, in an interview to rediff.com in 2000 described that ostensibly, Jayawardene's decision to request Indian assistance came in the face of increasing civil riots and violence within the southern Sinhala majority areas, including the capital Colombo that were initiated by the Janatha Vimukthi Peramuna and the Sri Lanka Freedom Party that necessitated the withdrawal of the Sri Lankan Army from the Tamil areas of northern Sri Lanka to maintain order.

THE INDIAN PEACE KEEPING FORCE

Originally a reinforced division with small naval and air elements, the IPKF at its peak deployed four divisions and nearly 20,000 men with one mountain (4th) and three Infantry Divisions (36th, 54th, 57th) as well as supporting arms and services. At the peak of its operational deployment, IPKF operations also included a large Indian Paramilitary Force and Indian Special Forces elements. Indeed Sri Lanka was first theatre of active operation for the Indian Navy Commandos.

The main deployment of the IPKF was in northern and eastern Sri Lanka. Upon its withdrawal from Sri Lanka the IPKF was renamed the 21st Corps and was headquartered near Bhopal and became a quick reaction force for the Indian army.

IPKF ORDER OF BATTLE

The first Indian Army troops to be inducted into Sri Lanka were a ten thousand strong force from the 54th Infantry division, composed of elements of the Sikh Light Infantry, the Maratha Light Infantry and the Mahar Regiment which flew into Palay airbase , from July 30 onwards. This was followed later by the 36th Infantry division. By August, the 54th Infantry Division under the command of Maj Gen Harkirat Singh and the 340th Indian Inf Bde had landed in Sri Lanka. By 1987, the IPKF consisted of :

- 54th Air Assault Division. (Major General Harkirat Singh (General Officer Commanding), Brigadier Kulwant Singh, Dy GOC):- Became an infantry division later duie to lack of airlift capacity within the Indian armed forces.
  - o 10 Para Commando. (Jaffna) - an attached unit
  - o 65 Armoured Regiment (originally with T-54 tanks and later with T-72s). - an attached unit, it was later determined that the T55 was a better vehicle for counterinsurgency operations. Listed by some sources as an independent unit.
  - o 91 Infantry Brigade (Jaffna)
- 5 Madras Bn
- 8 Mahar Bn
- 1 Maratha Light Infantry Bn
  - o 76 Infantry Brigade (Brigadier I.M. Dhar) (Munnar, Vavuniya, Mulliativu)
  - o 47 Infantry Brigade (Trincomalee-Batticoloa-Amparai)
- 36 Infantry Division.
  - o 115 Infantry Brigade.(Jaffna)
- 5th Bn The First Gorkha Rifles.(5/1 GR).(Battle Of Urumparai,Battle Of Nallur Temple Jaffana,Battle Of Manipai)
- 72 Infantry Brigade.(Jaffna)

- 4 Bn./5 Gorkha Regiment.
- 13 Sikh LI Bn.
  - o 41 Infantry Brigade. (Jaffna)
- 5 Rajputana Rifles
- 57th Infantry Division, trained in jungle warfare,
- 4th Mountain division, only two brigades used.
- Independent Units
  - o 340 Independent Infantry Brigade (Amphibious). (Trincomalee) The Indian Marines
  - o 18 Infantry Brigade. (Jaffna)
  - o 5 Para Battalion.

Indian Air Force

Soon after its intervention in Sri Lanka and especially after the confrontation with the LTTE, the IPKF received a substantial commitment from the Indian Air Force, mainly transport and helicopter squadrons, including:

- No. 19 Squadron- Antonov An-32s
- No 109 and No. 119 Helicopter Units - Mil Mi-8 helicopters.
- No. 125 HU - Mil Mi-24s.
- No. 664 AOP Squadron Chetak and Cheetah

Indian Navy

The Indian Navy regularly rotated naval vessels thru Sri Lanka waters, mostly smaller vessels such as patrol boats.

- Indian Naval Air Arm
  - o No. 321 Squadron of the Indian Navy- HAL Chetaks
  - o No. 310 Squadron of the Indian Navy- Breguet Alizé
- MARCOS (also the Marine Commando Force or MCF) - Took part in Operation Pawan (Hindi, "wind") in 1988 and in the raid on an LTTE base at Guru Nagar. MARCOS operators (including Lt Singh) boarded two Gemini rafts off

the coast of Jaffna City and towed two wooden rafts of explosives into a channel leading to the city's Guru Nagar Jetty. Avoiding mines, eight men and two officers shifted to the wooden rafts and paddled to the jetty then fixed demolition charges to the jetty and LTTE speedboats. The commandos were detected but laid down suppressive fire and detonated the explosives before retreating to the Geminis without taking casualties. Two nights later, commandos swam back into the harbour amidst heavy patrolling by the LTTE to destroy the remaining speedboats. They were again detected and sustained minor injuries. These actions helped recapture Trincomalee and Jaffna harbours from the LTTE. For leading these actions the 30 year old Lt. Singh became the youngest officer to receive the Maha Vir Chakra Award.

Indian paramilitary forces

Central Reserve Police Force

The Central Reserve Police Force (CRPF) is a paramilitary security agency/Force functioning under the aegis of Ministry of Home Affairs(MHA), Government of India. The CRPF's primary role lies in assisting the State/Union Territories in police operations to maintain law and order and contain insurgency. It came into existence as the Crown Representative's Police on 27 July 1939. After Indian Independence, it became the Central Reserve Police Force on enactment of the CRPF Act on 28 December 1949.

The Director General of CRPF is Mr.SIS Ahmed of 1970 IPS batch,appointed on 1 March 2007 who was earlier the Director General of CISF since 6 May 2005.

Besides Law and Order and counter insurgency duties, the role of CRPF in the General Elections, held repeatedly during the past few years, has been very significant and vital. This is especially true for the trouble torn states of J&K, Bihar and in the North East. During the Parliamentary elections of September 1999, the CRPF played a major role in the security arrangements. The CRPF is one of the largest paramilitary force in the world with 200 battalions besides various establishments. Of late, CRPF contingents are also being deployed in UN missions.

History

CRPF was originally created as CRP(Crown Representative Police) on 27 July 1939, with 2 Battalions. Its primary duty at that time was to protect the British residents in sensitive states. In 1949, Sardar Patel had it renamed as CRPF under the CRPF Act. The Sixties saw major expansion of CRPF in which many State Reserve Police Battalions were merged with CRPF. Today, the force has 200 Battalions. CRPF has been active against foreign invasion and domestic insurgency. On 21 October 1959, Dy.S.P. Karam Singh and his 20 soldiers were attacked by the Chinese Army, at Hot Springs in Ladakh. 10 were killed and the rest were taken prisoners. 21 October is now remembered across the country as POLICE COMMEMORATION DAY.In the 1965 India-Pakistan war, two companies (approx. 150 men) of the 2nd Battalion of CRPF defeated an infantry brigade (approx. 1600 men) of Pakistan Army at Kanjar Kot in Gujarat.

The CRPF guarded the India-Pakistan border until 1965, at which point the Border Security Force was created for that purpose.

On 13 December 2001, the CRPF troopers killed all five terrorists who had entered the premises of the Indian Parliament at New Delhi.

In 2005, the CRPF troops killed all terrorists who had stormed the Ram Temple at Ayodhya.

In recent years, the Central Government has decided to follow up on recommendations of the Cabinet to use each security agency for its mandated purpose. Therefore, the counterinsurgency operations in India has been entrusted to the CRPF. The CRPF is currently charged with securing the Kashmir valley. Recently CRPF have completely relieved the Border Security Force in the Kashmir Valley of its Internal Security duties.

Organization

The CRPF is headed by Director general and is divided into ten administrative sectors headed each by an Inspector General .Each Sector consists of one or more administrative and/or Operational Ranges ,headed by an officer of the rank of Deputy Inspector General of Police.Group Centres are headed by Addl DIGs. There are 200 CRPF battalions of 720 constables approximately each and commanded by an officer designated as Commandant and consists of seven CRPF companies.The Companies are in charge of Assistant Commandants.

The Rapid Action Force

The Rapid Action Force (RAF) is a specialised 10 battalion wing of the Indian Central Reserve Police Force. It was formed in October 1992, to deal with communal riots and related civil unrest. The battalions are numbered from 99 to 108.

Weapons

CRPF uses basic Infantry weapons such as:

1. FN 35 and Glock 17 9 mm pistols
2. Heckler & Koch MP5 replacing the Carbine 1A 9 mm sub-machine guns
3. INSAS 5.56 mm assault rifles replacing the FN FAL, 1A1, 1C, AKM and V.58 7.62 mm assault rifles
4. INSAS 5.56 mm light machine guns replacing the 7.62 mm FN MAG, Bren L4 and the .50 cal Browning M2HB machine guns
5. Dragunov, Mauser SP66 and Heckler & Koch MSG-90 7.62 mm sniper rifles
6. AGS-17 Plamya 30 mm automatic grenade launcher
7. M40 RCL 106 mm and Carl Gustav 84 mm recoiless rifles . CRPF also uses landmine detectors ; Light Machine-Guns and Heavy-Machine-Guns.strling carbine9mm

Women in the CPRF

The CRPF is the only Paramilitary Force in the world to have two battalions staffed entirely by women. The first battalion was raised in 1986 with its headquarters at New Delhi. The second battalion came into existence in 1996 at Gandhinagar, Gujarat.

The Green Force

Another specialised outfit of the CRPF is the Green Force. The force has been able to effectively check environmental degradation and sustain the regeneration of local flora and fauna. Every year Green Force personnel plant lakhs (hundreds of thousands) of trees in various parts of the country.

Indian Coast Guard

The Indian Coast Guard is a part of Armed forces (under Navy) of India created to guard Republic of India's vast coastline. Many people confuse the Indian Coast Guard as an Armed Force (akin to the Indian Army, Navy and Air Force) since it is placed under the Ministry of Defence. The Indian Coast Guard's structure is similar to the other Para Military Forces of India such as the Border Security Force (BSF) and the Central Industrial Security Force (CISF) which are all constituted as 'Armed Forces' of India (so is the Indian Coast Guard), wherein the 'Armed Force' means a Force which is authorised by the Government to Handle and use Arms in the legal discharge of their duties. It was created on 18 August 1978 as an independent entity as per the Coast Guard Act. It's primary objective is to guard India's vast coastline and operates under the effective control of the Ministry of Defense.

The coast guard works closely with the Indian Navy and the Indian Customs Department, and is generally headed by a naval officer of the rank of Vice-Admiral. India's coast gu rd has a large number of fast craft including hovercrafts and hydrofoils. They patrol the seas and river mouths. The coast guard has performed a number of commendable tasks of rescuing distressed personnel. It has also apprehended pirates on high seas and cleaned up oil spills.

Heavy patrolling of sensitive areas such as Gujarat, West Bengal and Mumbai have resulted in the nabbing of a large number of smugglers and illegal immigrants.

Unfortunately, the Indian Coast Guard was unable to intercept the heavily armed terrorists who came ashore from small boats during the seaborne November 2008 Mumbai attacks. After hijacking a fishing trawler to provide cover and avoid detection by the Indian Coast Guard, terrorists showed fake identification papers to Indian Coast Guard boarding officers and were allowed to continue on their way. Terrorist teams then sailed close to the Mumbai coast and deployed in small boats laden with arms and explosives. Once ashore, they killed and wounded hundreds in a standoff battle that went on for four days. After this attack decision was taken to improve the service by providing more assets and setting up nine more stations.

It's Responsibilities Include:

- Enforcing the provisions of enactment in force in the maritime zones.
- Assisting the Customs and other authorities in anti-smuggling operations.
- To preserve & protect the marine environment and control marine pollution.
- Measures for safety of life and property at sea including aid to mariners in distress.
- Ensuring the safety & protection of artificial islands, offshore terminals and other installations in MR zones
- Assist the Indian Navy in times of war

Motto: Vayam Rakshaamah -- "We Protect" in Sanskrit. (It is seen in Devanagari script on the coat of arms.)

The Coast Guard is responsible for the policing of over 2.01 million square kilometres of ocean. The area under its control includes nearly 1,200 islands and a coastline of 7517 kilometres.

History

In 1974, the Government of India set out to create an autonomous coast guard to protect the nation's long coast line. This coast guard was modelled on the lines of the British (HMCG) and American (USCG) coast guards. Like many coast guards around the world, the Indian Coast Guard has borrowed the white paint scheme and "racing stripe" from the U.S. service. The dress uniforms are similar to those of their counterparts from the Indian Navy.

An interim Indian Coast Guard was set up on February 1, 1977 equipped with modern weaponry and quick sea craft with the help of the Indian Navy. The duties and functions of the service were formally defined in the Coast Guard Act, which was passed on 18 August 1978, and came into effect the next day. The Indian Coast Guard conducts exercises with the other coast guards of the world. In 2006, the Indian Coast Guard conducted exercises with Japanese and Korean counterparts. In May 2005, the Indian Coast Guard agreed to set up liaison links with Pakistan Coast Guard.

RANK STRUCTURE

Coast Guard Rank Structure Equivalent Indian Navy Rank Structure

Director General	Vice Admiral
Inspector General Deputy Inspector General + Deputy Inspector General Commandant	Rear Admiral Commodore Captain Commander
Commandant (Junior Grade)	Commander
Deputy Commandant Assistant Commandant Assistant Commandant †	Lieutenant Commander Lieutenant Acting Lieutenant
Assistant Commandant ?	Midshipman

+ With three years seniority † Under training after completion of Phase III afloat training and during sub courses ? Under training after completion of Phase II afloat training

Bases

The Coast Guard is headed by a Director General from the Navy, of the rank of Vice Admiral. Coast Guard is presently headed by Vice Admiral Anil Chopra, AVSM. Although Coast Guard officers have previously headed the force (in the alternative rank of Director General), these have been naval officers on permanent deputation to the force. The force has a strength of 5440, including 633 officers. Its headquarters is based in the capital, New Delhi. It has:

- three Regional Headquarters at Mumbai, Chennai, and Port Blair
- one District headquarters in each of the nine coastal states and 2 in the Union territories of Andaman and Nicobar Islands and Lakshadweep Islands.
- Twenty nine Coast Guard stations[3] at places like Vadinar, Haldia, Kakinada, Okha, Tuticorin and Mandapam.
- two air bases, in Daman and Chennai
- Air enclaves at Goa, Kolkata and Port Blair.
- A new station has been recently commissioned in Pondicherry patrol vessels, aircraft and helicoptes into service.

Aircraft inventory

Aircraft	Origin	Type	Versions	In service	Notes
HAL Dhruv	India	Utility helicopter		4	
Aérospatiale SA 316 Alouette III	France	Utility helicopter	SA 316B	17	
Dornier Do 228	Germany India	transport search and rescue patrol	Do 228-101	24	18 built by HAL

COMBAT OPERATIONS

Indian Intervention in the Sri Lankan Civil War

The Indian intervention in the Sri Lankan Civil War (1987 - 1990) was deployment of the Indian military contingent Indian Peace Keeping Force intended to perform a peacekeeping operation in Sri Lanka. It was formed under the mandate of the Indo-Sri Lankan Accord signed between India and Sri Lanka in 1987 that aimed to end the Sri Lankan Civil War between militant Sri Lankan Tamil nationalists Liberation Tigers of Tamil Eelam (LTTE) and the Sri Lankan military.

The force was initially not expected to be involved in any significant combat by the Indian High Command. However, within a few months, the IPKF became embroiled in battle with the LTTE to enforce peace. In the two years it was in northern Sri Lanka, the IPKF launched a number of combat operations aimed at destroying the LTTE-led insurgency. The IPKF began withdrawing from Sri Lanka in 1989, following its military fiasco and the election of the Vishwanath Pratap Singh government in India and on the request of the newly-elected Sri Lankan President Ranasinghe Premadasa. The last IPKF contingents left Sri Lanka in March 1990.

The Indian Intervention

The LTTE had enjoyed support from India till the IPKF started getting inducted. However, not having been party to the negotiations leading up to the accord, it agreed to the truce only reluctantly. The Tigers had rejected the Provincial Council framework as inadequate and Prabhakaran had protested against the Indian military intervention. The Tigers resisted the spread what was deemed India's self-serving aim of binding Sri Lanka into India's geo political sphere of influence, as well as a symapthy for Sri Lanka's ruling Sinhala community in India outside the support-base in Tamil Nadu. With the induction of the Indian troops, the Tigers initially complied by surrendering arms along the terms of the truce. However, the opposition to the induction of Indian troops soon flared into active confrontation. Along with this, there developed an increasingly brutal confrontation within Tamil factions, with allegations that the LTTE, predominantly a Northern Tamil powerbase, was attempting to destroy both the PLOTE and the EPRLF, which represented more of the Eastern provinces. The LTTE boycotted the elections that were held in October and November 1988 along the lines outlined in the accord. The Indian administration had not expected opposition from the Tigers and was initially taken unaware. The support for Tamil Nationalism in India also raised the spectre to the Indian Govt. of a possible situation of Tamil secessionist movement in Tamil Nadu. However, faced with growing diligence from her erstwhile partner, India adopted a strategy of aiding alternative Tamil power bases, including the Eelam People's Revolutionary Liberation Front, which ultimately emerged strongly in the November 1988 elections, and at the same time continue negotiations with the LTTE. At the same time, however, Sinhalese nationalists, led by the JVP loathed the foreign presence on their soil.

Conflict with the LTTE

Two incidences that occurred in September-October 1987 marked the turning point of Indo-LTTE relationship. The first of these was the hunger strike and subsequent death of Lt. Col. Thileepan, a popular political wing leader of the LTTE, on 26 September 1987. Thileepan had begun his fast in protest against what was termed the failures of the Indian forces to satisfy the political demands of the Tamils, and his death was mourned throughout the Tamil community and fuelled a growing dissatisfaction and impatience with the pace of promised reforms. In addition it was a huge propaganda victory for the LTTE, which started taking an increasingly hard line in the negotiations for the Interim Provincial Council. The talks broke down. However, on 4 October 1988, the Sri Lankan Navy captured an LTTE boat off Point Pedro with seventeen Tigers, including some high-profile leaders of the movement, onboard. The Colombo government alleged the boat was involved in smuggling arms across the Palk Straits and on the grounds denied immunity to these captured Tiger rebels. The LTTE denied this claiming the rebels' movements were in accordance with the truce, being in the process of transferring documents for shifting the Tigers Headquarters from Madras to Jaffna. The Sinhalese government intended to bring a number of the rebels captured, including Pulendran, Kumarappa and others, to trial in Colombo for allegedly masterminding the massacre of a hundred and fifty civilians.

The Tigers, who were at the time still in negotiation with the Indian authorities, appealed for enforcement of protection by the IPKF. The rebels were at this time in IPKF custody at Palay Airbase pending transfer to Sinhalese authorities. Although the Indian authorities insist that they had explained the possible repercussions of such an action on the fragile truce and exerted considerable pressure on the Sinhalese authorities to desist from proceeding, ultimately the IPKF withdrew allowing the Sri Lankan forces to proceed with transferring the captured rebels to Colombo.

The detainees however, attempted mass suicide by swallowing cyanide- a common LTTE practice when faced imminent capture. This singular event marked a total break-down of the truce. The night of 5 October saw large scale slaughter of Sinhalese people who had returned to Jaffna, including eight soldiers of the Sri Lankan Army who were at the time being held hostages by the LTTE. These coincided with armed confrontations between the Tiger Cadres and the Indian Troops in and around Jaffna. On 8 October, the LTTE carried out a number of mortar attacks and ambushes on the IPKF.

In the face of this deteriorating situation, President Jayawardene threatened the visiting Indian Defence Minister and the Chief of Army Staff to re-induct the Sri Lankan Army to protect Sinhala interests if the IPKF did not take actions against the LTTE. The Indian government, already accused of inaction in the face of a failing accord, was forced into a position of having to enforce peace in Jaffna by force. By 7 October, the COAS had issued directives to the IPKF, laying down its operations parameters in the directive as:

- Seize/destroy the LTTE radio/TV transmission equipment in the Jaffna Peninsula;
- Seize or jam LTTE communication network;
- Carry out raids on LTTE camps, caches and strong points;
- Personnel manning LTTE offices in the East be detained and interrogated to gain information. In case of resistance,force to be used;
- Actions to further consolidate hold of IPKF in the region.

It was declared on 9 October that the IPKF was to launch a final campaign against the LTTE. This was the point of no return.

Operation Pawan

The first of the major IPKF operation was launched on 9 October 1987. Codenamed Operation Pawan (Hindi: Wind), it was expected to neutralise the LTTE operations capability in and around Jaffna. This included the capture or neutralisation of tne LTTE's chain of command. which was expected to leave the rebel movement directionless in the face of the impending assault on the LTTE strongholds by the IPKF. On the nights of October 9 and October 10, the IPKF raided and captured the LTTE radio station at Tavadi and TV station at Kokkuvil, while the printing presses of two LTTE sponsored newspapers were destroyed. These operations also led to the capture of nearly two hundred Tiger rebels. In retaliation, the LTTE ambushed a CRPF convoy near Tellipallai, killing four jawans, as well as an IPKF post at Tellipallai with automatic and mortar fire on IPKF post. Later that day, the Tigers hijacked a 10 Para Commando jeep on patrol, killing all five occupants.

On October 10, the Indian 91st Brigade, consisting of three battalions and led by Brigadier J. Ralli, began its push into the city of Jaffna.

The Jaffna University Helidrop

The first battle signalling the real beginning of Operation Pawan was the Heliborne assault on Jaffna University head-quarters of the LTTE by a detachment of Indian Para Commandos and the Sikh LI on the night of 12 October. Jaffna University was the tactical headquarters of the LTTE. This was planned as a quick commando raid to capture the top LTTE leadership and local commanders who, based on Indian Intelligence, were supposed to be in the building at the time. and was thus expected to cut short the Battle for Jaffna. The plan was to land a company of 70 men from 10 Para Cdo. to secure the football field. A second wave was to follow with a company of the 13th Sikh LI. The heliborne troops were to link up with 4/5 Gorkhas of 72 Brigade and the Sikh LI troops advancing on the ground. However, the operation ended in disaster as the LTTE, having intercepted IPKF radio transmissions, set up an ambush. The helidropped troops came under intense LTTE fire as they were inserted which, while increasingly vicious fire from LTTE positions hit and crippled the Mi-8s enough to force the insertion to be terminated midway through operation. Over the battle that lasted through the night, twenty nine of the entire Sikh LI contingent of thirty troops and six of the one hundred and twenty commandos were killed before detachments of the 65th armoured regiments were able to extract the Paras from their defensive positions. The Sikh LI radioman was shot by LTTE snipers early on, with the unit losing contact with the Indian High Command at Palay Air base and the lone survivor of the Sikh LI detachment, Sepoy Gora Singh was taken prisoner by the Tigers. It was not until his release later during the conflict that the fate of the unit was known.

Battle for Jaffna

As the battle for Jaffna proggressed, the IPKF advance came under intense and vicious opposition from the Tigers. Fighting in built-up and an as-yet unevacuated Jaffna, the Indian High command insists that the slow advance was, in addition to Tiger resistance, more a result of reluctance on the part of the IPKF to use heavy weaponry to clear LTTE defences. Furthermore all the approach roads had been armed with Claymore mines or explosives by the Tigers in its years of fighting with the Sri Lankan army. The Tigers also made extensive use of IED which could be remotely detonated from over a kilometre away. During this time, the Indian Navy, supported by the Coast Guards was key in establishing a 300-mile long blockade around the Northern Sri Lanka from October 1987 to disrupt the Tigers' supply and communications routes. In addition, it was around this time the MARCOS commandos of the Navy first went into action. Detachments of the IMSF (Indian Marine Special Forces, as the MARCOS was then known), along with a battalion of the 340th Independent Brigade of the Indian Army, provided beach reconnaissance around Jaffna and Batticaloa. The 340th Brigade was one of the first IPKF units to be deployed, and served until operations in the Trincomalee area were complete. The IMSF, at this time, also provided security patrols along the coastal road west of Jaffna until the 41st Brigade took charge later in November.

On October 15/16, the IPKF advance stopped its advance to stabilize the front. In addition, Palay, the major operations headquarters for the 54th Infantry Division, was secured from Tiger attacks. At this time the Indian Air Force undertook a massive airlift to reinforce the 91st with three brigades and heavy equipments including T-72 Tanks s and BMP-1 fighting vehicles. The improvised controllers worked round the clock to fly in troops and equipment. In addition, the Indian Airlines is said to have contributed, with its Boeing 737s transporting troops. In addition, this short interval saw the induction of the Mi-8s and the first induction of the Mi-25s of the No. 125 Sqn, along with the HAL Cheetahs. By end of October the IAF flew 2200 tactical transport and 800 helicopter sorties.

Now reinforced, the IPKF resumed the battle for Jaffna town. The tanks and armoured fighting vehicles are said to have been an effective protection against the anti-personnel mines. However, even with this protection, the IPKF advance was torturous in the face of the Tigers' sniper fire. The rebel snipers would take positions along rooftops of buildings, treetops and even coconut palms. Equipped with powerful telescopic infra-red sights, the Tiger snipers were able to selectively take out officers and radiomen, taking a heavy toll and bringing the advances to a grinding halt. In addition, Helicopters flying below 2000 feet also remained vulnerable, with at least five shot at and damaged before the Mi-25s took up their offensive role. The IPKF adapted quickly, with its officers taking off pips of their ranks, wearing slouch hats and carrying oversize back packs. However, as advances got bogged down, the battalions, instead of maneuvering around the defenders, were forced to commit more troops under orders from New Delhi. In addition, the LTTE increasingly started the use of anti-tank mines, taking a further heavy toll on IPKF casualties. A frustrated IPKF cut off power to Jaffna to counter these.

In addition, the IPKF communications lines were extensively mined by the LTTE, which further compounded the sometimes perilous situations that the Indian troops faced. It was not before the IMSF commandos broke out of the besieged Jaffna port and cleared the heavily mined Navanturai Coastal Road, that a crucial link up between 1 Maratha Light Infantry in the Jaffna fort and the advancing troops of 41st Brigade could be established that secured the Nallur area. On 21 October 1987, the commandos conducted a successful amphibious raid against a LTTE base at Guru Nagar. It was also toward the end of the Jaffna campaign that the IPKF started the use of Mi-25s for close air support when they flew against LTTE positions in Chavakacheri village on October 23, 1987.

Ultimately however, after two weeks of bitter fighting, the IPKF had wrested the control of Jaffna and other major cities from the LTTE, but operations were to continue well into November, with major operations coming to an end with the fall of Jaffna Fort on the 28th of November. Through the duration of Operation Pawan, the casualties suffered by the IPKF has been put at varying figures between 600 and 1200. In addition to the LTTE's defensive tactics alluded to above, the IPKF's problems were compounded by the fact that the Tigers, using classical guerrilla strategy, blended in with the local population. In addition, the IPKF came face to face with the child soldiers of the LTTE, something it had not expected.

By the time Jaffna fell, however, the LTTE had merely exfiltrated out of the town, moving south to the jungles of Vavuniya. Its hard core fighters moved to the safety of the jungles by skirting the coast of Jaffna from Point Pedro to Elephant Pass, sheltered by the impenetrable jungles and criss-cross waterways of the Nittkaikulam jungles.

This was however only the first of the IPKF's three year campaign to neutralise the LTTE.

The IPKF at this point still consisted mostly of an overstretched 54th Division. Following the Jaffna Operation, the 36th Infantry Division was inducted, along with two additional brigades, to take over the Vavuniya sector and the Trincomalee-Batticaloa axis. This relieved the 54th Division which, led by Brigadier Manjit Singh, could now focus on consolidating the Jaffna sector. The 4th Mountain Division and the 57th Infantry Division were inducted still later in February 1988 to take charge of Vanni and Batticaloa from the 36th.

Within Jaffna sector, although the LTTE had shifted out of the town itself, it nevertheless harassed the 54th's efforts to consolidate its positions using IEDs and anti-personnel mines. In turn, however, the IPKF was able to disrupt the LTTE's activities with regular raids that led to capture of large caches of Rebel weaponry. Brigadier Manjit Singh was later replaced by Brigadier JS Dhillon, under whom the 54th underwent considerable modifications of its operations routine. Small highly mobile units became the staple of the 54th's operations.

Operations Viraat and Trisul

The major force of the Tigers' fighting capacity had retreated to the jungles of Vavuniya following Operation Pawan. By December 1987,the LTTE was able to build up a network of a large number of camps in the jungles that allowed it to regain a position of power within the local population, instituting taxes and revenues. The Vavuniya sector was strategically and geographically key to accessing the North-South as well as East-West communications routes.

The LTTE was able to withstand the IPKF operations here as well, owing to natural cover from the dense jungles, an intimate knowledge of the terrain, and a low density of population which also probably held sympathy for the Tigers. The Vavuniya sector remained the most active sector throughout the IPKF's deployment and its casualties in this area were the highest after those suffered during the operations in Jaffna. The LTTE also managed to carry out a large number of successful ambushes against the IPKF patrols in the dense jungles. By summer the following year, the Indian High Command had evolved its doctrine from holding key strong points to conducting extensive search and destroy missions against LTTE strongholds and bases, denying them ground. In April 1988, the IPKF initiated two near simultaneous operations through the jungles of Northern Sri Lanka. These, codenamed Operation Viraat and Operation Trishul, were launched in the provinces of Mannar to Mullaitivu and Elephant Pass to Vavuniya and utillised approximately 15,000 troops of the IPKF, including armoured corps, Paratroops, as well as the infantry troops and army aviation. These achieved some success in disrupting LTTE operations, seizing weaponry and inflicting limited casualties among the LTTE cadres. During Operation Viraat, the IPKF uncovered well prepared LTTE defenses, including concrete bunkers with electric generators, as well as caches of arms and reserves. The IPKF also suffered in this unconventional warfare, with the LTTE frequently ambushing IPKF convoys and patrols. By the end of summer 1988, however, the Tigers were forced to move to another stronghold, when it started to operate out of Nithikaikulam and adjacent riverine areas.

Withdrawal from Sri Lanka

Ranasinghe Premadasa was elected President on 2 January 1989 and he on April 1989 demanded the IPKF withdraw within 3 months from Sri Lanka. In the 1989 elections both Premadasa and the SLFP wanted the IPKF to withdraw. They got 95% of the vote and Sinhala public opinion was against the accord. Consumed by his hatred for the Indians, Premadasa even opened up secret channels to the LTTE to arm them against the Indians. Premadasa demanded that the IPKF leave the island and asked the Sri Lankan Armed forces to throw them out. Any movement of the Sri Lankan forces outside their barracks would kill the still alive ISLA. Lt. Gen. A. S. Kalkat warned that the IPKF would retaliate if fired upon by the Sri Lankans. IAF squadrons moved to the South while naval units moved off the Sri Lankan coast. Thanks to the professionalism of the Indian and Sri Lankan armed forces a conflict was avoided. Rajiv Gandhi refused to withdraw the IPKF in a situation which clearly showed the failure of his Sri Lanka policy both diplomatically and militarily. Rajiv believed that the only way he could succeed was to politically force Premadasa and militarily force the LTTE to accept the accord. In December 1989 Indian elections V. P. Singh became the Prime Minister. He viewed Rajiv Gandhi's Sri Lanka policy as a miserable failure as it had cost over 1100 soldiers, over 5000 Sri Lankan lives and cost over 20 billion (2000 crore) rupees of Indian tax payers money in over 32 months and both politically and militarily it was a stalemate.V. P. Singh withdrew the IPKF and the last ship left on 24 March 1990. The Tamils were now paradoxically unhappy at the IPKF's departure but had to bear the start of a new ordeal. IPKF's arrival in India was boycotted by the Tamil Nadu government headed by Karunanidhi.

Analysis

Casualties

The IPKF suffered around 1,255 killed in action and several thousand wounded. After several years, the Sri Lankan Armed Forces realised the role of IPKF and proposed building a memorial to the Indian dead in Sri Lanka.

The LTTE casualties are not known reliably.The IPKF suffered around only 859 killed in action

Intelligence Failures

The Indian intelligence agencies failed to consistently provide accurate information to the forces. One example is the Jaffna football ground massacre. The LTTE's disinformation machinery leaked information to the Indian army that the LTTE leader Velupillai Prabhakaran was hiding in a building near the Jaffna university football ground. The operation plan was chalked out. It was decided to airdrop commandos on the ground while subsequent movement by tank formation ensured that Prabhakaran was caught alive. It was a good plan on paper. The formation moved out. Battle-hardened commandos were selected for the operation. The commandos started moving down from helicopter. But soon a rain of bullets from the LTTE fighters and sharpshooters perched on the tree tops started to fall on the commandos. The choppers also came under fire. The fate of the tanks moving in pincer formation on the ground was not much different. The LTTE had laid anti-tank mines in the way leading to the operational zone. And the football ground massacre was complete. The irony of the entire story was that the man they were hunting for was nowhere around the area on the day of the operation.

Impact

Whether it was successful militarily is an open question. On May 21, 1991, the LTTE assassinated Rajiv Gandhi for his role in sending the IPKF to Sri Lanka. The IPKF, although it shaped India's counter-insurgency techniques and military doctrine considerably, in the international scene, does not find significant mention in National and international military doctrines. The political fallout, the IPKF's casualties, as well as the deterioration of international relations has however shaped India's foreign policy towards the Sri Lankan conflict.

Assassination of Rajiv Gandhi

The decision to send the IPKF in Sri Lanka was taken by then prime-minister of India, Rajiv Gandhi, who held office until 1989. While he was campaigning for re-election during the 1991 Indian General Election, the LTTE assassinated him at a rally that he was attending at Sriperumbudur on 21 May 1991. The assassination was carried out by a suicide bomber named Dhanu, who was a member of the LTTE.

India's Foreign Policy

The debacle that was IPKF's intervention in Sri Lanka is raised at times in Indian political discourse whenever the situation in Sri Lanka shows signs of deteriorating, and there is a question of intervening; or, in Sri Lankan politics (particularly by the LTTE), when it is proposed that India, or, more broadly, other foreigners, ought to have a role in promoting peace on the island nation. As a result, relations between India and Sri Lanka became extremely sour and India vowed never to offer any military help to Sri Lanka again. This policy has not been changed since and no defence pact has been signed between India and Sri Lanka. India has never been directly involved in the peace talks between the LTTE and Sri Lanka but has supported Norway's efforts.

BIBLIOGRAPHY

Bellamy, C.: *Knights in White Armour: The New Art of War and Peace*, London, Random House, 1997.

Chandra, R.: *Judicial System in India*, Lucknow, Print House (India), 1992.

Davies .A.: *Telecommunications and Politics. The Secentralised Alternative*, London, Pinter, 1994.

Friedman, G.: *The Future of War: Power, Technology and Indian Army*, N.Y., Random House, 1996.

Heimanson, Rudolph: *Dictionary of Political Science and Law*, N.Y.: Oceana Publications, 1967.

Huntington, S.P.: *The Soldier and the Indian Army*, N.Y., Vintage Books, 1964.

Jones, W.H.: *The Government and Politics of Indian Army*, London, Hutchinson, 1971.

Kelly, John B.: *India and the Pakistan War*, Oxford, Clarendon Press, 1968.

Mary, W.: *Asian Power and Politics: the Cultural Dimensions of Authority*, Cambridge, Belknap Press, 1985.

Nair, A. M.: *Role of Indian Army in Kargir War*, Bombay, Orient Longman, 1983.

Posen, B.R.: *The Sources of Indian Military*, Cornell Univ. Press.

Rosen, P.: *Societies and Military Power: India and its Armies*, Ithaca, Cornell University Press, 1996.

Simon, D. : *Public Administration*, New York, Knopf, 1950.

INDEX

□□□